D1329884

HANNAH G. SOLOMON

FABRIC OF MY LIFE

FABRIC OF MY LIFE

The Autobiography of
Hannah G. Solomon

The National Council of Jewish Women
Bloch Publishing Company   New York

"If we could see the whole fabric of our lives spread out
What a wonderful weaving it might show;
Many a thread that we thought lost would re-appear
And form strange patterns of cause and effect.
But God holds the spindle and until He cuts the thread
We go on adding a bit each day."

THERESA G. LESEM

TABLE OF CONTENTS

PART III — TEXTURE

ILLUSTRATIONS

AN APPRECIATION OF HANNAH G. SOLOMON

EIGHTY YEARS AGO, when women's involvement in activities other than her home and family was totally unacceptable, Hannah Solomon staunchly believed that it was the responsibility of women, as well as men, to correct social injustice and combat the lack of humanism.

Today many things have changed, but the need to create programs for social reform has not. We have walked on the moon, developed long-range, button-operated missiles. But we have also had campus riots, racism, child abuse, and debilitating poverty. Ten million Americans go to bed hungry each night; millions more are inadequately clothed, housed, and educated. The elderly waste away from loneliness and neglect, and children's rights suffer in the very courts established to protect those rights.

The challenges facing an increasingly complex society have never been greater. And fully aware that strong motivation and good intentions are not enough, NCJW is forging a new path—leadership training. Volunteers throughout the country are being taught to develop action programs and problem-solving techniques with expertise equal to the most sophisticated corporate planners. In this way, Council women can effectively work toward eliminating patterns of poverty and injustice and improve the quality of life both here and abroad. Elliot Richardson, former Secretary of Health, Education and Welfare had declared, "Never before in our national history has volunteerism been so important to preserving what is best and most valuable in our society." His statement is a clear delineation of the broad role of the volunteer, whose function as a force to influence change will expand in the future.

Nearly eighty-one years ago, Hannah G. Solomon organized a highly-motivated nucleus of ninety-five women from twenty-nine cities. The Congress of Jewish Women evolved into the National Council of Jewish Women a year later.

It was an era of change, but social progress lagged far behind accelerating technological advances. Hannah Solomon led Council women into programs of aid to destitute immigrant families; promotion of child labor laws and public health regulations; and the furtherance of Jewish education and culture.

Delicate and petite, Hannah Solomon drew on a king-sized reserve of courage and faith. She sought and found ways to serve—but not behind a serving cart, as expected by a society that acknowledged the competence of its "fellow-men" exclusively.

Her place of distinction is assured as a feminist pioneer in history's hall of fame, but she disliked labels and resisted clichés. "Who is this new woman?" she asked at Council's first convention. "She is the woman who dares go into the world and do what her convictions demand."

Hannah Greenebaum Solomon—gentle revolutionary. She defied definitions; broke down barriers; stunned the establishment; and paved the way for a vital, expanded role for Jewish women.

Indeed, into the fabric of this extraordinary life are woven the hopes and aspirations of every woman who dares to do what her convictions demand.

[xii]

FOREWORD AND DEDICATION

WHY DOES ONE WRITE an autobiography? Chiefly for one's children and grandchildren, and it is at the insistence of mine that I begin this chronicle. All grandmothers have a tale to tell, for not only is the world of their youth full of charm and quaintness to succeeding generations, but there is ever a persistent desire on the part of one's young followers to have portrayed for them the life in which their forebears have participated. Then, too, grandchildren possess great faith in their grandmothers, whose wisdom and accomplishments are apt to loom large. On the other hand, have not grandmothers a peculiar insight into the potentialities of their grandchildren? It is the grandmother who oftentimes discovers the embryo of the genius that is to be. Her imagination gallops into space where float the colors of the rainbow ending in the pot of gold, and in her dreams she hears heavenly choirs intoning sweet songs of triumph and success. But, if fame or fortune really comes, it is the grandmother who has learned that the most enduring gratification results not so much from actual attainment as from the work in which there was participation with fellow-men, or in the consecration to and consistent effort toward a noble goal. It is this mature realization that a grandmother desires most yearningly to leave as her special message to those who follow her.

Thus, as I near my eighty-fifth birthday, I find I am glad to review the paths I trod, both for my grandchildren and for my children who have lived through so many of my experiences with me, sharing gladness or sorrow as they came, and the richness of each. I write, then, with a still firm pen, for Frank and Helen Solomon, my son and daughter-in-law, who are a tower of strength to me and whose home is as my own, and for Helen Levy, my beloved daughter, who has been at my side through all her life in perfect and indispensable companionship.

To my five dear grandchildren do I dedicate this book . . . to Betty, Henry and Frank Solomon, and to Frances Hannah and Philip Angel and their small Philip and Henry, my two delightful great-grandsons.

FABRIC OF MY LIFE

PART I

WARP AND WEFT

"Seeking Wool and Flax"

CHAPTER I

WHERE DOES A BIOGRAPHY BEGIN? Does the life story of an individual have its origin in the distant past and is any of that past crystallized in a new-born soul? Do we start our pilgrimage conditioned by patterns already ingrained and will the failures and the successes of an earlier generation and ancient preferences and prejudices play their part? How far do fate and chance mold our behavior and our lives? Is memory to be trusted, or has time, in passing, so obliterated the poignancy of experiences which distressed us or enhanced our joy that we are unable to record them in true proportion? Do we remember clearly those moments when inspiration was born through contact with rich minds; those in which courage was instilled and new insight kindled? Time, in a measure, blots out the tragic and the sorrowful that darken our lives for a space leaving, nonetheless, an irrevocable impress. How especially fortunate that memories of the pleasant recur and stand out in bold relief!

In Chicago, where I have lived eighty-four years, I have known five generations: the pioneers, among whom were numbered the contemporaries of my grandparents as well as of my parents, Michael and Sarah Greenebaum. Then

[3]

followed my own generation, now overtaken by those of my children and grandchildren. My relatives and friends, my city and country, my heredity and the traditions of a foreign nationality and of the Jewish faith sum up the influences that shaped my early life.

To the Jew, whether a voluntary or a forced immigrant, came the old call, "Get thee out of thy country . . . unto a land that I will shew thee." Many, of the pioneers' day, left Europe to escape religious persecution and to find freedom under a democratic form of government with a Bill of Rights as their shield; others departed to seek broader opportunities or to evade army service. All brought with them more than their bodily strength; they brought, in addition, talent and training and, oftentimes, wealth.

My father, Michael Greenebaum, was the first member of his family to come to America, thus paving the way for all who later came from Eppelsheim, a small German village in the Rhine Palatinate, as well as for relatives from far and near. He had reached the age when he was subject to military service. As there was no war at the time, soldiers for the standing army were chosen by lot and Father was fortunate in securing a number that freed him from conscription. My grandfather, Jacob Greenebaum, relates the episode, thus, in a short autobiography he wrote in 1859, at the time of his fortieth wedding anniversary:

"My Michael had learned the tinsmith trade according to his own wish, and he had worked for a time as apprentice after having learned his trade. His year of travel as a journeyman was due to begin as soon as he had completed his twentieth year and had been freed from conscription. Traveling as a journeyman is an absolute necessity for the artisan, without which preparation he would never be regarded as a

[4]

worthy master of his trade. The conscription passed luckily for him. In the meantime, he had planned with two young men, also Israelites, who were on the same train, to emigrate to America if they were freed from conscription. Michael agreed, on condition that his parents gave their consent. All three men really were freed.

"Now Michael revealed his plan to us and bade for our consent, with the promise to return in four or five years. The matter seemed quite feasible as there were then hard times in Germany, and his dear Mother and I saw him, in our thoughts, wandering from city to city with his knapsack on his back. Therefore, we gladly yielded to his wishes, thinking to see him again at home in a few years. Preparations for his departure were begun and, after he had made for me quite a stock of stovepipe, he entered upon his journey in July, 1845. Parting was hard, but the hope of a reunion helped us to bear our sorrow. When we received his first letter, however, we began to relinquish hope of his return, for he wished that one of his brothers would come to him and wrote that it might probably be advantageous for us all to come later, planning emigration for us as a matter of course."

Father remained in New York for about one year. He had not been very well, however, and thinking the climate in the west might prove beneficial, he set out for Chicago where, in 1847, we find his name recorded in Chicago's second city directory. Before Father's arrival there had been but few Jews in Chicago, the first city directory listing but four Jewish names: Benedict Shubart, Philip Newburgh, Isaac Ziegler and Henry Horner whose grandson and namesake became the able and honored Governor of Illinois in 1932.

Delighted with his choice of location, Father immediately recognized its possibilities and wrote back to Eppelsheim an enthusiastic account of this flourishing young city with a population of about twenty thousand which, because of its fortunate position at the head of one of the five Great Lakes was, he felt certain, bound to become one of the leading centers in America.

So it was that in 1847 my father's older brother, Elias, succeeded in persuading his parents to permit him to join Michael "for a few years." Of Elias' departure my grandfather wrote, "We could not resist his pleading despite the fact that we had enlarged our business and needed him very much, especially as we were always tormented by the thought that his brother was alone in a distant country, and we yielded to his wish. In July, 1847, he entered upon his journey and there were again troublous times for us until we received a letter and were assured that both brothers were together. ... Scarcely were the two boys together and settled in Chicago when they wrote that I should send their brother, Henry, with the promise to provide for his further education and to furnish funds for all his studies. This was asked repeatedly, and as I always complied with the wishes of my children insofar as I considered them to their own advantage, we at last fulfilled their request. We therefore took Henry out of school in 1848 and embraced an opportunity to let him travel, in September, with an estimable family from our town, which I would not have permitted if it had not been in the year of the revolution and I thought that this son, too, would be in a safe harbor for the present. As soon as he had taken his departure his dear mother and I began to repent of what we had done, and nothing in the world would have brought us again to this resolve if we could have had him back again. Restless days and sleepless nights now ensued in which our eyes were seldom free from tears. The reproach which my conscience always uttered, to have subjected a youth of fifteen to such dangers, brought me almost to despair. In this condition, we were obliged to wait three whole months until we received his first letter!"

Thus, in 1848, were the three brothers, Michael, Elias and Henry, united in America! 1848 — a notable year in the annals of the Greenebaum family, surely, and one of great historic significance to Chicago, as well. On January fifteenth, the first telegraphic message was transmitted via Milwaukee to Chicago, and on October twenty-fifth, the first locomotive, comprising two cars and a tender, puffed importantly out of the city.

My father was, at that time, a salesman in the hardware business of W. F. Dominick and Uncle Elias had found a position soon after his arrival in the Francis Clarke department store on Lake Street. Henry was to have studied law, but he was so intrigued by the opportunity of immediately entering into commercial life, that he joined my father at Dominick's, instead.

It was in this same eventful year that the Moses Spiegel family came from Abendheim, in Germany, to make their home in New York. Regina, the wife of Moses, was the sister of my grandmother, Sarah Herz Greenebaum, and since Abendheim was not far distant from Eppelsheim, the Spiegel children and their Greenebaum cousins had known one another in Germany. The deep family feeling which was so marked a characteristic of my father, caused him to travel to New York, in the year 1850, to visit with his Spiegel relatives. There, to his delight, he found in his cousin, Sarah, the answer to a perhaps sub-conscious quest. At any rate, the years proved it to be the happiest decision of his life, for he returned to Chicago, bringing Sarah with him as his bride! So, when Grandmother and Grandfather Greenebaum came to America, in 1852, they were welcomed not only by their three devoted sons, but by a new daughter, as well.

My grandfather chronicles his decision to leave Germany in this fashion: "The dear mother yearned for her sons; the children who were still at home, for their brothers. As there could be no further hope of a return and my children would remain separated for all time, some in Europe, some in America, I at last formed the resolve to accede to their wishes and go to America with all of them that they might live together in harmony with united strength. Although my business grew daily, I began in the year 1849 to prepare for departure and took three years to regulate my assets and liabilities. When my project became known, there arose on every side attempts to dissuade me. Everyone spoke of our prosperous condition and disapproved my leaving a safe harbor to go towards an insecure one."

With my grandparents, then, there came to America my father's sisters and brothers, Jacob, Isaac, Hannah (who later became the wife of Gerhard Foreman), Babette (later Mrs. Abram Wise) and David. Uncle Henry had returned to Eppelsheim to bring the family over, and Grandfather tells us that "Henry arrived after a perilous journey. The Captain became insane during the journey and the ship was nearly wrecked, but through the help of Providence it was discovered in time to avert the threatening danger and Henry arrived safely at our home." Of the family hegira he wrote, "The beginning of July, 1852, we bade farewell to our old home ... The sea voyage lasted thirty-eight days and was, on the whole, an agreeable one. There were three hundred and

[8]

fifty passengers of the boat, among them about seventy Israelites." The daily occurrences of the voyage were noted in a ship's journal edited by Jacob, Henry and their friend, Guttman, and contained, according to Grandfather, "some comic incidents and may be read to this day by anyone interested." Obviously, the Greenebaum urge to write was present in all generations!

Grandfather once said, "It may be seen that there was no necessity for emigration, in our case. Neither struggle for our existence nor anything that displeased us in our old home was the motive for this step." Later, however, he added this significant statement, "Although I enjoyed much there of which I am deprived, here, I have never for a moment desired to return!"

CHAPTER II

How well I remember our grandparents when, in later years, they lived on Hubbard Street! Their children had all married and Greenebaums occupied nearly the entire block of green-shuttered frame houses with surrounding gardens. We Michael Greenebaums dwelt on Union Street and there was, daily, a coming and going of grandmothers, grandfathers, aunts, uncles and cousins, all of whom had followed my father to Chicago. In fact, it was at his advice that many of them left their homes in Europe to come to the America they loved and where they prospered. There were Uncle Jacob and Aunt Hannah with their trio, Harry, Milton and Lina; Uncle Henry and Aunt Emily who, though childless, were like beloved second parents to a host of adoring boys and girls; Uncle Isaac and Aunt Matilda. All of those relatives were united by the closest family ties and their deep devotion to one another lasted throughout their lives. It was a firmly knit group and each shared to the full in the others' joys and sorrows, as was generally true with pioneer families who had left their childhood homes to establish themselves in America. So, there was reassembled in Chicago, a new population unit — the clan of Greenebaum.

Our name, Greenebaum, is said to have been acquired

at the beginning of the nineteenth century when, in 1805, by the decree of Napoleon, the Jews were ordered to take surnames. My grandfather's father, who was then the head of the family, adopted the name, "Gruenebaum" (green tree), suggested by the green tree painted upon a shield adorning the sign of an inn belonging to an ancestor. My grandmother's family name was Felsenthal, meaning hills and valley, and described the region in which they lived, where "high cliffs towered above the valley." Where my mother's name, Spiegel, originated, I do not know.

The house in which I was born, in 1858, was situated on the first land purchased by my father. The property was on the corner of Union Street, with about one hundred feet fronting on Randolph Street and extended to the next corner. Here, in one of the four dwellings my father owned, lived our cousins, the Beckers, while a frame cottage on the Union Street side was occupied by our relatives, the Harts, who had also come to Chicago from Eppelsheim, in the wake of the Greenebaums.

On the north corner of his property my father built our comfortable home. The dining room, on the first floor, extended across the entire width of the house, with the table placed near the windows at one side so that the rest of the space might serve as an ample playroom. In the basement there was a furnace — a rare possession in those days — but it was seldom used, as the house was well equipped with stoves, then more generally in vogue. The second-floor bedrooms were unheated, but all opened into a wide hall in which stood one of the stoves, and here we sisters, Theresa, Henriette, Mary and I would dress when we arose in winter. Each cold morning the windows were heavily frosted, but we all slept under feather beds and never knew that it was frigid. Our bedtime was six o'clock and before retiring we were lined up while each was given a tablespoonful of cod liver oil, followed by a piece of rock candy. Why is it, I wonder, that no modern confection, however delectable, quite equals in gustatory bliss the remembered delight of that rock candy? Afternoon coffee was an established custom, and if any of the children were at home they, too, were served, and not one suffered from insomnia!

We four sisters shared a room, Theresa and Henriette in one bed, Mary and I in the other. Each wide bed was placed before a large window, with bureau and mirror between. Here, in our room, we played our favorite games of 'school' and 'Indians'. Indians still lived near the west side of Chicago and occasionally they walked on Randolph Street, always in single file and wearing leather clothes with blankets over their shoulders. They fascinated us and we were never afraid of them. Indeed, we were brought up to be without fear of anything.

Randolph was the chief business street of the West Side. The section near us extended from Desplaines to Halsted Street and was known as The Haymarket — the same Haymarket which later became so important in Chicago history as a landmark in city labor situations, for here took place, on May 4, 1886, the famous Haymarket riot, at which a bomb was thrown and several policemen were killed.

We were not permitted to cross Randolph Street, which was very wide, unless we were accompanied by an older person. To us it seemed quite a thoroughfare and we saw its first cedar blocks take the place of the deep mud which formed the original roadway for Chicago vehicles. Later, when streets were being graded and the sidewalks raised, there was a continual going up and down stairs in the climb from one level to the other. One incident lingers reminiscently in my memory. On Union Street, the wooden planks were being laid several feet above the earlier ones. My sister Mary, always brimful of ideas, suggested to our cousin Viola Becker and me that we attempt to walk the planks all the way to our house, keeping our eyes shut tight. Unfortunately, our ringleader, Mary, miscalculated and lost her footing, and with a banshee shriek toppled over into the dirty, water-filled ditch that ran along the sidewalk. One of our uncles heard the outcry and recognizing its familiar ring, dashed out of his store, jumped down and fished out the dripping, grimy Mary, who indignantly accused us of the treachery of "peeking"; for how else, she reasoned, could we have avoided a similar dousing? It was years before we could convince her that we escaped only because she, the heroine, fell first! A warm bath and some hot milk soon restored Mary to her normal cheeriness, despite her misadventure, but after that experience we avoided the ditches except when they were frozen, in winter, and we took our first skating lessons on them, proudly wearing the ice-skates we each received upon reaching the impressive age of six.

Mary was as undaunted as she was resourceful, however, and found innumerable ways of entertaining herself, sometimes, alas, at the expense of others! She was only five years old when she invented a new game for herself which, though of short duration, she thoroughly enjoyed. She tossed her sunbonnet on top of a high shed and when it did not roll back to the ground she wept piteously for the benefit of a chance passer-by. First on the scene was a sympathetic lady who nobly and laboriously climbed up to rescue the bonnet before continuing on her way. This performance so delighted Mary that the bonnet was sent up again, for other helpful persons to retrieve. Unfortunately, our father soon came along! He witnessed Mary's game from a distance, then tiptoed softly up behind her and inquired in dulcet tones, "Little girl, shall *I* get your sunbonnet for you?" The "little girl" did not wait to respond, but flew home in what proved to be a vain endeavor to escape the painful aftermath of her mischievousness!

My sister Henriette, too, was ingenious beyond her years! Uncle Jacob was particularly devoted to Theresa, or Tress, as we called her, and promised to "wait for her until she grew up" to marry her. (I believe that all of us had similar promises made to us by faithless men before we were five years old.) Uncle Jacob bought Tress a lovely silk dress and a gold ring — a serpent rounded into a circlet, in the popular fashion of the day. Henriette was much enamoured of these riches, and when Grandfather Spiegel came to see us, later in the day, she complained to him, "Grandpa, I am so very poor! I have no silk dress and no ring with a tail!" Needless to say, her poverty-stricken state was remedied most speedily! I have reason to remember Tress' dress well, because it descended to Mary and later, when she outgrew it, I became heir to the same garment — the first of many hand-me-downs I can recall. Tress and Henriette were always dressed alike, as were Mary and I, and often, after the elder sisters outgrew articles of apparel before they had done sufficient service, they were passed down to us. Sewing was done in the home for all small members of the family and a dressmaker and seamstress were employed regularly, to make most of the children's clothes, boys' blouses as well as girls' attire.

One might dwell long upon the fashions of that day! One of my then most cherished hats was a leghorn with such a wide, floppy brim that an elastic, which I held in my hand, was sewn to the center of the front edge to prevent it from flying away in the breeze. How styles change ... without improving! What is "chic" in one decade is fantastic in the next! Our grandmothers, too, took account of the weather, and when they went out on rainy days they wore elastic bands buckled about their hips, through which they pulled their trailing skirts in order to prevent them from touching the ground. But, of course, they *never* exposed their ankles! Dear me, no!

As I look back, it seems to me that, in my youth, a grandmother was a beloved member of nearly every household. This was true, perhaps, because that was before the time when thousands of grandmothers lived in hotels and constituted a large part of the tourist armies invading Europe and other portions of the globe. They aided in the daily home tasks and were highly esteemed by the children of the family. Respect for elders was taken for granted and such a thing as questioning the absolute rights of parents was reserved for a later generation.

Parents had real jobs at that time, and large families provided fathers with serious business days, while mothers knew, and expected, no union hours. Married couples were partners in home-building, with the father the undisputed "head of the family" and the mother the supervisor and worker in the home. Such partnerships existed even though, as frequently happened, husband and wife had been brought together, originally, in a most impersonal manner. In the immigrant communities a man might be told, "I know just the wife for you!" An introduction followed, and after a short courtship a marriage was arranged. The girl's parents usually made the decision, sometimes with a professional marriage broker participating in the transaction, and the young couple "lived happily ever after" — almost always!

In our house on Union Street there were, in addition to the immediate family, a sturdy maid-of-all-work and a nursegirl who helped with the children. The nursegirl told us the most fantastic fairy tales, specializing in those of particularly gruesome qualities, full of witches, goblins, wicked stepmothers and fiendish monsters. To these we listened in amazement, but none of us batted an eye, deciding among ourselves that the poor thing simply didn't know any better. Our nursegirl's mother was the "Shabbos goya" — a necessary adjunct to every Jewish household at that time. It was her duty to come on the Sabbath, to light the fires and do such chores as the day of rest prohibited the members of a Jewish family from performing. All Jewish homes were strictly kosher in my childhood, and no one, however radical, would dream of questioning the custom in those days.

One of the most memorable incidents of that time was a visit from our Ohio relatives, when Uncle Marcus and Aunt Caroline Spiegel came with their four children, to spend the summer with us. This period of happy companionship so impressed itself upon our childish minds that a long, long time elapsed before we ceased referring to it as "two years ago." This early visit, punctuated with the most amusing games and hilarity, cemented a lifelong friendship between the children of the two families, and when the Marcus Spiegels settled in Chicago, a few years later, we became inseparable. It marked, in fact, the beginning of the close association and devotion of the eldest daughter, Lizzie, and myself who, ever afterward, played and worked together in complete harmony and understanding, each relying with utmost confidence upon the other.

Lizzie's father, Colonel Marcus Spiegel, was one of the first Union volunteers of the Civil War. He was wounded at Vicksburg, in 1863, and was brought through Chicago, on his way home. I can distinctly recall the dramatic scene when he was carried into our dining room on a stretcher, and how the doctor made him rest there, without speaking, before he was taken to the train which would transport him to his home in Ohio. He recovered from his injury only to return to his post where, some months later, he was killed in action.

It was in 1864 that I first became aware of politics, as we children listened, with interest, to the slogans of the National political parties. I especially remember the one that began, "Lincoln on a white horse, McClellan on a mule ... " And how dreadful and awe-inspiring was the grim day when Lincoln was shot and the entire neighborhood, regardless of political belief, was plunged into grief! My mother made black-and-white draperies for the front windows of our house and I shall never forget the atmosphere of gloom pervading the city though I was then too young to realize its implications.

Years later I heard the story of the contest between Abraham Lincoln and Stephen A. Douglas for the senatorship of Illinois, as well as tales of Lincoln and his candidacy for President. My father knew and greatly admired Douglas, who was a close personal friend of Uncle Henry Greenebaum. Lincoln, too, was a friend of Uncle Henry, who later became the Civil War President's staunch follower. Years later, when our third generation was old enough to appreciate Lincoln, we gathered all the children together in our home on Michigan Avenue, to hear Uncle Henry tell his great-nieces and nephews of his friendship with President Lincoln, and how he had requested Uncle Henry to be present at the station when he left Springfield to take up his residence in Washington. Despite the many years which had passed, there were tears in Uncle Henry's eyes as he told of the beauty of the historic speech delivered by President Lincoln from the train platform on that memorable day.

Although I have only a vague recollection of the Civil War, I clearly remember hearing my father speak of slavery and denouncing it. He disliked any defiance of established law, but had an equally firm conviction of man's right to personal freedom; a conflict that once, at least, might have had troublesome repercussions. Here is the story, quoted from Madison Peters' book, Justice to the Jew: "As early as 1853, a fugitive negro arrested by a United States Marshal was liberated by a crowd of citizens, led by Michael Greenebaum, and on the evening of the same day, a mass meeting was held to ratify the act." Father was an exceedingly strong man and had started to batter down the door of the jail in which the negro was confined. A crowd soon gathered and rallied to Father's support, freeing the negro from captivity.

That Father was a member of "Engine Number One" of the volunteer fire department, in those early Chicago days, stirred the imaginations of his grandchildren, most of whom, in their young years, knew the last word in horse-drawn hook-and-ladder and puffing hose-cart. Now, both horse-drawn and man-drawn types are Chicago Historical Museum exhibits, appearing to boys and girls of today more like toys than genuine fire-fighting equipment.

Nevertheless, even in our formative years, we children of Sarah and Michael Greenebaum were unconsciously affected by their spirit of joyous citizenship in a beloved country whose reverse side, our parents never forgot, imposed civic obligation.

CHAPTER III

IN 1864, AFTER THE BIRTHS OF MY BROTHERS, Mose and
Henry, Father sold our Union Street house, and the family moved to Chicago's south side, to the corner of Fourth
Avenue and Polk Street. We lived near the Jones School and
there, in the circular room on the top floor of the building,
I began my education. My most vivid Jones School recollection goes back to the day when one of the older boys proudly
bore a flag through our schoolroom on his way to the roof,
where it was to be raised to celebrate the taking of Vicksburg.
I remember, too, that we school children were taken to the
Sanitary Fair — a huge bazaar organized by Chicago women
to raise money for the care of our Civil War soldiers. This
was my first exposition experience, but I must have enjoyed
it, if the long list of those I attended, subsequently, is any
criterion!

Though we remained on the South Side for only two years,
that period is marked by an unforgettable occurrence! My
brother, Henry, then but four years old, wandered away from
home, and a thorough search of the entire neighborhood
failed to locate him. How awe-stricken we were when Father
then employed a "crier"— a man who, with his little dog,
walked block after block, from corner to corner. He rang a

bell to attract attention, and cried out, "Child lost! Child lost!" Then he proceeded to describe, in grisly detail, the child and his clothes. He finally succeeded in locating Henry, who had fallen asleep on a doorstep and been carried into the house by a woman who lived there and who, strangely enough, proved to be one of our former maids! Henry slept soundly as he was borne triumphantly homeward, and when he awakened his only plaint was, "I want my supper!" Obviously, for him, the experience was not as harrowing as for the rest of the family.

When, in 1866, the West Side again beckoned my parents, we went once more to dwell on Randolph Street. Here, my brothers, Gus and Ben were born. We were now a family of goodly proportions, needing plenty of room in which to grow. My father, accordingly, purchased a new house on Adams and Morgan Streets — a home which, ever after in the annals of the Greenebaum family, has been known as "the Adams Street house". Here, our little sister, Helen, was born in January, 1868, and here, too, the arrival of the baby, Rose, in 1870, completed our family circle, bringing the number of children to a good round ten! Theresa, Henriette, Mary and I, Mose, Henry, Gus, Ben, Helen and Rose! Babies, in those days, were a special brand of surprise and a variety of fairy tales accounted for their arrival. Mary, with her usual competence, somewhat prepared me for the event of Rose's birth, however, by taking me into Mother's room and showing me a big feather-bed on the top shelf of the closet, with the statement, "See that feather-bed? Well, whenever it comes down from the storeroom, it means we're going to have a new baby!" Our small brothers and sisters were highly prized and, after a few months, when they began to develop real personalities, became members of the clan with which to reckon.

"Children are a heritage of the Lord"

(Left to right; standing) . . . Mose, Henry, Henriette, Theresa, Mary, Gus
(Seated) . . . Ben, Father, Hannah, Rose, Mother, Helen

Our substantial red brick house on Adams Street stands out pre-eminently in our memories and was the scene of a joyous procession of experiences for many years. It was spacious and comfortable, for Father had become a prosperous hardware merchant, able to provide all that a family of ten children could require. One of the most important demands of well-adjusted children was plenty of room for company, and accordingly, the Adams Street latchstring always "hung out." Mother and Father never failed to extend a most cordial welcome to all our friends and our dining table was seldom surrounded only by members of the family. Mother always managed to have enough food on hand to provide for any number of "droppers-inners" and there was, at all times, an extra fowl roasted and cooling in the larder so that, as someone once remarked, 'At Greenebaum's, those who come late get chicken!''

Mother was a remarkable mater familias, yet, in spite of her many home duties, she found time to befriend all who needed her. In 1883, she called together a group of women to form Chicago's first Jewish Ladies Sewing Society, where they made garments for the poor and aided the unfortunate. It was a source of deep gratification to us that Mother's ability and quality of leadership were recognized and honored when a sister branch of the Jochannah was organized in 1907, and named Sarah Greenebaum Lodge.

Strength and gallantry were outstanding characteristics of my mother, yet she had a natural buoyancy of spirit and a gift of quaint expression that made her evaluations unique. She met life courageously at every turn, and to this day we quote the many original sayings — so wise or so witty — with which she habitually punctuated her conversation. Once, when we were discussing the vicissitudes of life, she said,

"One must never allow conditions to master him; he must always master them." At another time, she remarked, "The good Lord should not bring us all we can bear!" Not mere expressions, these, but phrases which embodied the philosophy by which she lived.

In the Greenebaum family, anything and everything called for a "party"! Upon the slightest provocation — or none at all — the clan would gather for a celebration. As I look back through the years, I realize how firmly that pattern was set, for from our earliest youth, we were never happier than when we, with our parents, relatives and friends, embarked upon some simple but thoroughly enjoyable adventure. Family picnics, particularly, were highspots of our summer vacations. How eagerly we scanned the skies as we awoke, and with what joy we greeted the sun that augured well for a bright, clear day. Huge hampers would be filled with hearty goodies, and then the entire family would swarm into the carriages in which we would ride out to the woods or pleasant open places which surrounded Chicago, "the Garden City", as it was then called. One especially eventful Sunday picnic comes to my mind when, in two carriages driven by Father and Uncle Isaac, respectively, we set out for Lincoln Park, in Lake View, then well outside the city limits. There had been a heavy rain the day before, and as we neared our destination, our carriage, weighted down with Greenebaums of all ages, sank deep into the mud of the unpaved road. What a dismal groan arose as we felt ourselves sinking lower and lower, until the wheels were rutted in mire almost to the hubs! For almost an hour the men of our party struggled to free us, with the aid of sturdy planks which they put under the wheels, and finally, with much pushing and pulling and grunting, egged on by plenty of encouragement from the "back-seat drivers", we emerged. Just at that very minute, Father — always the most considerate of men — saw another carriage approaching. Without a thought for himself or the snowy white linen suit he was wearing, he ran to warn the newcomers, so that they might avoid our misfortune. He succeeded in heading them off, but not before he, himself, sank into mud to the knees! How we unsympathetic youngsters laughed to see our usually immaculate father in a state all too familiar to the small members of the family. Fortunately, Father joined in the merriment, and no one was gayer than he as we dined, al fresco, in a nearby vacant lot, accepting philosophically that substitute for Lincoln Park.

In the winter, one of our favorite forms of diversion was sleighing, then so much in vogue. The large bob-sled used in Father's business, by day, would be filled with our friends, on bright moonlight nights, as we embarked upon long, jolly rides. The bottom of the sleigh would be covered with hay and we bundled ourselves up in our heaviest clothing with thick robes of fur and wool as further protection from the blasts of Chicago's chilling winds.

But always, throughout our lives, the home pleasures have lingered most tenderly in our memories. In about 1867 we acquired the piano which became, virtually, a member of the family, and ever after, as we children learned to play and music assumed an increasing importance in our household, it proved to be a most treasured adjunct to the home.

The festivities incident to the observance of the Jewish holidays were looked forward to with great eagerness, from year to year: in December, the feast of the Maccabees, which we celebrated with the burning of the Chanukah lights; Purim, in the springtime, brought its merry pranks and masquerading, in commemoration of Queen Esther and the destruction of Haman; and Pesach — the Passover — with its Seder service was especially loved! Jewish home festivals were solemnized thoughtfully, indeed, and woe to the child whose decorum failed to measure up to standard! To Jews who came from lands where the hand of the oppressor still palled, these observances were of tremendous significance and importance and the home, as well as the synagogue, was a center of religious life.

At the same time, the synagogue shared in the secular life. In connection with Zion Temple, there was a school to which many of the Jewish children were sent in preference to public school. Mary and I, Mose and Henry, all attended for a time. The services in the synagogue were conducted in German and Hebrew and so these languages were made part of the school's curriculum. As there were only six or seven grades, many of the pupils who attended went on to public school for further instruction when the course of study at Zion was completed. Tress and Henriette were already too advanced in their studies for attendance at Zion and so, in 1867, after a year or two in public school, it was decided that they be sent abroad to complete their schooling. Father, always progressive, believed that girls, as well as boys, should be given educational advantages, and since his faith in a German education was unbounded, Tress and Henriette were permitted to enter the Jewish boarding school conducted by the Misses Loewenthal and Blum, in Frankfort-on-the-Main. Here they received a thorough continental education in a course of studies that included languages, music and sewing as well as history, geography, Greek mythology and German literature. Henriette, who was especially gifted in music, was provided with the finest teachers in Germany, and returned home a most accomplished musician.

In 1869, Father took Mary to Europe, to enter her in the school in Germany which the two older sisters attended, and when he returned he brought Tress home with him, where she immediately assumed charge of the younger children, becoming Mother's most dependable assistant.

Mary's departure deprived me of the sister whose constant companionship began in infancy. What did I not owe to her interest in my education! When the Washington Street tunnel was completed, in 1869, she took me through it — neglecting, in her own inimitable way, to mention the excursion to our family whose anxiety regarding our whereabouts mounted higher and higher during our absence. Upon our return home, she was dumbfounded to learn our elders had been alarmed, and in response to their concerned questioning said that she thought they, too, would realize how important it was for Hannah to see the tunnel right away! Another time, she piloted me to the top of the Court House with the excuse, on this occasion, that "Hannah had never before had the opportunity of visiting the building." Surely, without her, I might well have missed many of the highspots of early Chicago!

I continued attending the Skinner Grammar School after Mary's departure for Germany, graduating in 1871. I preferred an American education to study abroad, electing to learn Latin and mathematics rather than modern languages. On Monroe Street, between Halsted and Desplaines, was West Division, Chicago's only high school, which was entirely adequate at that time, since many children carried their formal education no further than eighth grade. Only a high school course was required for those wishing to embark upon a teaching career, and boys planning to engage in the professions began their specialized studies immediately upon completion of four years high school training. Comparatively few went to college.

My introduction to West Division High School is indelibly impressed upon my memory because of the frightful tragedy that swept Chicago at almost the same time. Little did I dream, as I prepared my lessons just a few hours before, that the Chicago Fire, on October 9, 1871, would prove so grim a test of the courage of Chicago pioneers! It was a gruelling experience for every inhabitant of the city, and although we lived outside the devastated area, we — along with all our neighbors — shared in the terror and heartache it brought in its wake. All through the night we stood at the windows and watched the flames and smoke; all of us fully dressed so that we might be ready to flee to the prairies if the fire came our way. All citizens aided valiantly in protecting people and their possessions, and officials and police were tireless in their staunch efforts to be of service wherever and whenever needed. Our house was thrown open and filled to capacity, thus providing lodging to many persons whose homes were gone, and every room was piled high with the possessions of others, as were our yard, barn and shed.

The desolation of the city after the conflagration was almost as numbing as the fire itself, and it was some time before normal living could be resumed. Throughout the demolished district temporary shacks were erected for business firms and, little by little, in a new Chicago, old wooden structures were supplanted by sturdier ones of stone and brick. The fortitude and resilience of the Chicagoans who suffered such terrifying dangers and losses at that time can never be described adequately, but their spirit still serves as inspiration for many of us who have been called upon to face experiences stoically.

As the city was rebuilt, the playhouses on the West Side

were reopened, and favorite Saturday treats were the exciting melodramas and light plays presented at the Globe Theater, located on Desplaines Street, in the building which earlier had housed the Zion Temple. To this day I still see Kate Field, tied to her horse, in "Mazeppa", and bethink myself of how I thrilled to her joys and chilled to her woes! The curtain of the Globe Theater bore these words: "Westward the Course of Empire Takes Its Flight"— a sentence that impressed me profoundly, and which I interpreted to mean that the Jews would continue going west until they reached Palestine. So it is clear that in my very young years, at least, I was a Zionist, albeit unwittingly.

The theaters of that day had excellent stock companies, worthy of supporting the great and famous stars who came to play the leading roles. Shakespearean plays were prime favorites. The performance of As You Like It, I saw in 1873, with Adelaide Neilson as Rosalind and James O'Neil as Orlando was brilliant and unforgettable — a glorious introduction to the works of the English bard. For my sixteenth birthday I was taken to hear my first opera, Les Huguenots, with Christine Nillson, the renowned Swedish prima donna and my delight was unbounded when, entre acte, was produced an exquisite ballet dance — the first I had ever seen! In retrospect, I realize that Mother and Tress, who accompanied me, were — in the approved attitude of the day — more than a little perturbed at my witnessing so "daring" a performance!

When Henriette returned from Europe, in 1871, she brought with her copies of many of the great German classics. The following year Mary, too, returned bringing still more books, and we had a grand time over the plays and stories. Mary read Hauff's tales aloud to me, and how we enjoyed them, replete as they were with the doings of the Devil and his grandmother! Later, a French teacher was added to my tutors, and I studied until I could master the French novels by myself. My, but we took them seriously ... those books of Dickens, Thackery, Scott, Emerson, Oliver Wendell Holmes, Carlyle and George Elliot (and if we ever "skipped" a few pages of description or philosophic musing, you may be sure we didn't admit it, even to ourselves!) The study of history held first place in my interest and I enjoyed, especially, Macaulay's History of England and the biographies of historic characters in his essays. But I was wholesomely undiscriminating and indulged most freely in reading *everything* I could find, literary or otherwise, including The Fireside Companion—the "pulp" magazine of the day — which I bought every week during my youthful years, Almanacs full of witticisms, the novels of Mary Holmes and Miss Evans, as well as the really fine works of distinguished writers. There were not so many extraneous distractions for girls of that time, and the romance and thrills provided by the motion pictures of today came to us from between the covers of popular books of the moment which, in our naivete, seemed simply breath-taking in their excitement and colorfulness.

CHAPTER IV

IT WAS A FRUITFUL MOMENT for the traditional questioning of an adolescent.

Important and rapid were the changes in thought that occurred during the period of the pioneers and their children. Up to this time, philosophy, science and religious interpretation had been reserved for clergymen, rabbis and scholars and the result of their study and research was received and accepted without question by their followers. Piety was founded upon an accepted Faith in the Universe and its Creator and Ruler, rather than upon the personal conviction of a layman and science was considered authentic only if it agreed with religious belief. Later, with a more general knowledge of the laws of evolution, a new attitude developed. Sciences were then judged on their own merits and religion was no longer the yardstick by which were measured their truth or value.

Religious disagreements also existed between the various sects of Protestants, as well as between Catholics and Protestants or Jews and Christians. The rift between Christian sects was wide, though the points at issue were based largely upon some specific detail, rather than fundamental religious tenets. As the study of Biblical criticism and of comparative

[29]

religions became more general, however, a new understanding emerged. In this the sciences, too, played a part, contributing toward the development of a kindlier spirit. Respect and appreciation, though by no means universal, slowly replaced many prejudices. Nevertheless, since the social life of that day centered largely around the church, Catholic and Protestant groups mingled but little and the Jews, with few exceptions, formed their associations among their own people. In our younger years, our social contacts were entirely with Jewish girls and boys, but when we began attending public schools we found congenial companions among the families of other faiths, many of whom have remained our friends through the years.

When the children of the Jewish pioneers started to attend public schools, English soon replaced German in the homes and, some time later, in the synagogue as well, to the point where a third generation scarcely realized that German ever had been used in religious services. Many national groups, however, remained loyal to their native lands, and it was taken for granted that this should be so. The name of a mother country was given to many enterprises by men who were most devoted to the United States, and who loved its form of government. Banks were known by such titles as Scotch, Hibernian or German; societies like the early musical associations also followed this practice and many were named for similar organizations existing abroad. As long as the laws were respected and local customs not neglected, no one objected to this carrying over of old-world atmosphere. A conflict did occur, however, when the Germans, who represented about one-sixth of Chicago's population, wished the right to keep their beer-gardens open on Sunday. The English-American heartily disliked what was known as a "Continental

Sunday", and a serious controversy arose. Uncle Henry Greenebaum, who was a very prominent citizen, was named spokesman for the Germans, and finally succeeded in winning permission to enjoy the gardens and halls on every day of the week.

Our family belonged to the Reform Jewish group, for my father was most progressive — even radical in many ways. One of his strongest convictions was the importance of adapting religion to the needs and welfare of the people, and long before they were actually adopted, he advocated Sunday services so that men who were occupied with business on Saturday could have the benefits of the teachings of the pulpit. I remember a discussion he had on the subject, with Mother, who asked him, "Would you do such a thing to your old Mother as to change the day of the Sabbath?" This was a powerful point, at a time when honoring father and mother implied a life-long duty and old customs were frequently retained out of deference to parents, despite one's own earnest convictions. Reform congregations, however, continued the Saturday services even after Sunday morning worship was introduced.

Father also urged that the Prayer Book be translated into English. Made up of portions of the Bible, of traditional prayers from older works, poems from Jewish literature, as well as original lessons, the early Prayer Book was written in Hebrew, which was readily understood by practically all of the pioneer Jewish group. It took much persuasion to have the English substitution made, but once translated, it spread rapidly to all Reform congregations and soon even the more Conservative synagogues, in other countries, adopted their own languages for services.

In the early days, there were no choirs in the synagogues,

and prayers were chanted by a cantor. Men followed the prescribed practice of wearing their hats and the talith at services, and continued to use phylacteries for prayers in the home. Though the Reform Jews omitted many of the traditional customs, never did they discard the recital of the Kaddish, a prayer in praise of the Creator, repeated for a year after death by mourners in memory of departed members of the family. Even the most lax in synagogue attendance continued this rite, though the observance sometimes consisted merely in arriving in time for the Kaddish and departing immediately thereafter! The celebration of the Barmitzvah for a boy upon reaching the age of thirteen was general, too. In honor of this event, the youth was privileged to read a portion of the Temple service on the Sabbath Day, and the occasion was both important and impressive. The boy was then considered eligible to be a member of the congregation and to be reckoned one of the ten men necessary for a religious service. Needless to say, girls and women were never permitted to count among the required ten. Later, in Reform temples, upon completion of the Sabbath School course, confirmation was adopted for the boys, in place of the Barmitzvah, and for the girls, as well.

The attitude of even the most Reform Jews was that of the Fundamentalists as far as the Five Books of Moses was concerned. The Creator was a positive Personality who had inspired Moses to give the Ten Commandments as the Divine Law for all men. God had no stepchildren; all, alike, were in His keeping, but to no group had He shown more favors than to the Jews whom He had saved, time and again, from their enemies.

To Jews in a strange land the need to worship together was a vital one. For the observance of the Day of Atonement in the fall of 1845, it was barely possible to recruit, in Chicago, the ten men traditionally required for the holding of Jewish public services. Two years later, however, there were twenty who were ready and eager to establish Chicago's first Jewish congregation, Kehileth Anshe Ma'ariv (Congregation of the Men of the West). By 1855 it was a firmly established Temple which my grandfather, Jacob Greenebaum, was chosen to represent at a convention of Jewish congregations, in Cleveland, Ohio. It was there that a resolution was adopted which declared the ordinances and practices laid down in the Talmud binding upon American Jews. How my grandfather voted upon this resolution, I was never told, but I do know that his sons belonged to a small group of men who were extremely liberal for their time, and for whom such a pronouncement could not hold. A story is told of Uncle Henry's declaration to his father one day, that he intended to remove his hat at Temple services the following Friday evening — a procedure hitherto unheard of! My grandfather was horrified, but was unable to dissuade Uncle Henry from his revolutionary purpose. However, history has it that, a few weeks later, my grandfather, too, removed his hat for services.

In 1858, Dr. Bernard Felsenthal came to live in Chicago, and under his leadership, a group of men who had veered from orthodoxy, organized a Jewish Reform Society (Judische Reformverein) in which they discussed, with ardor and conviction, changes in religious belief and attitude. In 1860, Reform was made an issue at the annual meeting of the Temple, Kehileth Anshe Ma'ariv (K.A.M.) to which they all belonged. My father was among the officers elected, all of whom were of the Reform group. Under protest, an organ was purchased for the Temple, and a committee was appointed to consider changes in the wording of the ritual for the serv-

[33]

ices, with — as might well be imagined — highly emotional reactions on both sides. The committee, however, brought back as its report a recommendation that, since there were many in the congregation to whom a break with orthodoxy would bring real distress, the Reform group should resign and organize a new congregation. This course was agreed upon. On June 20, 1861, Reform Judaism, in Chicago, was officially born. Sinai Congregation was incorporated, with Dr. Felsenthal as its first rabbi. One of the controversial differences was settled without argument, thanks to a dramatic journey made by my father and Uncle Henry, in the dead of the night. They drove up to K.A.M., with a horse and wagon, and removed the organ to the new Temple, and music, thenceforth, became an integral part of the revised ritual.

CHAPTER V

M Y GRANDPARENTS CELEBRATED their golden wedding anniversary in 1868, with a tremendous affair given at the Concordia, then the most popular Jewish social club, of which Uncle Henry was a founder, as well as its first president. All of the pioneer Jewish families of the community were invited, as well as many friends and relatives from other cities, all of whom joined enthusiastically with the children and grandchildren of the family in the celebration. It was, indeed, a most memorable occasion, beginning with a dinner at two-thirty in the afternoon, and the festivities continued until late into the night. Grandmother was lovely in a gown of rustling taffeta silk, made in the style she always wore, with very full skirt and short waist adorned with a beautiful lace collar. The inner sleeves, of filmy tulle, were edged with lace, for that was the period when white inner sleeves were a fashionable adjunct to all elegant silken costumes. Everyone agreed that Grandmother was exquisitely gowned and perfectly accoutred but, to my youthful eyes, the piece de resistance was the exquisite snuff-box, intricately wrought in carnelian set in gold which each grandparent carried — and used! No jewelled compact or flashing lipstick or novel accessory, now in vogue, has ever impressed me so forcibly, and I longed for the day when I, too, might indulge in so adult a habit. Needless to say, though adulthood came, in the usual course of events, my ideas of "grandeur" changed with the times, and so hasten to acknowledge that the snuff habit is one I acquired only in those childish thoughts. The use of snuff was a custom probably adopted at the time of my grandparents' marriage, when Napoleon was master of their country, and ante-dated the cigarette habit of later generations.

It was a source of deep satisfaction to my parents that the golden anniversary was so joyously celebrated, for just two years later, in 1870, Grandfather Greenebaum died. He had been held in high esteem in the community, and I can remember how moving and impressive was the tolling of the Court House bell as his funeral procession passed.

The autobiography he had written for his children, and which was later translated into English by my sister Henriette, ended with these words: "You can also gather from this narrative, with what care we brought you up and nurtured you, and with what exertions and even privations we provided for your education, as far as our circumstances permitted. And finally, that you might not be separated on different continents, and only for this reason, we took the perilous journey to America. For all this I demanded nothing of you except unity among yourselves . . . Therefore, follow my admonition . . . it is the only one I recommend to you. I do not know how long it will be vouchsafed me to call your attention thereto, but when my last hour strikes, and the power of speech fails me, this will be my last thought."

Surely this message, fraught with the most perfect parental devotion, carried on through generations after, for Grandfather's "admonition" in which he "demanded nothing . . .

except unity among yourselves" has ever been exemplified in our Greenebaum family life.

The beautiful and ever-present examples of marriage set by both our parents and grandparents were, perhaps, responsible in a measure for the fact that romance budded early in our home on Adams Street. It swept through the family like a welcome contagion, and all of us, with the exception of the youngest brother and sister, Ben and Rose, left it for homes of our own. In 1873, our beloved Tress was married to Marx Lesem after the only two months in which our whole family had dwelt together under one roof, and in May of the same year, Henriette became the wife of Henry L. Frank.

Scarcely had we recovered from the excitement attendant upon the weddings when our household was diminished still further, and Henry and Mose were sent abroad, to school in Heidelberg. Meantime, I had become engrossed in my musical studies and time was entirely too inadequate for me to accomplish all I wished. So, after two years at High School, when I was given the choice of going to Germany or continuing my studies at home, I asked that I be permitted to leave school in order to devote more time to my piano. My parents consented, and arranged for me to take lessons from Carl Wolfsohn, a remarkably fine piano teacher but recently arrived in Chicago. Mr. Wolfsohn's star pupil, at the time, was none other than Fannie Bloomfield, whose magnificent piano artistry was developed under his guidance and who, later, became the greatest woman pianist of her day — Fannie Bloomfield Zeisler.

Though never aspiring to such heights, myself, I nonetheless devoted three hours a day to practicing, performed in public at Mr. Wolfsohn's frequent student recitals and accompanied many young violinists, cellists and singers.

George Upton, in his biography of Theodore Thomas, Chicago's first great orchestra leader, wrote a most interesting history of musical development in Chicago, which local musicians will find enlightening from many standpoints, and in which he pays tribute to Mr. Wolfsohn and his whole-hearted efforts to make Chicago a musical center.

Music was just then beginning to assume importance in Chicago, and an early edition of The Chicago Tribune announced the coming of "Theodore Thomas and His Troupe".

Thomas concerts were presented with great regularity throughout the summers, in the old Exposition Building which stood near the present site of the Art Institute, and annexed to the concert hall was a restaurant where the serving of soft drinks and suppers added a welcome social aspect to each distinguished performance. The warmth with which the orchestra was hailed, even then, presaged the city's enthusiasm for the later years of glorious concerts given, originally, in the great Auditorium Theater. Then came the thrilling day, in 1904, when for the first time, Theodore Thomas conducted at the new Orchestra Hall, specially built for his "troupe". The following January, Mr. Thomas became ill, and died, and despite their grief at his loss, all Chicago music lovers rejoiced that he had been spared long enough to realize his dream of conducting his orchestra in its own new home.

The Apollo Choral Society was foremost among the many amateur music organizations existing in those early days, particularly among the German-born groups. The Beethoven Society, another of the leading singing associations, was the one to which Mary, Henriette and her husband, Henry Frank, and I belonged. No affiliation brought us greater pleasure than those hours we devoted to singing with the large mixed chorus, preparing for the public concerts and oratorios we presented from time to time, and in which many renowned musicians participated. The organization was founded in about 1873, by Mr. Wolfsohn, whose profound admiration for the great composer was loyally expressed, both in the name he bestowed upon it, and in his gift to the city of Chicago, of the beautiful Beethoven statue in Lincoln Park, the work of the sculptor, Gellert.

Uncle Henry Greenebaum was the Beethoven Society's first president. Indeed, it would have been difficult to find a roster of any educational, cultural or philanthropic organization of that day which did not include his name. This short little man, with his silvery goatee and ready smile, more than compensated for his physical handicap by his great heart, noble spirit and remarkable abilities. His wide interests brought him prominence in civic affairs, as well, and he was a leader, too, in Jewish and German circles. After the Franco-German war, in 1870, he was made Field Marshal of the peace parade; he was appointed Chief Marshal for the festivities celebrating the dedication of Humboldt Park, and was among the promotors of the Chicago City Library, serving on the committee that went to the state capitol, at Springfield, to arrange for the library's permanent establishment. Often, he and Aunt Emily took me with them to see the plays at the German Theater with which he was affiliated, and he worked actively with those who arranged to bring the opera to Chicago. He was the first president of Zion Temple, serving for a number of years and when, in 1895, Isaiah congregation was founded with Dr. Joseph Stoltz as rabbi, Uncle Henry became its first president. What a colorful, benevolent and lovable man was "little Uncle Henry", as he was affectionately known, because of his noticeably small stature. Though he was a great historical figure in all pioneer activities, we like best to remember him for the many years he devoted to the collecting of funds, to which he donated generously, himself, to provide adequate training and education for promising young artists and musicians. As long as he lived, this was his most absorbing enterprise, and surprising is the number who, having achieved fame, gladly acknowledge, with appreciation and gratitude, that they owe their successful careers to "little Uncle Henry". His portrait hangs, today, in the Chicago Historical Museum's gallery of Chicago personages, as does a painting of Uncle Elias in recognition of his similar noteworthy participation in many important civic projects.

Music remained, for a number of years, one of our few prescribed means of self-expression, until — in 1877 — my father proved again his understanding of youth and his instinctive gift of answering its needs. He called a meeting of all the young Jewish folks of the West Side and organized, for us, the Zion Literary Society. It was so delightful an addition to our social life that we enjoyed the memory of it long after it had outlived its usefulness and ceased functioning. I served on its first board, as did a most interesting and — to me — appealing young man, Henry Solomon. Levy Mayer, who became one of Chicago's eminent lawyers, was editor of the "Zion Lit", a carefully prepared news journal that was presented at each meeting. I was made assistant editor.

Our meetings were held in the basement of the Synagogue and the programs consisted of recitations, lectures, theatricals, music and original contributions by members. Large affairs were arranged, from time to time, and especially vivid memories remain of the Purim masquerades. There was one particularly memorable ball at which my father, who had just learned to dance, was what the young people of today would call "the life of the party". The recollection of the general amusement and astonishment when his identity was finally revealed was mirth-provoking to the family for a long, long time.

Our whole circle of associates were active members of the Zion Literary Society until it was disbanded in 1892, and we attended all of the jolly reunions. Many of the young men of the group were in the professions, later distinguishing themselves as physicians, lawyers, musicians and authors. Some were the sons of pioneers who came from lands where, in the villages, times were difficult and opportunities few. The second generation had aspirations, ambition, industry and courage, and aided their families in achieving higher standards of living. Only to their own abilities and efforts did they owe their success; a rich reward which cannot be acquired through fortunes inherited from ancestors. Many of the pioneers felt keenly the desire to protect their children from the hardships they had endured and, with the wealth they had acquired so recently, purchased ease and comfort for their sons and daughters, too often weakening, rather than strengthening them. Of this generation, a number drifted away from the orthodox views of their parents and waited until a calamity roused them to some form of religious expression. They did not realize, alas, that faith can be achieved only through hours of calm reflection — that it is not a prop or a soporific, to be conjured up, magically, in time of trouble. If it is to be sustaining, it must be, in truth, a part of the fibre of one's own being, embodying a philosophy with which to meet the problems of daily living.

As I look back upon my life's adventure, this period appears as the beginning of my career — if I ever had one — and it started with an amusing experience. In 1877, Henriette and I were honored with an invitation to join the Chicago Woman's

Club. It had been founded the year before and numbered thirty of the representative women of the city, of whom Mrs. Murray F. Tuley and Kate Raworth (afterwards Mrs. Kate Raworth Holmes) were among our good friends. The summer before, when Henriette and I had vacationed at Beaver Lake, Wisconsin, Mrs. Tuley had also been there, and had spoken to us of the Chicago Woman's Club and of her desire to have us enjoy its membership. Long after we learned that when our names were first proposed, the members thoughtfully and seriously considered whether the presence of women of a different faith might prevent frank and open discussion of certain important issues. It was finally decided that a member should visit us in our home and bring back a report! The woman delegated arrived one morning at about eleven o'clock. She was charming, and Mother — as unsuspecting as we of the object of her visit — invited her to prolong her stay so that she might meet the rest of the family at dinner. She spent the entire afternoon with us, remaining, indeed, for supper, as well! Her day was evidently quite satisfactory, since we soon received notice that we had been elected to membership in the Chicago Woman's Club. I was the youngest among them — just eighteen when the matter of membership was broached — and I am now the only woman still living who entered in the Club's second year. At that time, we had but one study group which later became the Art and Literature Department. There were eight in our class and as we devoted ourselves to the subject of Egyptian sculpture, little did I dream I should see the marvelous remains of the early art we then studied, after I was sixty years old!

Our entrance into the Chicago Woman's Club was significant for the organization as well as for us, as we were not only the first Jewish women invited into it, but were probably the only Jewesses many of the members ever had met. To join an organization of "women"— not "ladies"— and one which bore the title "club", rather than "society", was in itself a radical step, but my parents approved, for they whole-heartedly endorsed its educational value. We met either in a hotel or in private homes; occasionally at that of the president and founder, Mrs. Caroline M. Brown. That Mrs. Brown was a woman of keen foresight is evident from the fact that she built the earliest apartment house in Chicago.

Those were the days when politics (including, of course, woman's suffrage) and religion were taboo as subjects for discussion in the Club but in 1892 the program committee asked me to present its first paper on religion for which I chose the subject, "Our Debt to Judaism". Tolerance, now a word in none too good repute with those who feel that men must do more than tolerate one another, had advanced sufficiently so that various members of the Club invited me to present my paper before other organizations to which they belonged. Its subject aroused a lively interest and it was subsequently published in "Unity", the magazine of the Unitarian Church.

Miss Herma Clark has gathered some of her "Dear Julia" letters, originally appearing in a Chicago newspaper column entitled "When Chicago Was Young", into a delightful volume she calls "The Elegant Eighties", in which an imaginary character, Martha Freeman Esmond, pens to an out-of-town friend intimate accounts of Chicago happenings. In a letter purported to have been written in the eighties, she wrote, "This has been a busy day, for I have spent the morning at the Chicago Woman's Club, where I heard an interesting paper on religion given by Mrs. Henry Solomon. This is the first time such a subject has been presented at the Club, and we were all much interested for it was so well done. She is the youngest member ever taken in by the Club, for she was barely eighteen when she was admitted, with her sister, Mrs. Henry Frank. However, it is not surprising that she should have been so heartily welcomed, for her father and mother, Mr. and Mrs. Michael Greenebaum, have the organizing spirit. Mr. Greenebaum has founded a society called Zion Literary Society, in which such promising young people as Levy Mayer, Jacob Newman and Joseph Schaffner are leading spirits. Will was lately invited to speak on a legal subject before these young Jewish men and was much impressed by their earnestness.

"Mrs. Sarah Greenebaum, mother of Mrs. Solomon, is hardly less public-spirited than her husband, and has organized a sewing society which has done much good. With such unselfish parents, my lovely young friend could hardly be other than the fine person she is. But I forget that you met her when you were last here and so don't need to have her qualities set out before you. She was the girl, you know, who played that duet with her sister, Mrs. Frank, at the musical given by her uncle, Henry Greenebaum. You thought them both very talented. ... The Michael Greenebaum home on West Adams Street has always been a social and cultural center for the Jewish settlers in Chicago."

And then, bless her heart, Miss Clark goes on to describe me as I appear in a photograph taken at about that time. "Mrs. Solomon was wearing a lovely gown today, a basque of plain cloth above a figured silk skirt. The waist was cut very plain, with a row of small buttons fastening it down the front, while a shoulder bow relieved its severity. A white linen collar finished it at the neckline and about this was knotted another ribbon. Her hair was prettily arranged, the

My "First Public Appearance" costume in which
I read the first paper on Religion ever presented
before The Chicago Woman's Club

back part brushed away from the front and defined with a band of silver. Her bangs were worn in soft ringlets — some people call them 'spit-curls', odious word!"

It was good of Miss Clark to preserve my elegance for posterity — an elegance that the young lady of today, in her informal sports togs, can scarcely picture and surely would not envy!

Continuing her picturesque letter, Martha Esmond wrote, "After leaving the Club meeting, Mrs. Solomon and I stopped by invitation at the home of her sister, Mrs. Charles Haas, where we met at a "Kaffee-Klatch" a group of fine women." The sister mentioned is, of course, Mary, and the "group of fine women" formed our circle of intimate friends. We were known to one another as "the girls"— yes, even after three of us, Mrs. Charles Liebenstein, Lizzie Spiegel Barbe and I, had reached what some people consider the age of discretion, but what we preferred to think of as a very youthful eighty!

CHAPTER VI

"... THY PEOPLE SHALL BE MY
PEOPLE ..."
(Ruth i:16)

MARY'S MARRIAGE to teasing, lovable Charley Haas, in 1878, was in itself a most exciting occasion. The fact that I became engaged to Henry Solomon at her wedding made it, of course, the most entrancing and memorable event of my twenty years! I did, however, by dint of the utmost self-control, manage to keep my joyful tidings a secret throughout the wedding festivities, and it was not until the following morning that I prepared, shyly and tentatively, to share Henry's and my newfound happiness with my mother.

I found her, that next morning, busily restoring to its normal tidiness a house much disordered by the crowd and gaity attendant upon a wedding. As she bustled from room to room, straightening rugs, moving chairs and re-living, again, the highlights of the previous day, I followed in a daze, seeking the psychological moment for imparting my great news.

Suddenly Mother stood erect and with a far-off look in her eyes, said, "Well, it was a beautiful wedding, wasn't it? And now, I don't want to hear of another engagement in the family for a year, at least!"

"Oh, but Mother!" I gasped, "Henry gave me a ring last night!"

Needless to say, Mother was only too happy to find a

special niche in her ample heart for my Henry. Father, too, rejoiced in the new son, and we were married on May 14, 1879.

It is almost impossible to write of one's happiness and contentment in the home. My husband and I were most sympathetic in our tastes, and in our social life we enjoyed the same friends. Henry was one of the amateurs who "strutted the boards" for the Zion Literary Society, being cast usually as the romantic lover, for he was not only handsome but an able actor, as well, with a rich deep voice of unusual beauty. Edwin Booth was his ideal and we rarely missed any of the performances he gave in Chicago. Henry's volumes of Shakespeare were among his most prized possessions and from them, in later years, he would often read aloud to our children, to their delight. One of my sisters called him "Brutus"; some of his friends spoke of him as "the noblest Roman of them all", and no description better expresses his character and nature than Shakespeare's words, "His life was gentle, and the elements so mix'd in him that Nature might stand up and say to all the world, 'This was a man!'" He once remarked, "I would like to have the words, 'His life was gentle', engraved upon my tombstone." They are there inscribed.

After my marriage, my husband's mother and sister, Mrs. Fanny Peyser, became members of our household, remaining with us throughout their lives, as did a brother, Joseph Solomon, who came to us some years later. Those were the good old days — now almost legendary — when most of us had large homes with plenty of spare rooms. Kitchenettes were then not even a dream of the future, and it was not at all unusual for family groups to live together under one ample roof.

Never think, though, that to the Henry Solomons two gene-rations, numbering five adults, would compose a large enough family circle! To us, our house only became a true home when our son, Herbert, and our daughter Helen, were born during the early years of our marriage, each contributing an individual and special quality of joy to our household. Frank, the adored little brother, completed our trio of children who, from the first, shared in all activities and responsibilities of family living and were never relegated to the seclusion of a nursery.

Our first home, on Morgan Street near Van Buren, was built in the approved architectural style of the era. Those were the days of "basement" houses and both ours and my parents' were of this type. On the ground floor were located kitchen, dining room, maids' quarters and "furnace room"; the second floor contained two parlors and what served in our house as a guestroom and was used, in the Adams Street house, as Mother's and Father's bedroom. Frequently, in other dwellings, this third room was utilized as a library. We had no separate library on Adams Street, but I remember our overflowing bookcases, there; especially the one filled with Grandfather Spiegel's many German and Hebrew books on Jewish subjects. Some years after Grandfather's death, Mother invited Dr. Felsenthal and Dr. Joseph Stolz to select any vol-umes they wished to own; the rest were sent to Hebrew Union College, in Cincinnati, where they were installed in an alcove as the Moses Spiegel collection. Once, years later, when I visited Rabbi Stolz, he read to me from my grand-mother's Saturday Afternoon Storybook, a chapter relating to the time when Jews might still be polygamous, and giving sage advice as to the kind of wives men should choose! To a confirmed woman's-rights-er, like me, there was consola-

And so — Henry and I were married, and lived happily, ever!

tion in the knowledge that what he read was all ancient history!

Our house was, of course, furnished in the fashion of the day; yes, even to the ubiquitous hat-rack and chatty cuckoo clock in the hall. Red damask-covered furniture with carved walnut frames filled the parlor with its Brussel's lace curtains and "what-nots" bursting with bric-a-brac (that had to be dusted, painstakingly, every single day!) The crowning elegance was a large easel upon which rested a picture of Beethoven. The wallpaper in our dining room I can never forget, for the part it played in starting our oldest off "on his own"! It happened on the morning that Mary Haas brought her little daughter, Valerie, over from her neighboring home on Jackson Boulevard, in order that we might see the small girl — just a little older than Herbert — take her first, tottering steps. Herbert, not to be outdone, immediately imitated her performance, and to our great astonishment and delight, the two youngsters launched out, simultaneously, upon their great adventure, smelling at the large red roses on the dining room wall paper as, together, they walked for the first time!

When Herbert was six, and Helen four, a huge crayon portrait of them was given to me as a surprise upon my birthday. No household was complete without family portraits, and I confess that I wept in surprise and delight when I received the one of our children. It was promptly hung in the front parlor and it never lost its charm for me even though it seemed to grow longer and broader with each succeeding home into which we moved.

My life was exceedingly full of household tasks in those days and, indeed, from the time of the coming of the children until they were well along their way, I had divorced myself from outside activities. My interest in education naturally related itself, first, to the rearing of my children. It was our desire to permit them the greatest possible latitude, and I truly believe that they never felt restricted in any sense, though our household was so complicated a one. Consideration for the widowed aunt and the bachelor uncle who were always a part of their background was taken for granted, and this added necessity for courtesy and thought for others was, I am sure, an important factor in the development of their ability to adapt and adjust, readily, to varying conditions in their lives.

Music continued to be a source of greatest pleasure to us. One evening each week amateurs gathered at our house and violins, cellos and two pianos brought the classics familiarly into our home. We became well acquainted with the masters and they contributed one of our most significant recreational joys, for those were the times when we who loved good music had to do much of the singing and playing, ourselves. We had been encouraged as we grew up in "the Adams Street house" to value such gatherings. Indeed, my father felt there should be no card playing, lest that pastime be substituted for hours of music, conversation and happy companionship. Our children, too, grew up in the tradition of music and I, myself, gave them their first piano lessons. Later, Herbert turned to the violin and devoted himself to its study with the same faithfulness and scholarliness he brought to all his work. Helen, also, was greatly interested in music and, when she grew older, was able to play in our eight-handed family quartettes. "The Awakening of the Lion" or Schubert's "Unfinished Symphony" brought great delight to us and our appreciative audiences as we performed them together, my sisters Henriette and Helen at one piano, my daughter Helen and I at the other. But sister Rose was most frequently the "star" of our evenings, for her glorious mezzo soprano seemed to us the loveliest we knew, and about her there was ever an aura of radiance . . . a glow reflecting to all whom she met her zest and joy in living.

Busy as I was in those first years of my married life, I was able, nevertheless, to continue reading regularly, and I rarely missed spending at least an hour at it each day. Many of our friends shared my interest, and the discussion of novels and essays afforded us much pleasure and intellectual stimulation. At the same time, a neighbor and I embarked upon a study of astronomy. Surely, we thought, a liberal education should include knowledge of the things surrounding us, and nothing seemed closer than the heavens where sun, moon and stars made their rounds. In my many travels, the friendly stars were my companions and, as the planets rose, the fact that I could always recognize and locate them gave me a feeling of being "at home", wherever I might be. The Book of Job provided one of my favorite passages: "Canst thou bind the chains of the Pleiades, or loose the bands of Orion?" Words which have always served to strengthen my faith in a Divine Order.

As I read and studied, often the question came to my mind, am I what I am, and do I act as I do, because of heredity and training, or do intuitions come, perhaps, from Force and Spirit surrounding me? I had, for the most part, devoted myself to the works of those who were of a scientific school of thought, believing that I could best preserve, thus, the balance I sought. Now I added Darwin, Huxley, Renan and Tyndall to my list, but I also read much of the mystics, undecided whether these would not show me more of truth than the practical thinkers toward whom I naturally inclined.

Desiring, however, to be a person of action, I therefore soon eschewed, completely, the field of the esoteric.

In 1891, the Chicago Woman's Club members devoted themselves to reviews of books on ideal states: Plato's Republic, Moore's Utopia, St. Augustine's City of God. To me fell the task of discussing Spinoza's Theologico-Politicus which, because no English translation was available, I was obliged to read in German. In the Club's Philosophy and Science Department we studied, also, the history of the philosophers who had made their precious contributions, each following the special path illumined for him. This study, more than any other, tended to aid me in my classification and appraisal of members of the human family, and I finally decided to my own satisfaction that heredity was the cause that shaped tendencies in men, but that environment influenced their course. Talents were either fostered or stunted, but the great powers with which each man is endowed seldom reach their highest fruition because of the limitations imposed by circumstances. One must differentiate, however, between talent and genius, for the latter appears to flourish, regardless of environment.

The mind is a universe in itself!

CHAPTER VII

WERE I A FAIRY-TALE HEROINE, I am sure the story would record that my god-mother had touched me with her wand, at birth, predestining me to a love of travel which would prove one of my most frequent indulgences! For, truth to tell, I have been ever an inveterate traveller, starting, they tell me, 'way back in 1858 when I was plucked from my crib at the tender age of six months, to visit Mother's family in New York, then a journey of two nights and a day.

But for the fact that I have promised myself that this book shall be a faithful and true chronicle, I might attempt to insinuate, here, some "recollections" of that first journey. Alas, such a precocious babe I cannot claim to have been, and that trip must go unrecorded, therefore, save for the one tangible souvenir still in existence: a wee bonnet of mull and lace which a proud relative presented to me, along with a resplendent French robe, to adorn me fittingly for my visit. The robe must have been worn out by my younger sisters, but Mother gave me the bonnet on my tenth birthday, to use for my favorite doll and I, in turn, have passed it on to succeeding generations to whom it is now a quaint and cherished heirloom.

My next travel experiences were really only dire threats, and began at the age of four. Whenever I was displeased at the way my family managed affairs at home or neglected to consider my sage advice, I became very haughty and announced that I could no longer remain with them, but would get on the "brumlibus" and go off to stay with Uncle Marcus Spiegel, in Ohio. Upon one such occasion my father decided to put me to the test. Giving me a few pennies and a bundle of clothing, he escorted me down the steps and realistically started me on my way. Kind-hearted and loving Mary, a year and one-half my senior, burst into tears and pleaded with me to stay at home. Disgusted at her display of softness, I responded with a muttered, "Go back, you goose! I'm just going to the corner to buy some candy!" Never again, though, did I threaten to abandon my family. And so it came about, that for all my day-dreams, my first *real* travels did not begin until 1886 when, with my husband and his brother, Joe, I journeyed to the East.

Every incident and impression of our trip was conscientiously written into the diary I kept as we went along ... forerunner to many similar volumes I have since filled. In fact, I suspect that the travel diaries of the "Michael Greenebaum girls", if placed end to end, would encircle the globe, for it was our custom, when away from home, to record each day's happenings and many were the delightful occasions when, upon our return, we would come together to read aloud the experiences one of our number had enjoyed. My diary of 1886 is typical, even to the painstaking mid-Victorian flavor we find so thoroughly amusing today, and through it one can picture, readily, the mustachioed gentlemen of the eighties and their ladies whose swirling skirts swept the ground and whose bonnets tied pertly under their chins.

In the pages of my diary we find, "At parting with my children I must confess to a slight feeling of remorse at leaving them from choice ... I trust to a merciful future to restore them and all our dear ones to me well and happy.

"We are going at the rate of fifty miles an hour ... along the lake ... here and there a little country town comes into view and vanishes; wild flowers grow along the road and seem happy to grow in their own artless way without being cultivated.

"It is a difficult task for anyone but an agent or a reporter to write up a railroad, so let this short description suffice. I would say, anti-monopolist that I am, I must admire the railroad monopoly for the excellence, comfort and general success of its undertakings. One of its chief features is the dining car. One can now sit down to dinner as cozily as at home, not taking the old 'twenty minutes for breakfast' at a station, but have an excellent meal while whirling along. ... By the way, for comfort's sake, one's baggage on such trips as this should consist of a grip-satchel. ...

"From Fall's View we first beheld Niagara Falls. The air was bracing, and altogether a sense of supreme delight filled us as we beheld the beautiful scene, a feeling of awe for a Creative Mind that clothes Itself in such wondrous beauty. ... How to convey an impression of Niagara's grandeur, I do not know. No words, no picture, can portray its majesty, its power or beauty. It would be like breaking a piece of marble from the Venus de Milo and asking you to imagine the statue from that fragment."

So I write on, in the manner of 1886, detailing the succession of events and the procession of scenes that delighted and enthralled me. The Suspension Bridge — wonder of wonders of the American eighties; the new Cantilever structure; the rapids and the whirlpool and the endless leaping of the spray, the color of the waters changing from white to gray, from dark blue to black and green to rose; the eternal rainbow at the foot of the Falls all come in for wordy description. So, also, did the paradoxical and unpoetical cries of the photographers who insisted upon producing a picture for posterity, as they posed us, in the stiff, startled-fawn manner of the day, against the background of the Falls! There, then, for one moment one might forget how puny is the frame of man beside the mighty Niagara, for the photographed male of that era was a truly impressive figure!

Amusing in the light of present-day achievements is the paragraph from my diary telling of our ride down an "endless shaft. One drawback I must not forget to mention is the 'talking machine' at the bottom. It tells you, in the most monotonous tone, of all the suicides of the place." The use of the talking machine — forerunner of the Victrola — as a substitute for announcer, guide or advertising medium must have seemed a modern and wonderful innovation to us, then! There is no indication in my diary, however, of a vision of the gigantic future accomplishment of the harnessing of Niagara's water power.

To my diary, too, I confided my thrills as I viewed, for the first time, Lake Ontario, the Thousand Islands, the St. Lawrence River and Montreal; of the ecstacy of the mountain air in the Adirondacks and the patriotic fervor awakened at Fort Ticonderoga where "only a few ruins remain to remind us of its stormy days." The towering mountains that make of Lake George a spot of secluded beauty struck me with deepest awe, and it was almost with reluctance that we drifted down the Hudson River to New York — the New York of 1886 — a metropolis then, as now; but with what a difference!

The following, according to my diary, is what the sight-seer of sixty years ago considered of importance there:

[56]

"We had been prepared for New York by the advertisements high up on the Palisades, but how could we have visualized a city of such proportions? We were unprepared for what we really found. We drove through Fifth Avenue and saw the residences of those whose wealth is fabulous. The street itself is a mass of brown-stone houses, monotonous in architecture, many of them closed for the summer, and their occupants away at the seashore. What a relief it was to arrive at Central Park. . . .

"We enjoyed the scene along the Hudson as we took a carriage and traversed a pleasant road called the Riverside Park that leads to Grant's tomb and the monument. At the tomb we gaze with reverence upon the structure that holds the remains of the celebrated hero. . . .

"We plan to see old New York, made famous by Oliver Optic and other writers of our youthful days, who told of Baxter and Division and Chateau and Hester Streets and the Bowery. Thither we went next day. Baxter Street was packed with human beings, groups of varying types and children so numerous that they seem to grow under one's feet. Division Street is the Broadway of the East Side. On one side of the street there are only millinery stores, one after the other, at least a hundred, and since everyone seems hatless, who will ever wear the hats? Chatham Street is very respectable as is also Five Points with its old reputation gone. Having satisfied our curiosity, we drove to see Brooklyn Bridge, the great achievement of its day. Then on to Coney Island. At one end the poorer classes enjoy their sports just as much as the more prosperous group, at the other. Brighton Beach is the west end of Coney Island. As soon as one arrives at Brighton Beach one sees the elephant, an immense creature made of wood, fitted out as a large beer saloon. Brighton's five carousels and numerous beer saloons with orchestrians all combine noise, and the strains of music bewilder one.

"At seven we took the boat for New York. . . . It was just dusk. In the distance we saw Brooklyn Bridge which, with its lights resembling a diamond necklace, seemed but a short distance away. We caught a glimpse of the fortifications of the harbor and saw the place where the Bartholdi Statue of Liberty will be erected.

"This morning, after packing our satchels, we started out for Tiffany's, the wonderful jewelry store. . . . We were told not to miss the Eden Musee, copied from museums abroad, showing historical happenings and persons, and depicting, in wax, a Chamber of Horrors . . . Garfield's Death . . . celebrated persons . . . the crowned heads of Europe . . . also our presidents. We visited the Jewish Synagogues and some charitable institutions, among them Temple Emanuel . . . and the Mount Sinai Hospital.

"One day we visited friends at Long Branch, the most popular of resorts, and had our first view of millionaires' summer homes. We saw the cottages of President Grant, the house in which Garfield died, Garrison's Cottage and many others. We took a ride through the countryside along the Hudson River and visited the piers where the big boats leave for Europe. Will we ever take one of them? How I longed to be of the crowd on the Westerland, bound for Bremen! . . .

"We did quite a little shopping in New York, most of it at Macy's, where we purchased toys for the children. We also went to Strauss' Crockery House and bought some presents. We met old Mr. Strauss and Mr. Nathan Strauss, both of whom gave us a cordial greeting.

"We have been most favorably impressed by New York, especially by its fine charitable institutions and by the places nearby to which all can go for Saturdays and Sundays. The means of gratifying the desire for recreation which the rich and poor share alike seems far ahead of all other cities. On Saturday at one o'clock all business ceases and everyone from proprietor to clerk rushes in search of rest and pleasure. We carry away from New York the pleasantest recollections. Brother Joe holds as his fondest memory a glimpse of the residence of Samuel J. Tilden whom he so greatly admires."

Joe, who was much interested in politics, lived at that time in DuQuoin, one of the larger cities of Southern Illinois, and was its highly honored mayor. He became a confirmed Democrat, when Benjamin Harrison was elevated to the presidency of the United States, supposedly defeating the Democratic candidate, Tilden. Tilden would never allow the result to be investigated, thus becoming a hero in the eyes of many who believed the election unfair and open to question.

We left New York for Washington, going by way of Philadelphia, and much enjoyed our stay at the Willard Hotel which was then famed as the home of many senators and congressmen. We were fortunate, in Washington, in visiting all the places of interest there, and in being introduced to many of our statesmen, including the Secretaries of State, Navy and War; Bayard, Whitney and Endicott. Attorney General Garland and Postmaster General Vilas we met, as well, and were, in each case, extended the utmost courtesy.

But for me, the most impressive moment came when we were taken to the White House to meet President Cleveland — the first President I had ever seen — and whom we found both pleasant and cordial. We were invited to inspect the White House at our leisure, and were provided a guide to show us through the various departments, including the President's second-floor office. Later, the wife of one of our congressmen took us to Mrs. Cleveland's reception which was one of a series given on Tuesdays and Fridays for members of Congress and their friends. But let my diary tell the story for me: "We arrived at twelve o'clock and found that many others had preceded us. The reception, held in the Pink Room, lasted from twelve to two. Mrs. Cleveland is a beautiful young woman, gracious and lovely. We went then into the Blue Room, noted because President and Mrs. Cleveland were married there. The long parlor of the White House in which large parties are held is furnished in olive color and has beautiful mirrors and chandeliers, as well as pictures of George and Martha Washington. The room has the atmosphere of a private house."

Though, in later years, I was privileged to visit the White House many times and to meet almost all our presidents since Cleveland, I need no diary record to bring back most vividly the breathlessness of that first momentous experience!

After Washington, as we turned homeward, I confided to my diary (with apologies to the railroad company), "But, oh! the ups and downs of the B. and O., in 1886!"

CHAPTER VIII

"EVERY MAN TO HIS TENTS"
(2 Samuel xx:1)

I N THE SPRING of the year, 1890, Mother and Father left the much-loved Adams Street house for one on South Park Avenue, near Thirty-Third Street, and Henry and I moved our household from Morgan Street to Lake Park and Fortieth — the last of our clan to become residents of the South Side.

Our departure from Morgan Street was considered, more or less a matter of course. I had gone there as a bride, and there our three children were born. In this same house, too, Henry's mother — a gentle, noble soul to whom I was deeply attached — had died, in 1887. Our life on Morgan Street had rounded itself out; we were ready, now, to begin a new cycle in a more modern section of the city and this move, we felt, would bring advantages to each of us.

But . . . abandoning the Adams Street house — ah, that was different! And what a wrench it was to part, with such finality, from that beloved home of our youth which had been, throughout the years, the port and harbor for the Michael Greenebaum children and their families. The hold this dwelling had upon us is best illustrated by a story we grin about, to this day. For many years, our father and brothers worked together in their hardware store and each day they rode home together, at noon, for dinner. One day one of my married brothers arrived with the group and assumed his accustomed place at the table. When Mother turned to him to inquire about his wife and baby, he jumped as if shot from a cannon, aghast and dismayed to realize that he had automatically reverted to the old custom of coming "home to Adams Street" for his noon-day meal, forgetting, for the moment, that he now had a home, a wife and a child of his own! To the credit of his wife, be it reported, she, too, found it amusing.

By this time, other marriages had brought added joy to our family circle, and new, deeply cherished sons or daughters to our parents. My brother Mose chose Rose Simon, a beautiful young woman, to be his wife; Henry brought us Esther Loeb whose rare selflessness enriched the lives of everyone of us; to our delight, Gus married Leah Friend. All these charming young girls had been members of our social circle and each was most happily welcomed into the clan. The last wedding in the Adams Street house was that of Helen, to Henry Kuh, and thus only Ben and Rose remained at home to move, with Mother and Father, to the South Side.

Yes, the Adams Street house was dear to all of us!

After we married, Friday of each week brought us together there for our special evening reunion. When we left to return to our respective homes, Mother always refused to allow the chairs to be set back in place that night, because she loved to come into the parlors the next morning and picture each of us as she had seen us seated the night before.

But now our families were settling on the South Side of Chicago, and it was only common sense for our parents to move into a smaller house in the heart of the area where most of us were locating. We Solomons, in the Oakland district which began at Thirty-Ninth Street, were the farthest away. We found the neighborhood ideal for the children because it was like a small suburban community and the rela-

The Ten Little Greenebaums and How They Grew Up!

(Left to right, standing) Henriette, Mose, Theresa, Henry, Mary, Gus
(Seated) Father, Rose, Hannah, Mother, Helen, Ben

tionships established with others of their age seemed right for them. The Oakland School ranked exceptionally high, and the name of the principal, Mr. Speer, remains important in modern pedagogy

My sister, Rose, married Joseph N. Eisendrath shortly after moving to South Park Avenue, and she and her husband rented the house next door to ours. Their outdoor back-porch stairs were adjacent to ours, and the separating fence at the top was cut away so that we could run back and forth. Inside our houses, the wall partitions were not thick and a knock from either side brought us flying to the front windows for interchange of messages. One evening our son, Herbert, had a particularly difficult arithmetic problem which so intrigued his father and uncle Joe that they worked over it, at our dining table, the entire evening — but to no avail! Long after the Eisendraths had gone home, Henry continued with the figures, to meet with success, at last! Jubilant, he pounded on the wall and though Rose and Joe were already asleep, the knocking brought Joe flying to the window. "I've got it!", cried Henry. "You've got what?" blared Joe. "The answer to the problem," gloated my husband. "Well! Of all the blithering nerve!" Joe complained, as he shuddered and shivered in the cold, "So you've got the answer! But what I'm getting is tonsilitis! For this important news item I could honestly have endured waiting until morning!" And with a bang of the window he dashed back to the comfort of his bed.

At the corner of our block lived Lyman Trumball, a great statesman and one of the most distinguished United States senators ever sent to Washington from Illinois. He had served three terms in the Senate and would have been reelected again, without doubt, had he not had the temerity to cast the vote which saved President Andrew Jackson from impeachment. When the Senator died, the whole neighborhood was stirred. My daughter's first community enterprise consisted of the collecting of money for a floral piece from the boys and girls of the block. With a feeling of participation in a patriotic situation, the children were then permitted to file past the coffin, most of them a bit terrified, since it was, for them, in many instances, a first experience with death.

The simple Trumball house still stands, its wooden exterior now stuccoed, and bearing a bronze placque that gives it dignity.

In the block below ours, on Lake Avenue, were the fine homes of the McWilliams family. President McKinley once came to visit in one of them and the children of the Oakland School were taken there to march past their President and shake his hand. Frank, and a few of his little friends, missed the school parade but, with the dauntlessness of youth, they determined to go by themselves, and actually won the opportunity of seeing the President, alone!

Mother and Father did not live long in their house on South Park Avenue, for soon after Rose's marriage they came to dwell with the Eisendraths, next door to us. Here, on September seventeenth, 1893, my father passed away as the result of a severe mastoid infection which the limited medical skill of that day could not overcome. Then, even with all her devoted sons and daughters about her, our mother was alone! On March twelfth, 1897, at Mary's home, she too died.

At the time of the dedication of the new Sinai Temple and its Center, in 1912, there was a special service for the women's organizations that had met regularly in the old Synagogue's vestry rooms. As he referred to the Sarah Greenebaum Lodge,

Dr. Emil G. Hirsch spoke these cherished words about my mother: "Sarah Greenebaum! Who knows it not that the name here in Chicago recalls a noble woman's life; a Jewish woman to whom must be applied in sober truth the Biblical description of the ideal woman said to have been written by a kingly author. A 'woman of power' was Sarah Greenebaum, and although we may say of her daughters that they have done valiantly, of her we shall sing, 'Thou, the mother, hast outrisen them all'. ... she was an exemplar and incarnation of the genius of Jewish womanhood, Jewish piety and Jewish loyalty."

Mother and Father happily saw all of their girls and boys, with the exception of Ben, married, and Mother lived to rejoice in the lovely, thoughtful young woman, Hattie Weil, of Youngstown, Ohio, who had promised to become Ben's wife. At the time of Mother's death, there were already thirty-three grandchildren to carry on, into the future, the Greenebaum tradition.

CHAPTER IX

THE LAKE AVENUE HOME was ours until 1897 when we
packed up our belongings, put our furniture in storage and
arranged to spend the summer in Rogers Park which, though
now a thickly populated section of the city, was then a wooded
suburb. From the beginning of May to the end of the school
year we, with our children, went to live at the always hospitable home of the Charley Haases, on South Park Avenue.

Those were, indeed, gala days! My husband and Charley
Haas had been intimate friends for years, and Mary and I
were now, as in childhood, constant and sympathetic companions. Because we held in common almost every enterprise
in which either of us embarked, we and our families were
accustomed to being much together. It was natural, therefore, that when we departed for Rogers Park, the Haas children, Gus and Rose, should accompany us while the Haas
home underwent a renovation. And what a re-decoration it
proved to be! Those were the days when one was not satisfied with a mere freshening coat of the latest shade on one's
walls. So simple a procedure was then unthinkable! No,—
a real artist was engaged to paint friezes on the walls, to
festoon the ceilings with posies or to lend a woodsy touch

[66]

by means of flocks of birds and hovering butterflies! And sometimes, as a finishing, enterprising touch — the epitome of decorative elegance — would be added an entire scene, all in the favorite Delft blue of the day!

The red-brown stone house at Michigan Avenue and Forty-Fourth Street, which was to become the property of the Henry Solomons, was likewise re-decorated to the last square inch, with aesthetic motifs reflected even in the wash basins. Spacious rooms and the last word in trappings of the era were ours, thereafter.

Our Herbert was attending St. John's Military Academy and we had been in our new home but a few days when a telegram from his school informed us that our son was ill and was coming back to us.

For two years following that fateful message the special thought of our entire household hovered about this beloved boy. He had seemed, always, to have been fashioned of material that was not merely of this earth. He was gentle and thoughtful, intellectual and musically gifted. Joe Eisendrath has set up a laboratory in his basement where he experimented with chemical processes for the treating of leather, and Herbert often accompanied him there. He went to concerts at a time when it was not usual to see boys of his age in attendance, and practiced on his violin with diligence, playing a violin solo at his graduation exercises in grammar school. Many years later, one of his Hyde Park High School teachers told me that in speaking of their outstanding pupils of the past, one of their number said, "And of course, we haven't forgotten Herbert Solomon!"

We were called upon to part with him in 1899. His nineteen years had been a constant blessing and his loss was difficult to bear. But, as one matures, one learns to let gratitude for what has been compensate, as far as possible, for the sorrow that is inevitably meted out to each of us, and Herbert's life was, we know, a happy one.

Just as, during my parents' lifetime, Friday nights found us all together at their home, so Friday evenings at the Solomons, now became an established custom. The Haases were always expected, and our other brothers and sisters, too, all came in turn.

My sweet-sour fish brought me culinary fame in the family circle, and it gave me secret delight to hear a brother-in-law exclaim, "Hansie certainly has a way with a goose!" Consequently, Fridays always found me hovering between desk and kitchen.

We did a great deal of entertaining, and my thoughts return with special insistence to the recurrent picture of our long table, twinkling with candlelight and fragrant with massed flowers and festively arrayed with the "best" china, glassware and silver. But the crowning happiness was, of course, to be found in the dear relatives and friends whose presence provided the real fillip to the gathering.

At different times some of our family moved away from Chicago. Each such occurrence brought a pang at parting, and their visits home were always a source of great delight and occasions of joyous gatherings of the clan. Especially was this true when Tress would travel back to us, all the way from California! Many of these celebrations were held at the Solomons, and I love to review them in retrospect, recalling with each name the qualities and characteristics that made each member of the family so special and so dear.

Tress was a remarkable woman — dynamic, for all her fragility; wise, spiritual and courageous. Her letters to us were brilliant and we treasured every one. Our good friends, the Israel Cowens, deeply impressed with a paragraph in one of them, had it beautifully illuminated and framed for me. This is what Tress, in her wisdom, wrote: "If we could see the whole fabric of our lives spread out, what a wonderful meaning it might show — many a thread that we thought lost would re-appear and form strange patterns of cause and effect. But God holds the spindle and until He cuts the thread, we go on adding a bit each day." It is not to be wondered at, is it, that the many miles separating us, physically, from our oldest sister never, in any way, tended to diminish the bond between us?

Henriette, our scholar, comes next to mind. In addition to her very great musical talent, she had notable literary gifts, and the capacity for leadership, as well. She was a member of the committee for the Jewish Women's Congress of the Parliament of Religions and she became the second president of the Chicago Section of the Council of Jewish Women. At the time of her death, she was especially interested in the Illinois Training School for Nurses, serving as secretary of its board. Many contemporaries considered her the most intellectual Chicago Woman's Club member of her day. Its fifth president, she was, in fact, the only Jewish woman ever to have held this office, and it was during her presidency that the organization acquired the first club rooms of its own.

In Mary, it was her sagacity and quality of heart as well as her strength of character that made her outstanding. She was honest and outspoken, yet so heavenly kind that people of all ages just naturally sought her out as comforter, advisor, friend. Her generosity carried everyone along with her to participate with enthusiasm in whatever project or pleasure she proposed. Mary was a member of our World's Fair Congress Committee and served on the first national board of the Council of Jewish Women. She became particularly active in the Jochannah Lodge, where she and Lizzie Barbe shared in the highest expressions of affection that the members of an organization can give, either personally or as a group. Mary is never forgotten! If a woman ever enjoyed immortality on earth, it is she, and though she has been gone for many years, probably no woman in Chicago has left a greater impress on our Jewish community and her name is always recalled with living gratitude and joy.

Our "little sisters" were Helen and Rose! Rose, I most frequently picture, standing at the piano, singing to us; enchanting with her beautiful voice and lovely face. And Helen, the skillful accompanist! Helen, so gentle yet so purposeful, so serene yet so firm; so fearless, forthright and intelligent. Helen and Rose — each so decided a personality, yet each so devoted to the other that we invariably group them together in our hearts. The vocation of each was the rearing of four children, their avocations and interests were many. Helen was, with Henriette and me, an active member of the Chicago Woman's Club and was chairman of its Education Department when it called together persons and organizations to discuss the formation of the Joint Committee on Public School affairs. Rose devoted much of her time and interest to the Infant Welfare Society.

And my brothers! Ben, the youngest, became the beloved confidant of old and young, alike. At his office each day, one found friends who were legion, or children of the family, waiting to go to luncheon with him and "talk things over". Although he was a man of affairs, he was never too busy to help them solve their problems, ever ready to discuss and advise, to solace and to aid. Gus, the next older, lived in

Danville, Illinois, for a time, where he entered fully into the civic life of the community. He was a member of Governor Deneen's staff and he looked very impressive in his official uniform. He, like our uncle, Henry Greenebaum, was steadfast and untiring in his work for the B'nai B'rith.

Brother Henry was so rare a soul that when one says, "Heaven lies about us in our infancy", one feels that more must be added for him. He carried heaven with him through his entire life!

Our brother Mose's attitude toward little children was an attribute that brought rich returns from them to him. Had he been a Pied Piper, I am sure the young people of the family, as well as countless others, would have followed where'er he led. He, as well as all the others, was meticulous and scrupulous in his honesty.

Beyond what these brothers were as individuals, it was their quality as a group that was most noteworthy. All for one, one for all, and all for all the rest of us, they remained a closely knit unit, and the bond that had held them so firmly under our father's roof, continued strong and changeless. Their wives, all exemplary, were not alone helpmates to their husbands, but encouraged their continued family allegiance and themselves joined in with it. So it was, also, with our brothers-in-law, each contributing his share of loyalty and devotion. Everyone who married into the family, having received a royal welcome from those who already belonged, was then made part and parcel of "the clan". And it is a joy to look back from the vantage point of eighty-four years and realize, anew, that harmony was, at all times, the keynote of our family life. And better still, to be able to record with veracity that it was a harmony of the heart rather than of the mind; a one-ness of the spirit which was the host at every

[71]

gathering. As one of my sisters-in-law remarked to me the other day, "I have been a Greenebaum for over forty years, now, Hansie, and never once have I heard a single discordant note!" Perhaps a contributing factor was a natural gayety and a gift of enjoyment. We loved to laugh together! Nevertheless, a new member of the Greenebaum clan never lost any of his close associations with his own group by this incorporation process, for — be it said to the wisdom of our parents — their children as sons and daughters-in-law became an integral part of, and a source of strength to the family into which each entered.

And so, we Greenebaums possessed an immense capacity for celebration, and so large a family that there was always, in the offing, some reason for it. If there was no legitimate excuse, we were quick to invent one!

Harry, Milton and Lina Greenebaum, the children of our Uncle Jacob, were orphaned when they were young, and had been cared for by "little Uncle Henry" and Aunt Emily, who loved and nurtured them as though they were their own. These cousins were always included in the clan get-togethers, as were Lina's husband, Alex Bergman, and their two children.

Numbers never daunted the hardy Greenebaums, and so each birthday, as it came along, was celebrated with great festivity. The younger generation, too, knew that each could count on their aunts and cousins making much of their special day, and some of the older ones could remember when my mother and father also came; Father always bringing a large round shining silver dollar as a birthday gift. Nor dare one overlook the occasional "noodle parties", so-called for the prescribed menu of chicken, noodles and ice cream; and woe betide the aunt who attempted a substitute in the form of rice or apple sauce! We thought them an exceptional group, that coming generation. Some of them did, too! When, during their engagement, Ben brought Hattie Weil from Youngstown to become acquainted with us, one of our nieces overheard Hattie express her pleasure in her new sisters and brothers. "Hm-m-m," murmured the youngster, "just you wait till you get to know us children!"

The family picnic tradition carried on, meantime; the August crop of birthdays was always sure to produce some. One especially gay affair was marked by a ride to Lincoln Park, atop a huge tallyho. Then, in Washington Park by the pavillion was a spot we considered ours, as well as a large three-cornered plot with huge shady trees, in Jackson Park. This lovely picnic space was beside Lake Michigan, known to some of the older children as "Grandma's lake", because my mother specially loved it and delighted to be driven there by Mary, in the Haas surrey. What an important accessory Mary's surrey proved to be! Many a time it carried some of us off on a pleasure jaunt and often we drove to the bandstand in Washington Park where, of an evening, Chicago enjoyed open air concerts.

Perhaps most unique of all our family "doings", however, was the family auction! I know that some people do not like to wear the garments of others, but with a quirk all our own, we always did, and so this event was hailed, unanimously, with greatest glee! It was an invention of my sister, Rose, and as long as the Eisendraths lived in their Grand Boulevard house, the auctions — one in spring and one in fall — were held on their top floor. Later, we all took turns at having our houses the scenes of these mirth-provoking and glorified rummage sales and no functions of which I have ever heard, contrived by any other family, have equalled the ridiculous and gay possibilities of our "auctions". A strictly "For Ladies

Only" affair, each participant was expected to bring articles of apparel with which she was willing to part, and these were auctioned off to the highest bidder. Once a garment was up for sale, no last-minute change of heart was tolerated, and it frequently happened that a member of the group would have to buy back an article she, herself, had contributed and decided — just too late — she'd prefer to keep! In fact, one niece had to pay a pretty penny in order to re-purchase her brand new spring hat, inadvertently included among the auction merchandise! Mary and Rose were our most effective auctioneers and some of the nieces made very attractive models as they paraded in our fashion show. No money ever was paid to the seller, for all proceeds were donated to some charity; originally, to Rest Haven, the convalescent home sponsored by Sarah Greenebaum Lodge. Before the auction itself, luncheon was served, and sometimes the men of the family were permitted to join us for coffee, at four o'clock.

In the Michael Greenebaum tradition, however, our annual New Year's Eve celebration was, by all odds, the most elaborate and gala occasion! In this festivity, all the children who had attained the age of fourteen were allowed to join, and so eagerly did they anticipate this gathering that none ever dreamed of accepting invitations that would prevent their attendance. On the contrary, they used to plead with their parents to lower the age-limit in order that they might be privileged, earlier, to join in the fun, and many who, as they grew up, married out of town, would make every effort to return to Chicago to celebrate the coming of the New Year with the family.

For the program, a sort of vaudeville performance was instituted, and each person attending was expected to make a contribution, either individually or in groups. Each year there were a few serious features, Henry Frank always preparing a timely and scholarly essay; Henriette a newspaper which she called The Sylvestor Echo, and I wrote the "Minutes"— a recording of the history of the year's happenings.

On this one night each year, an unwritten law provided opportunity for affectionate fun-poking at individual foibles and idiosyncracies, with the guarantee that no one's feelings could be hurt and no sympathy would be wasted on touchiness. And what eye-openers some of us experienced as we were given glimpses of ourselves "as ithers see us"!

Since most of the acts were composed within the week between Christmas and New Year's Eve, perfection was not expected of the finished productions and as much fun went into the preparation of our "stunts" as in the program, itself. The younger generation performed in a troupe and managed to create, with original costumes and ingenious props, a show of no mean proportions. The brothers and their wives always astonished and delighted us with an elaborate topical skit which they acted, together, and there were always letters and messages from those who, perforce, must be absent. Midnight usually found us — sixty strong — at supper, greeting the New Year with toasting, speeches and song. Always, as the hour for parting drew near, we ended the evening by singing the family song which Mary had written for one of Mother's birthdays. This we sang in German, to the tune of "Laute Schöne Leut Sind Wir" ("Fine People Are We") — a ditty that grew, in time, to awe-inspiring length, as a verse was added for each person who married into the family. Nor dare I overlook mention of the grab bag! For this everyone brought fantastically wrapped packages and, as a grand finale, we each in turn drew out a gift. And what a comparing of "grabs" then ensued . . . and what a trading, as one of the boys, perhaps, "swapped" his powder box for a girl cousin's pipe!

At the New Year's Eve party shortly before his death, Father said to us, "Breaks in our family ranks are inevitable ... but these gatherings must be uninterrupted." And so there was never any question in our minds about continuing these celebrations. When, from time to time, death visited one of our homes and saddened our entire family, the members of that household were with us on New Year's Eve, even though the day of bereavement had been very recent, and grief found its own solace in the comfort of being together. In our midst, just as happiness was shared, so, too, was sorrow, and I remember only twice that our New Year's festivities were suspended; once because of the Iroquois Theater Fire when, on December thirtieth, 1903, so many lives were lost so tragically, and again when Charley Haas died, on December thirtieth, 1928.

Thus, "in the hearts of those who cherish their memories," have we ever kept vibrant the spirit of our loved ones, in remembrance that continues to gladden our lives.

PART II

PATTERN

"Laying Her Hand to the Distaff"

CHAPTER X

"HAVE WE NOT ALL ONE FATHER?"
(Malachi ii:10)

IT WAS 1893 . . . a year when a world's fair was to commemorate the four-hundredth anniversary of the discovery of America, and though many rival cities sought the privilege of being named the Fair site, it was Chicago to which the United States government granted the honor.

"Chicago", groaned some members of Congress, in vociferous and angry protest. "Chicago? How can a city where people sit out on their front steps in summer be a proper place for so great an exposition?" The violent objections were coupled with the gloomiest predictions and complete and dire failure of a Chicago fair was prophesied in many quarters. Now, it was quite true that in those days Chicago boasted no country clubs, and a paucity of diversion spots, and it was, indeed, the custom, on warm evenings, to drag hall rugs out of doors, allowing them to trail down the long stone steps in front of the houses. Upon these the younger members of the family would drape themselves, while the oldsters swayed in rocking chairs on the verandahs, trying to fan away the heat. That did not mean, however, that they were strangers to the amenities a great exposition imposed! Yes, even though royalty might attend, Chicago was confident she could hold her own!

It was 1893 . . . the year for a world's fair! And a year

that marked the beginning of women's collaboration with men in civic projects in Chicago.

Preparations for the World's Columbian Exposition entailed many exciting obligations on the part of the Chicago Woman's Club. Two of its members, Mrs. Potter Palmer and Mrs. Charles Henrotin, were made chairman and vice-chairman of the Board of Lady Managers, which included representatives from every state in the country, and under their supervision women's participation was to be organized and established. A special building for women's exhibits was planned, and an auxiliary to arrange for women's congresses was formed. In addition, the Chicago Woman's Club was appointed to act as official hostess at receptions scheduled in honor of the many distinguished guests who would participate in the congresses. So it came about, that we met not only the noted women of our own country, but many from abroad, as well. Club members served on committees of all congresses and, beginning our work in 1890 and continuing until the Fair was history, were enabled in this way, to make our contribution toward the great impetus then given to Chicago's artistic, spiritual and educational life.

I was honored, by those who were planning the women's congresses by being made representative of the Jewish women, and was further authorized to call Jewish women together under whatever division or divisions I thought best. Since I believed then, as I do now, that when we use the word "Jewish" it must have a purely religious connotation, I felt that our place should be with the Parliament of Religions which was to be one of the great features of World's Fair year. A women's board was organized to aid in furthering the Parliament, and I was made chairman for Jewish women's participation.

Today, with our ready telephonic communication; with radio messages flashing across the continent in the twinkling of an eye; when airplane travel permits one to lunch in Chicago and dine in New York; when every organization publishes printed membership lists of easy accessibility, the task confronting me in the early nineties seems, perhaps, a fairly simple one. To me, in 1891, it appeared colossal — and with reason! Somehow, some way, I must gather together America's outstanding Jewish women. But how could I go about it; how reach the right women? Not only were there no organization lists available . . . there was not even a federal organization! The problem of establishing contacts was a poser that gave me the utmost concern. After much thought, however, I determined to write a personal letter to leading rabbis of the larger cities and communities, requesting them to send me the names of the women in their congregations whom they felt would have the most to offer to such a Parliament, in the way of ability, interest and leadership. First, of course, it was necessary to secure the names of these rabbis — a process entailing much time and energy. Then, when I received a response from each of these spiritual leaders, all of whom proved most genuinely interested and cooperative, I wrote ninety letters (all by hand, and each one personal!) to the women whose names had been suggested. I began to work toward this end in 1891, and it was almost a year later — a year of planning, conferring and incessant letter-writing — before I was satisfied that we could, indeed, present a Jewish Women's Congress worthy of the stirring Parliament of Religions. The gratifying results and the enthusiasm evidenced at the end of this year's work more than compensated, however, for any effort expended.

Two questions were at first involved: one,— should we

have a congress; two,— would it have permanence, or would it be a brief bright tale in which was written, "they met and parted"? In a flash, my thoughts crystallized to a decision: we *will* have a congress out of which must grow a permanent organization!

It was a moment of real elation when I was able to announce to the Woman's Board that the Jewish women would convene, and to present our plans.

The first step had been to appoint a committee chosen from among the leaders of our local Jewish organizations, augmented by representative women from other cities. Invaluable and sage counsel was given me by my constant advisors, Dr. Emil G. Hirsch and Mrs. Charles Henrotin.

How gratifying the day when I could report definite progress and request two places for Jewish women on the general Parliament program. We had selected two remarkable speakers: Henrietta Szold, then secretary of the Jewish Publication Society, who chose as her topic, "What Judaism Has Done for Women", and Josephine Lazarus, a brilliant thinker who wielded a powerful pen, and who elected to discuss "The Outlook for Judaism." Both papers proved scholarly and paved the way for Jewish women, magnificently opening up for them many opportunities to speak on Judaism before women of other faiths.

When the Jewish men of Chicago gathered to make plans for their congress, I was invited to attend the meeting. After some preliminary business, the chairman turned to me, asking,

"Mrs. Solomon, will you Jewish women cooperate with us in our sessions?"

"Well", I replied, "our plans are already far advanced, and assignments have been given our representatives in the general Parliament. We will, however, be very glad to join with you if you will accord us active participation in your program."

The program committee then retired to deliberate, and when they returned, lo and behold! not a single woman's name appeared in their recommendations!

"Mr. Chairman", I inquired, "just where on your program are the women to be placed?"

"Well," hemmed and hawed the chairman, "the program seems complete just as it stands."

"Very well," I replied, "under these circumstances we do not care to cooperate with you, and I request that the fact of our presence at this meeting be expunged from the records."

Does it seem that I spoke hastily in saying, before, that this year of 1893 marked the beginning of women's collaboration with men? Though it is obvious that every forward step met some such stubborn resistance, we really dare not be too critical of these Jewish men, since their attitude was the accepted one of that day. After our Women's Congress proved to be something of a triumph, however, a number of them condescended to acknowledge that we knew better than they the achievments of which Jewish women were capable.

Early in 1893, I journeyed west with my husband and, as we traveled, attempted to arouse interest in the Jewish Women's Congress and augment the success of correspondence so assiduously carried on during the past two years. In Denver, one of the leading women invited a large circle of friends to hear me tell of our work for the Congress, and of the plan for a national organization. Through this fortuitous meeting, I secured for our program an admirable speaker on philanthropy in the person of Carrie Shevelson Benjamin.

Returning to Chicago at the end of May, I again plunged into preparations for the congress, with an increased realization of its great value and historic potentialities, for it would represent the very first attempt of Jewish women, anywhere, to assemble together as an entity, in a great religious gathering.

Even as I think of it I thrill to the remembrance of my first view of the Parliament! Men of every clime had come together, under the banner of religion. From Orient and Occident they had journeyed, to meet, to teach and to learn. Representatives of every country, all joined in unison, lifting their voices to sing, "Praise God from Whom all blessings flow"! Years of preparation had resulted in this great bringing-together, and never has there been more inspiring evidence of the spiritual achievements of the human race. Followers of Confucius and Buddha, of the Jewish prophets, of Jesus and his disciples, as well as founders of other great faiths spoke, as one, the challenging words, "Have we not all one Father? Hath not one God created us all?" These words, at the suggestion of Dr. Hermann Adler, chief rabbi of the British Empire, became the keynote of the Parliament, and its motto. Dr. Henry John Barrows, pastor of the First Presbyterian Church of Chicago, was chairman of the magnificent conclave, and our most prominent Unitarian, the Reverend Jenkin Lloyd Jones, its secretary. Outstanding religious leaders presided over the meetings and rapt attention was accorded the brilliant addresses. Thousands thronged the halls of the new Art Institute in which the Parliament convened before the pictures were installed, and for seventeen days audiences proved too large for the rooms assigned and speeches frequently had to be repeated to overflow audiences.

Harlow Higgenbotham, President of the World's Fair, wrote to me at its close, "I think the whole world has reason to be proud of our effort. . . . I agree with you that our Parliament of Religions was the crowning glory of our Exposition and, in fact, of all time. It did more to unify the peoples of the earth and make them more kindly than any other event in all history."

Today, in the light of the burning flame of hatred so recently ablaze in every corner of the globe, one wonders just when, and by whom, the small candle kindled by the Parliament in the interest of world harmony and kindliness was snuffed out! One may rejoice in the knowledge, however, that at least one group ... our own ... became unified at that congress and will never lose the inspiration there engendered!

Glorious consummation of long months of preparation was the opening of the Jewish Women's Congress! Through it all, my own household had been dedicated to the cause. Little Frank had added the lisped word, "Juda-ithm", to his vocabulary, and Helen and Herbert had labored assiduously at the important tasks of sealing envelopes and posting letters. I must confess, they seemed remarkably unimpressed by the Congress, itself! The focal point of their admiration centered about my gown of heavy white satin embroidered with large golden bowknots, which I wore at the evening reception given at the Standard Club, in honor of our delegates. How Jane Addams chortled as she told us, later, of a conversation she and Mary Rozet Smith had with Herbert and Helen after the one session they were permitted to attend. "Aren't you proud of your mother?" Miss Smith asked the children. "Oh, yes," replied Herbert. "Helen, wouldn't you like to do what your mother has done?" queried Miss Addams. "Oh, no," Helen immediately responded, "when I grow up I'm going to be a lady, like my Aunt Rose!" And here, philosophied Miss Addams, was mirrored the distinction of the day: on the one hand, a "lady", and on the other, a woman interested in "causes"! Rose was, indeed, a lady, but she was also a servant in the cause of humanity, brightening in her charming and unobtrusive way the lot of many who were in need.

My husband's unabated interest in our Congress, and his staunch encouragement continued throughout, and when I delivered the chairman's address at the opening session, I am sure he felt that a truly historic moment in world affairs had been achieved! There, too, sat my father; but my mother remained away; a sacrifice she made because it was so difficult for me then — as always — to speak in public in her presence. There was for me a self-consciousness which I am sure many other women experience from a platform when a mother is in the audience. Father, however, never missed a session of the Congress of Jewish Women, and he and Mother were among those most concerned and interested in its outcome.

With these words, Mrs. Henrotin opened the Jewish Women's Congress on the morning of September fourth, "The great number assembled in response to the call of the committee testifies to the universality of sentiment on the point of holding a congress among Jewish women. That this meeting may result in a national organization is my earnest desire." She especially delighted my husband, however, when she introduced me as the presiding officer, saying, "Mrs. Hannah G. Solomon, to whose courage, energy and devotion the success of this congress will be due."

The congress was, indeed, a success! In developing the program, our thought was to present subjects relating to the Jewish woman, to Jewish problems and the Jewish woman's part in their solution. The evening of September sixth was especially outstanding. Larger rooms had to be obtained for all our sessions, but for this one it was necessary to provide a second hall, and to repeat the program. Minnie D. Louis, of New York, read a paper on "Mission Work Among the Unenlightened Jews" which was discussed by Rebekah Kohut. It was of "humanitarian endeavor" among the underprivileged that they spoke, and of integration into American life. Mrs. Louis ended her moving speech, thus, "You Jewish women of Chicago, all Israel honors you! You have inaugurated a new mission of enlightenment! Like unto Samuel, you have gathered us together to unite us, that we may gain strength, to arouse in us a thirst for better knowledge of our people and our trust, with a more loyal allegiance to both, through which we may become invested with that holiness that will make even our enemies worship with us." These words might, indeed, have been used as the platform upon which the permanent organization we were to plan would rest. Mrs. Kohut voiced a stirring challenge: "We must not be clannish and narrow-minded. Down with the wall that divides us from our Christian brother! High up with the standard of Judaism in the other camp! Act in every sense of the word as American Jews. This is the great lesson we must teach. It is a glorious privilege to be a Jew, but it is also glorious to be an American!"

The other topic of the evening, "How Can Nations Be Influenced to Protest or Even Interfere in Cases of Persecution?", was presented in a paper by Laura Davis Jacobson of St. Louis, and in the discussion which followed Jews, Catholics and Protestants took part, among them Archbishop Ireland of St. Paul and William Onahan, Jenkin Lloyd Jones, and Dr. Hirsch of Chicago. All were sympathetic, but none could find solution for the insane course taken at that time by Russia, whose persecution was then driving the Jews to our shores, just as did Germany's, later.

It was also at this session that presentation was made of the "Collection of the Principal Melodies of the Synagogue from the Earliest Time to the Present." This beautifully bound book of traditional music had been gathered for us by a number of noted cantors and compiled by the Reverend Alois Kaiser of Baltimore and the Reverend Sparger of New York, and touching, indeed, were the words spoken by Mrs. Emma Frank who introduced it, thus: "When first the subject of a religious congress was spoken of, the idea suggested itself to a few of our ardent workers that no more fitting time or opportunity would ever present itself for the revival of our forgotten and scattered hymns than at this first Jewish Woman's Congress. That it is peculiarly woman's sphere to introduce divine and sacred music into the household is self-evident; why should not we, then, deem it a duty to become familiar with the beautiful echoes of the past and the histories that surround them? .... To many, these revised melodies will bring memories of the sweet and pathetic incidents of their past lives when, surrounded by those who have long since departed, they knew no greater pleasure than to make their Sabbaths and other holidays perfect so far as their simple mode of living allowed."

"The present volume", wrote Cyrus Adler, then the Librarian of the Smithsonian Institution in Washington, in his preface to our hymn book, "is the first fruit of the organization of the Jewish Women's Section of the Parliament of Religions." The "second fruit" was to be a national organization; the natural outcome of our gathering for the first time as a body of Jewish women. The members of the committee and I had carried on an extensive correspondence during our several years of work. No less than two thousand letters had been written, and I still treasure some of the replies to mine. Of special significance was the fact that we announced in all our communications that, following our congress, permanent organization would be attempted.

Women in the United States, whom we had contacted, were requested to call meetings in their communities to choose delegates prepared to consider plans for the future, and in our congress, twenty-nine cities were represented by ninety-three women.

The presentation of the final plans for organization was to conclude the congress. All the material we had gathered and the outline we had charted and discussed were therefore turned over to Sadie American, of Chicago, who would present them at the meeting. On September third, we met at the home of Mrs. Emmanuel Mandel, and framed a resolution of organization to be prepared in case none more desirable should be forthcoming.

The closing session terminated in a business meeting, and in the resolution brought in by Julia Richman of New York, we read, "the visiting essayists and delegates pledge themselves to the support of any permanent organization which shall be the outgrowth of this congress."

Naturally, the question of a name aroused general interest, and several suggestions met with only lukewarm response. Then came the dramatic moment when Julia Felsenthal of Chicago rose to her feet and said,

"Madame Chairman, I suggest the name 'The National Council of Jewish Women' for this organization!"

Instantaneous and enthusiastic acclaim greeted Miss Felsenthal's words. Immediately, a motion from the floor, followed by a quick "second", put the question before the assembly. A vote was taken and passed unanimously! Our organization had a name!

A committee was appointed to draw up resolutions defining the purposes of the new association. After deliberation, the following program was brought back to us, and accepted:

"Resolved, that the National Council of Jewish Women shall (1) seek to unite in closer relation women interested in the work of Religion, Philanthropy and Education and shall consider practical means of solving problems in these fields; shall (2) organize and encourage the study of the underlying principles of Judaism; the history, literature and customs of the Jews, and their bearing on their own and the world's history; shall (3) apply knowledge gained in this study to the improvement of the Sabbath Schools, and in the work of social reform; shall (4) secure the interest and aid of influential persons, wherever and whenever and against whomever shown, and in finding means to prevent such persecutions."

A brief statement, that, and simply worded; yet sturdy enough to bear throughout these years, the ever-growing structure of which it is the keystone.

And so was born the National Council of Jewish Women ... living symbol of world progress as demonstrated by the World Columbian Exposition.

The Chicago Fair of 1893! How I wish I might write words that could convey even a suggestion of its glory! Of all the world's fairs I have seen, none has equalled it. Jamestown, St. Louis, San Diego, New York, Philadelphia's Sesquicentennial and Chicago's own Century of Progress ... all of them I attended ... all were superb ... but Chicago's exposition of 1893 was peerless in beauty! Unlike most fairs, the World Columbian Exposition did not convey the impression of the temporary and evanescent as many subsequent fairs have done. It possessed an air of distinction and a feeling of substance that made it difficult to realize it was but a transitory creation, not intended to endure. And surely, it *has* endured for those of us who saw it, for great architects, great sculptors, great painters and great artists in every field had been brought together to create it. The location, in Jackson Park, was perfect for the "White City", as it was often called, and the wonderful buildings, the landscaped gardens, the fountains and statuary provided exquisite vistas in every direction. And the marvelous murals! And the splendidly arranged exhibits! Indeed, it was not merely a materialistic world we surveyed, but one built about a core of idealism and beauty.

At the Fair, I spent much of my time at the Art Palace, for I was especially interested in pictures and sculpture. Fortunately, at the close of the exposition, our own Art Institute, which had served to house the congresses, became possessed of many paintings that had been imported to hang in the Art Palace. Today it harbors some truly renowned examples of the great masters and affords an opportunity for a wide education in art. Many new schools have been added since those days when "Impressionism" was a breath-taking departure from the classic and when "Breaking Home Ties" represented the ideal in art to a wondering World's Fair public!

Literally millions flocked to Chicago during the period of the Fair and all agreed that the way the city met the exigencies of the novel situation was little short of miraculous. Yes, Chicago vindicated herself brilliantly! Chicago — frowned upon by some of our Washington solons as ill-prepared to merit the great honor bestowed upon her by the government — found herself crowned in triumph as the glorious exposition closed.

CHAPTER XI

MANY OF MY CONTEMPORARIES look backward with nostalgia to those "good old days of the gay nineties". But, in retrospect, I vision always a different Chicago. My mental picture of 1893 is that of a city of such rapid growth that its problems were a constant challenge to its citizens.

There were lacking, as yet, adequate organized means of solving these problems. Oh, yes, we had desultory groups like the Ladies' Aid and Benevolent Societies; we had Orphan Asylums; we had a Home for the Friendless and many individual "ladies bountiful; we had huge Charity Bazaars and philanthropists! But the heightened necessity of more intensive associated and cooperative organization was becoming increasingly evident.

Perhaps it was the great need of the moment that brought forth so remarkable a galaxy of brilliant women, foremost among them such notable leaders as Jane Addams, Mary MacDowell, Louise de Koven Bowen, Mrs. Charles Henrotin, Lucy Flower, Mary Bartelme, Celia Parker Wooley, Ella Flagg Young and Julia Lathrop. Certainly, it was the era of a sweeping change of technique in civic endeavor!

Mrs. Henrotin, realizing that expositions always leave numbers of stranded women and children in their wake, took the initiative, as chairman of a committee of the Chicago

Woman's Club, and again called me to her assistance. Inviting the cooperation of other organizations, this committee opened an emergency workroom in December, 1893, where seventy women were given employment. In stores and offices we were able to find positions for many more. As did other members of the board of the Woman's Club, I assumed charge of the workroom one day each week. Not all those in need of aid had been World's Fair participants, however. One day, when I was in command, an assistant asked me to accompany her to a side room where, she said, were women who were "speaking a German no one could understand". To my great surprise, I realized that these women were talking Yiddish which, up to that time, I had rarely heard. Fully one-third of them were Russian; part of the large group forced to flee from Russian persecution.

It was unusual, then, to find Jewish wives at work, but the husbands of these women were without employment, and their families badly in need of money. With other members of the Club, I undertook to visit their homes, and thus was inaugurated, for me, a new and practical philanthropy which resulted in a continuous and constructive cooperation with the many Russian Jewish women of Chicago who labored so conscientiously and untiringly for their unfortunate friends. I realized that it was necessary to create a more general interest in the recently arrived immigrants, in order to help them solve the many problems presented by the new language and unfamiliar customs of a strange country.

In the winter of 1895–96, the Chicago Section of the Council held a one-day bazaar at which we realized two thousand dollars. Half of this I requested. and obtained, for the establishment of a bureau through which women's organizations could project a much-needed personal service effort.

Thus was created, in 1897, the Seventh Ward District Bureau of the Associated Charities of Chicago, non-sectarian! It was later renamed the Bureau of Personal Service, and I served as its chairman for the thirteen years of its existence, after which it became a part of the Associated Jewish Charities In the beginning, we asked for space with the Jewish Charities, but our request was not granted because the Charities Board did not wish, at the time, to extend its work. We then established ourselves in the heart of the so-called "Ghetto" district. Though we were non-sectarian, we referred all our non-Jewish cases to another branch of the Associated Charities located not far away. They, in turn, sent all Jewish cases to us. In planning, we decided that those people requiring relief be directed to the Jewish Charities and only emergency assistance be given in situations which, for other reasons, necessitated the Bureau's attention.

The Council instituted the Bureau as a separate entity, apart from its own work, since it believed better cooperation with other agencies would be secured if it functioned as an independent body. Minnie Low, who had been my secretary, became its executive director, and Minnie Jacobs (later Mrs. Minnie J. Berlin) her assistant. The Bureau afforded legal aid to the Jewish poor, and for this we were able to secure, gratis, the services of Chicago's finest lawyers. No work that we did was more satisfactory than that which was accomplished through the courts. Every judge and every official before whom we appeared gave us the most courteous treatment and invaluable assistance, and cases in which we were interested were never lost. Indeed, our advice was often sought. Later, we established a direct prison contact, in connection with which, Mrs. Berlin did an outstanding service.

Working in the West Side locality, the Bureau established

relationships with all possible agencies, including churches, synagogues and schools, both public and private. Cases were investigated for the Woman's Loan, for the School Children's Aid Society and for some of the settlements. Hull House and Henry Booth House applications for coal, distributed by Henry Lyton, were also passed upon by us. We aided in a study of tenement houses and worked for better laws relating to them, as well as for their enforcement. We organized and supervised, for a time, a Jewish woman's workroom, founded upon the plan of the one directed by the Chicago Woman's Club.

By the time the Bureau became a part of the Associated Jewish Charities, it had established a record of splendid achievement. Our first report, for the year 1896–97, contained a survey of the Jewish district where many interesting facts came to light. It was found, for example, that there were fourteen Loan Societies operated by the Russian group, alone, and that in the seven public schools, a great majority of the children were Jewish.

It must be remembered that when the Bureau was opened, there were few trained social service workers, even among the superintendents, and nearly all women assistants were volunteers. There was little scientific administration of charities and practically no collaboration among the different agencies. Our methods of administration were entirely inadequate; a fact I realized even at that time, and expressed thus, in my first Bureau report: "We can no more run charities on the old lines than a business house can chalk the names of its customers on the barn door."

During the existence of the Bureau, higher levels were reached, a uniform system of records was adopted and a copy of all cases aided by Jewish women's organizations was kept.

[95]

New assistants were constantly added to grapple with the steadily increasing load. Beginning with our survey, the work extended until there was no institution that housed Jewish dependents, delinquents or defectives that did not have regular Friendly Visitors, in addition to necessary attention from the paid staff of the Jewish agencies interested in each case. How far that little candle threw its beam!

In 1904, the Bureau secured a summer playground for the district. Its director was Sydney Teller, who later became head of the Irene Kaufman Settlement, in Pittsburgh — a development of the center originated by the Pittsburgh section of the National Council of Jewish Women. Great was the rejoicing when, still later, a small park, whose location I had helped to select and in behalf of which I had used such influence as I could, was opened. Known as Small Park Number Two, or Stanford Park, its location was especially satisfactory, for at one corner stood a large public school and at another was Henry Booth House, the settlement established by the Ethical Culture Society of Chicago. Shortly after, on yet a third corner was erected a beautiful building, the gift of Mr. and Mrs. Levy Mayer, which housed The Helen Day Nursery, an organization which had been undertaken by my daughter, Helen, at the suggestion of Jane Addams. There was, at the time, no Jewish day nursery, and Hull House, in the adjoining district, was unable to care for the growing number of children whose mothers were obliged to work. Helen, just out of college, was ready and eager to be of service and she was president of the nursery board until her marriage. This board was unique in that it was composed, for the most part, of women of financial means who had never before participated, personally, in the establishing and conducting of any philanthropic institution. From this beginning, however, may of them developed markedly, contributing greatly in other far-reaching branches of social service.

My first acquaintance with Hull House began when it was still the home of Captain Hull and his sister, dating back to the days when Halsted Street was a residential avenue lined with beautiful trees. The Hull House we know today, however, became a social settlement in 1899 and I was privileged to know its founders, Jane Addams and Ellen Starr, as well as Julia Lathrop, Florence Kelly and Laura Dainty Pelham who were among its first important workers. All of these women gave signal service, but always Miss Addams was their leader. For me, any work which she undertook required no questioning, and I was always happy to be among her devoted followers, feeling honored to be her friend as well as her co-worker. Associated with Miss Addams in her efforts were many whose accomplishments cannot be overestimated and heading the list were Mrs. Henrotin and Lucy Flower, women of rare mentality and broad vision. Every institution for children won their interest and assistance, as did all helpful legislation.

Hull House started as a home in which Miss Addams and Miss Starr established themselves as friendly participants in the life of a neighborhood inhabited by foreign groups. Now, with its many buildings, it occupies one entire city block and its influence extends far beyond its physical boundaries.

The section of Chicago adjoining Hull House developed into the Jewish Ghetto. In a report of the Bureau of Personal Service for the 1897-99 period, I wrote, "Hull House, our neighbor, a beacon-light, carries its cheering rays throughout the district, and I venture to say that seventy percent of those who love to cross its threshold to receive its inspiration are of our faith." In 1892 a meeting was held at Hull House to

[97]

discuss the possibility of establishing a social center in the Jewish community, and it was then that the Maxwell Street Settlement was brought into being. The Jewish Training School, in which my brother-in-law, Henry Frank, was deeply interested and of which he was president, had been opened in 1890, in the same neighborhood. It had a remarkable curriculum and a most progressive pedagogic basis, offering a program of manual training for the children of immigrant families, and proving to be a significant factor in the lives of many who are, today, outstanding citizens. In another district inhabited predominantly by Jews, an exceptional institution, quite unique in character, was established in 1903. Its object, according to its charter, was "The promotion of education, civic training, moral and physical culture, the amelioration and social advancement of the Jewish residents of Chicago." In a sense, it serves its immediate locality, but at the same time it draws interest from persons near and far. Originally called the Chicago Hebrew Institute, it is now known as the Jewish Peoples' Institute, and is a center of widespread influence.

With the widening scope of women's civic and philanthropic activities, it became necessary, in 1895, to evolve some effective method by which the various organizations might function cooperatively. Consequently, I asked my cousin, Mrs. Martin Barbe, to assist me in calling together all the presidents of the Jewish women's associations in order that we might discuss the advisability of creating a meeting ground for furthering work we all seemed to be advancing more or less independently. Lizzie Barbe was then president of the Jochannah Lodge, of which she is, today, the beloved and honored dean, and I knew that her interests so closely paralleled mine that she would realize, as I did, the crying need

[98]

for such action. She had been one of the most enthusiastic delegates to the Jewish Women's Congress, in 1893, and at one time served as national vice-president of the Council, later becoming an honorary vice-president. Her influence in the Chicago section, of which she was the third president, has been noteworthy. Through the long years Lizzie and I worked in harmony, and the association has made pleasanter and more successful every task undertaken jointly. It was natural, then, to turn to Lizzie Barbe at this time, and it was with characteristic zeal that she, too, went to work.

Mrs. Henry Adler was, in 1895, president of the Young Ladies Aid Society, later known as the Chicago Woman's Aid. She and a number of others joined with us to create the first Conference of Jewish Women. Twenty-six groups came together to take the initial steps in bringing about co-ordination, and resulted in "a Conference Committee of the Jewish women's organizations . . . . . formed for the purpose of specializing the charity work of these organizations, to prevent duplication in the distribution of relief."

This, I believe, constituted the first attempt in the country to unite diverse women's groups together in an association dedicated to the serving of common goals, and we disbanded only when the Associated Jewish Charities came into existence.

It was in 1900 that the Jewish men of Chicago effected an affiliation between the Jewish charities in order to create a body which would have the confidence of the public and to which direct contributions for the affiliated agencies could be made. It was hoped that fine institutions, laboring under the difficulty of raising sufficient funds for maintenance, could thus be adequately financed and their boards relieved of the gruelling burden of meeting deficits. In April of 1900, therefore, the Associated Jewish Charities became permanently established and four officers and eight trustees were selected. I was the one woman trustee, chosen to represent the women's societies on the board, and I worked among these to gain support for the federation, since most of them had little interest in any philanthropies but their own. For one year I also served on the board of the Associated Jewish Charities, until a ruling was made that no one might be a member of that board and continue to sit on the governing board of any of its special units, since it was felt that the obligation of the Associated's board should lie in securing funds for all. Consequently, I withdrew, in order to continue as chairman of the Bureau of Personal Service.

In 1910 it again seemed desirable to create a conference of Jewish Women's organizations. The initial meeting for its re-establishment was called under the auspices of the National Council of Jewish Women, during the presidency of Mrs. Emily Weinberg. The Conference of Jewish Women's Organizations is, today, an important, if not an indispensable association, acting not only as a clearing house, functioning to prevent duplication and overlapping of projects and preventing as far as possible conflicting meeting dates, but serving, further, in establishing our groups in friendly, sympathetic contact. It creates opportunities for the interpretation of each unit to the others, thereby providing a medium through which all advance together in the interest of the many causes they espouse. It is a living refutation of the hackneyed argument that women cannot work constructively and in harmony, together.

CHAPTER XII

WHAT MOTHER DOES NOT WATCH with mingled hopes and prayers her child's each new development? With what an intertwining of joy and fear does she see him take those first uncertain steps! And proverbial is her expectation that her offspring is destined to become President of the United States! We Council mothers followed that immemorial and traditional pattern. And, as always, the future for us, too, was only a bright hope! For how could we be certain, despite our zeal and confidence, that our child would one day leave a noble impress in its wake? That it would boast not one, but many presidents? That our infant organization, lusty though it seemed, would grow in time to span even the dividing oceans? No, these things we could not foresee! And perhaps it was just as well that we could not penetrate, in those early days, into the misted future, with a consequent growing impatience at the necessarily slow development of what we sensed, even then, as the logical and limitless potentialities of our organization. For, just as careful nurturing and wise direction are first requisites in the constructive growth of an individual, so, we knew, it would have to be with the Council. If, as we hoped, it would unite all Jewish women — orthodox, conservative and reform; if it was to make a vital contribution to the religious, educational and philanthropic work of Jewry, each new step in its development must, of necessity, be painstakingly planned and carefully considered. It was with this thought foremost in mind that I approached, with enthusiasm and humility, the gigantic task of perfecting the framework of the National Council of Jewish Women, devoting myself to this unfinished work for the entire period, from the conclusion of our congress to the end of the year, 1893.

Rich returns followed immediately!

In her report of the congresses, Mrs. Henrotin wrote, "As to the permanent effect of so much effort, several associations, councils, and innumerable clubs were organized. Without doubt, the National Council of Jewish Women was the most successful. It practically took on an international character .... it was a power for good, not only in America, but all over the known world. Mrs. Solomon labored from the inception of the Woman's branch to make her congress a permanent association, in organizing the Council of Jewish Women."

The Council's first national officers had been chosen at our closing session in the Art Institute. All were Chicago women, and I had been honored by election to the presidency; Mrs. Emanuel Mandel was made vice-president, Sadie American, corresponding secretary, Mrs. L. J. Wolf, recording secretary and Mrs. J. Harry Selz, treasurer. Mrs. Mandel, now ninety-three years of age, has been at all times one of the Council's staunchest supporters, and her name is revered in the Chicago section. She is one of whom it may be said, in truth, "Her works praise her in the gates".

It had been decided that there should be a vice-president for each state, some of whom had been elected at the congress.

I was empowered to appoint the others, as well as to complete the board of nine directors. The members of the board were, of necessity, Chicago women, since we realized the need of frequent consultation.

After the selection of the board and the national committees, my initial task was to plan the first draft of the constitution, which was then presented, as a working basis, to a committee who, in turn, would prepare it for submission to the national board. It was accepted as a provisional constitution to function for three years, at the termination of which our first convention was scheduled to take place.

Chicago's was the first section of the Council, founded in January, 1894. A post-card invitation had been sent out to the Chicago women who had evinced a particular interest in the congress, and one hundred and sixty-four members joined, at once! Speedily there followed the formation of other sections, so that at our first triennial, fifty cities in twenty-two states were listed.

The greater part of the work of organization fell, naturally, upon the president and the corresponding secretary. The task was arduous but the fullest cooperation was forthcoming from leaders in each community, for women who were known throughout the country were enrolling, with enthusiasm, under the Council banner, and their zeal enabled the organization to secure a firm footing. Thus, the Council's success is due to thousands of Jewish women and their loyalty to Judaism and all that it imposes.

How I wish that I might include in these pages a detailed story of the Council of Jewish Women! That, unfortunately, would require a volume all its own. Impossible, too, is the complete recording of all the highlights of the thirteen years of my presidency and the four splendid conventions over which I presided. But especially do I regret having to leave unmentioned, here, the names of many of the fine women who have helped make Council history. In our Triennial reports they all appear and in my memory, too, all are appreciatively inscribed!

The constitution of the Council permitted freedom in activities to all sections, in order to meet the individual needs of each community. It provided, however, for two national committees: one on Religion and one on Philanthropy. Soon a third, on Sabbath Schools, was established. The program for the first three years planned study classes in both religion and philanthropy. Pamphlets written by leaders in both fields stressed newer methods for religious training as well as in the approach to and organization for philanthropy. We advocated professional social service workers and were among the first to urge training for "Friendly Visitors". The report of the philanthropy committee revealed that none of the sections had entered the sphere of alms-giving, but it listed many charitable ventures, classes and clubs for boys and girls and every possible aid to immigrants and their families. A number of Jewish Sabbath schools were organized for communities in which there was neither rabbi nor synagogue and at all times we urged the use of professional teachers.

My first report, as president, was printed in 1895, and in that I stressed the necessity for cooperation with other established agencies in philanthropy and personal service and the importance of introducing protective measures against delinquency and indigence. There were few precedents to follow so that in both our philanthropic and religious undertakings we were obliged to experiment.

Since we had agreed to assemble triennially, the first convention of the National Council of Jewish Women was to be held in 1886. We were now an organization with fifty sections and over thirty-three hundred members, and New York was selected as our first convention city. So much publicity had been given to us that some of the country's larger newspapers sent special reporters to New York. Still Victorian in their evaluation of women's activities, headlines in a leading daily announced, "Meeting of Fair Ones", "Princesses of Israel Gather" and "First Convention of the National Council of the Daughters of Judah"! Papers were not yet printing photographs, but they produced delightful pen-and-ink sketches of the "daring" women attending, copies of which are still preserved in my scrap-books.

It was at the New York convention that our Council motto was adopted. The desirability of having one had been discussed by the board in 1895, and suggestions from the sections had then been requested. Philadelphia's suggestion was "Faith and Humanity", and this recommendation received the most votes and was adopted, forthwith. It was decided, at the same time, that we have a "badge" and Katherine Cohen, a Philadelphia artist and sister of Mary M. Cohen who had read a paper at our congress at the Parliament of Religions, was commissioned to design a seal and pin. The simple but effective pin she produced, with its white and blue ground and gold lettering, is worn, with pride, by Council members today.

The 1896 response of the male sex to the participation of women in discussion of subjects outside the home is very revealing. A perfect example of this decidedly "superior" attitude was evidenced by a leading rabbi of the day, following a scholarly address by my sister, Henriette, who spoke these words at an evening meeting of the convention: "The Sabbath is one of the best gifts of Israel to humanity. The

Sabbath idea is essential to Judaism", she said, "but" (referring to the controversial question of the acceptance of Sunday) "not the choice of the calendar day, but the manner of its observance makes of it the Sabbath." In a newspaper report of the meeting the following day we read, "Rabbi ———— created a little stir at the close of Mrs. Frank's paper by declaring that women should not meddle with such matters. 'This is a matter for rabbis to decide', he declared."

The proceedings of the convention, the first in which our women had assembled as a distinctly Jewish organization, was printed by the Jewish Publication Society where the report of the Jewish Women's Congress of 1893 had also appeared.

It was not to be expected that so large a group of women, with varying backgrounds and different traditions could always see eye to eye! So it was not surprising that a controversy should arise at the convention, as it did, over the question of my re-election to the presidency. A number of the delegates were orthodox and, believing in the observance of Saturday as the day of worship, felt that the president of the National Council of Jewish Women should be one who adhered also to this custom. When, therefore, this issue was raised, a speaker from the floor stated that she thought the president of the Council should be "one who consecrated the Sabbath". Immediately, I countered with, "I consecrate every day of the week!" This statement was hailed with touching acclaim, and I was duly re-elected.

My return from New York, therefore, assumed the proportions of a triumph in our home, and when I arrived in Chicago, my husband and children had prepared a royal welcome! There, above the piano, all decked out in smilax and evergreen, was a huge floral piece on which was written, "I consecrate every day!", while on an opposite wall hung an equally impressive tribute, proclaiming, "Faith and Humanity."

My husband's interest and cooperation in everything that I undertook was of greatest importance to me. In fact, without his constant encouragement, I could not have continued, satisfactorily, on my way. He was my chief advisor and many a time his ready financial assistance eased the way. Often, when problems arose, he aided in their solution, buoying up my flagging spirits, sharing in my every endeavor with quick understanding and wisest counsel.

In accepting the invitation of the National Council of Women to become an affiliate, in 1894, the Council of Jewish Women took a most memorable step, thereby becoming associated with other women of the United States as well as with women of the world who were united in a desire to work for all humanity. The National Council of Women was composed of many organizations and belonged, as a body, to the International Council, as well. Both had been organized in 1888 under the direction of Mrs. Elizabeth Cady Stanton, pioneer of pioneers, who as early as 1886 had urged an international convention for the cause of woman's suffrage. It was, in fact, the Woman's Suffrage Society which took the initiative in calling for a union of the large national and international women's organizations and both had been invited to hold meetings at the World's Fair Congresses. Thus, through arduous effort, influential leaders of thirty-five foreign countries were brought together in 1893. These representatives voiced the belief that organizations which differed in outlook should present their points of view in joint meeting, calmly discussing their differences and establishing agreements. Here, then, was one of the first efforts to effect large associations for the

[107]

purpose of improving world conditions, developing mutual understanding and goodwill and attaining increased purpose in action.

The National Council of Jewish Women was invited, likewise, to become a member of the General Federation of Women's Clubs. Since the Federation's constitution did not provide for the inclusion of religious groups in its membership, we were asked to join nationally, on the basis of our philanthropic work, but because we considered ourselves primarily a religious body, we refused. The General Federation held its first convention, in Chicago, in 1892 and a year later a great impetus had been added by newly formed organizations, and joint efforts and cooperation became important features. In 1894 the federation began to form state federations, and these the Council's sections were urged to join. I assisted in organizing Illinois, and in 1896 attended the General Federation convention in Louisville, as delegate from the Illinois State Federation and as honorary delegate of the National Council of Jewish Women. Many of our sections had, by that time, affiliated with the State Federations and enjoyed delegate representation.

In 1895 the Council participated in the convention of the National Council of Women, in Washington, sharing an evening program with the Women's Temperance Union of which Frances Willard was the illustrious president. Temperance was then one of the burning issues of the day, and Miss Willard presided at the first half of the meeting, I at the second. The convention, of course, brought us into contact with women who were leaders in the other large national organizations, and there I became acquainted with Susan B. Anthony, the greatest woman's suffragist, forming a friendship that lasted as long as she lived. Later, I had the pleasure of knowing Carrie Chapman Catt, the remarkable and energetic woman who succeeded Miss Anthony as president of the Woman's Suffrage Society and who remained at its head until its object was achieved. Then, with characteristic vision, Mrs. Catt devoted herself to efforts in other important fields and has continued her blessed work throughout the years. Her National Committee on the Cause and Cure of War has labored unceasingly in the interest of international understanding and peace.

The fight for suffrage constitutes a long and interesting chapter. Even without the ballot, the influence of women had been a factor in the enactment of laws that aided women and children, but it was conceded that not until we could vote could our strength be exerted to the fullest. The earliest crusaders had secured the right for women to hold joint guardianship of their children. Before that time, in case of a divorce, decisions were entirely the father's prerogative, with the mother having no claims in relation to her offspring! A married woman could not inherit property from her parents; it all belonged to her husband! She could find no employment except as a teacher or a servant and she had little opportunity for higher education. Now these injustices had become things of the past, and women were free to direct their attention and energy to obtaining suffrage.

It is almost impossible to gauge the great influence of the 1893 women's congresses! The cause of women's suffrage is surely a case in point. Its congress of representative women converted a surprising number of people, men included, to the point where suffrage actually became fashionable! Many thinking people realized that it was impossible to make headway against unscrupulous politicians without women's votes. When a new constitution was being drawn up for Illinois, the section which would have granted suffrage to women was beaten by just one vote in the committee drafting the document. Meantime, the sentiment in favor of suffrage had become so strong that, because of this single omission, the whole constitution was rejected when it was presented to the people in the election! In 1913 Illinois granted limited suffrage to women, but they were compelled to wait for full ballotting privileges until 1917, at the time of World War I.

The historic women's suffrage parade of Chicago was one of those unique occasions in which an almost tangible unity brought stimulation such as is rarely experienced. Though it was held on a miserable, rainy day, our spirits were not affected in the least, and we proceeded down Michigan Avenue with intense enthusiasm, some in carriages, some on foot. Our chic uniformed women of today would be heartily amused at the suffragette's brand of feminine militancy, but our cause was won, nonetheless!

In its strides toward progressive development, the National Council of Jewish Women was keeping in step with the times, as was clearly evidenced at its second Triennial held in Cleveland in 1900. Because of the illness and death of my son, Herbert, the convention which would normally have been held in 1899, was postponed until the following year.

Many changes in which we were deeply concerned were then taking place. The Jewish population had increased, greatly, through the arrival of refugees from Russia. In the larger cities a number of philanthropies had assumed civic importance, and the sections of the Council, themselves, had created some of the most outstanding. The Columbian Settlement, with free bath house facilities had been established, in Pittsburgh, later becoming the Irene Kaufmann Settlement, a model institution. The New York Section had opened a fine

Our Three Children, Helen, Herbert and Frank

recreation room for girls in the crowded Jewish district; Cleveland carried on a splendid piece of work in a Council building, for the benefit of immigrants, and other sections were engaged in similar activities on a smaller scale. In Chicago, the Seventh Ward Bureau of Personal Service had been started with money contributed by us. The Denver section had requested that the Council undertake the management of the National Jewish Hospital for Consumptives, and though we did not adopt this as a national enterprise, the fact that it was suggested is worthy of note. Permission was given to the Denver section, however, to circularize our entire membership for funds toward the hospital's maintenance.

Certain significant affairs of the day are mirrored in my report at our Cleveland Triennial: "As your representative, I signed a petition to the President of the United States in the interest of peace, but that failing and war being declared with Spain, we devoted our energies to do our share toward the alleviation of suffering". Also: "Several letters regarding our position on the Dreyfus matter were received, but none were answered until after the trial had ended, as we felt satisfied that we could not assist, but might greatly harm the cause. After the trial had ended we sent a letter to Mrs. Dreyfus in the name of the Council." This, of course, refers to the celebrated Dreyfus case in France, and I find that in my address, as President, to the third Triennial, in 1902, I said, "We remember gratefully Emile Zola, a departed hero and champion, who conquered by force of the honest word, the just demand. Nor, for the Jew alone, did Zola bring deliverance. He wrought far more for France in dispelling the gloom, in bringing to her the opportunity of blotting from her pages the record of a great crime."

It was Dr. Emil G. Hirsch, great and learned rabbi of

Sinai Temple, who accorded me a signal honor when, in 1897, he invited me to address his congregation. It was the first time a Jewish woman had ever been accorded the privilege of occupying a Jewish pulpit, though Jane Addams had spoken there, previously. But Dr. Hirsch's example was soon followed in this, as in other important innovations, by many congregations throughout the country. A clipping from one of the Chicago newspapers records that, "Mrs. Hannah G. Solomon, the first woman in the history of Judaism to act as rabbi, filled the pulpit of Sinai Temple yesterday morning. It could have happened in no Jewish Temple but Dr. Hirsch's, and the congregation predicts that the incident will put it farther from orthodoxy than any other innovation which it has been its pride to make. It makes Sinai and its leader the talk of the Hebrew world.... There was not a vacant seat in the gallery, or elsewhere. There did not seem to be a voice from the congregation save one of praise for the woman."

The fact that this approbation was entirely too fulsome in no way minimized the delight with which it was received in our home.

As each year passed the Council influence grew more marked. And now it was 1899, and the organization was beginning to think in international terms! Since I was unable to go to England when the International Council of Women met in London, our corresponding secretary, Sadie American went as our representative.

A highlight of the conference was an evening meeting at the home of Mrs. Leopold De Rothschild where a group of English Jewesses assembled to hear of the plans and attainments of the National Council of Jewish Women. When Miss American presented the chairman of the evening with a gavel made at the Jewish Training School, in Chicago, she learned to her surprise that "a gavel was an instrument unknown in England!"

Mrs. Frederick Nathan and Julia Richman of New York were also in attendance. Miss American told of the origin and purpose of the Council; Miss Richman discussed religious schools; Mrs. Nathan told of work in the field of philanthropy and the Reverend Maurice Harris, of New York, described "Circle Study". Mrs. Hermann Adler, wife of England's chief rabbi, responded in behalf of the English women. Claude Montefiore, one of the great liberal Jews of our day, said, in closing the meeting, "In many senses, this is an epoch-making meeting!"

At the time of our Cleveland Triennial, Mrs. Nathaniel Cohen, who had presided at the London gathering in the Baroness De Rothschild's home, sent this message: "The possibilities of self-improvement and helpful educational and philanthropic work opened out by the American Council of Jewish Women and brought to the notice of English Jewish women by your kind and able efforts last summer, have made a deep impression on many members of our community here. A definite effort has resulted, to try and found a society on kindred lines in this country and there are great hopes that it will shortly be definitely started." The society founded was the Jewish Study Society, out of which developed the Union of Jewish Women of England. This, then, marked the beginning of our attempt to suggest organization to Jewish women abroad.

Meantime, here at home, the Council was growing year by year. At the second triennial, ninety-three sections and a membership of five thousand had been reported. At the third convention, held in Baltimore in 1902, the recorded membership was seven thousand! There had been, also, a steady growth in the scope of our endeavors. Among the projects reported in Baltimore were eighty-two study groups, a number of lecture courses, new Sabbath schools, new settlements with clubs and classes, kindergartens, personal service groups, work in juvenile courts and many other splendid activities. Two new committees had been created: one, on Peace; another on Juniors. It was at the Cleveland Convention that a Junior Auxiliary had been ordered and there, too, it had been decided that an executive conference of the Council's board should be held annually, the first taking place in 1901, at New Orleans. Here, we adopted a provisional constitution for the Junior Auxiliary, and by the third triennial Junior sections were already flourishing.

One of the most memorable features of our Baltimore triennial was the presence, there, of Chicago's own Jane Addams, who presented an inspired address on "The New Social Spirit" . . . a spirit which she, in truth, best exemplified! It was in Baltimore, too, that a meeting at which Henrietta Szold spoke was held, most appropriately, in the Temple whose pulpit had been occupied for forty-three years by her distinguished father. In recognition of this, as she stepped upon the platform, I placed a bouquet of roses upon the chair that once had been his.

Miss Szold's address was most thoughtful, and rich in the best at her command. She had not yet assumed the position she now holds in Palestine, nor given her strength to furthering its splendid achievement, but for Henrietta Szold I held always the most profound admiration; her figure is outstanding in modern Jewish history.

Throughout these years of organization work, there were many individuals upon whose interest and help I counted. In addition to those whom I could approach, personally, in

Chicago, I conferred through correspondence with three eminent Jewish men: Cyrus Adler and Louis Marshall, who gave most generously of their valuable time and sound advice, and Max Kohler, whom I considered one of the ablest men I knew, and to whom I wrote, especially, on the subject of Zionism. I found that he, too, shared my misgivings over the Balfour Declaration. My highest esteem and admiration goes to Chaim Weizmann who wished no personal reward in the first World War for his great service to England when he, a chemist, developed an explosive of inestimable value to the war effort. He asked, rather, for what he considered a gift to his people, the Jews . . . the gift of the Balfour Declaration. This unselfish act constitutes a glorious page in the annals of Jewry. I have always feared, however, that the sentimental hope of a return to the beloved land, born immediately after the destruction of Jerusalem, could not result in a reality that would be practical in the modern day world. Should Palestine become a Jewish State in a world already overburdened with national boundaries? It is my hope that it may be a refuge for the oppressed now, and for years to come, and that the remarkable regeneration brought about by the Zionists may never be destroyed. I must confess, however, that — for me — Zionism has never seemed more than the despairing cry of a forlorn hope and I still believe that Palestine is destined to be a buffer state in which nothing can, or will, count to other nations but its usefulness to them. Nevertheless, I consider the achievement of the Zionists the greatest of all accomplishments during the peace years after World War I. Those Jews who have continued, by their efforts or their assistance, in turning a wasteland into one of indescribable beauty and promise, a haven of refuge for thousands, have earned universal gratitude and praise.

CHAPTER XIII

"DOWN TO THE SEA IN SHIPS"
(Psalms cvii:23)

O N MAY FOURTEENTH, 1904, Henry and I celebrated the completion of twenty-five years of perfect companionship and harmony with a dinner in our home which was attended by one hundred guests. All silver wedding anniversaries are notable, of course, but as we reviewed our years together and counted our blessings, one by one, we were both humbly conscious of the most profound gratitude for the richness and beauty with which our marriage had been crowned. A devoted family, loyal friends, firm faith and the opportunity to serve . . . what more could we ask, or need? The sorrows that had come to us with the death of loved ones were in direct proportion to the joy each, in life, had brought, and so — deep as was our sense of loss — even there we felt we had been rarely blest.

"Girls," I said to my sisters and sisters-in-law, after the other anniversary dinner guests had departed, "some of you will simply have to come back here for lunch tomorrow and help eat up the mountains of sandwiches and salads left from the party! Honestly, there's enough food for another reception!"

And with that innocent invitation, I set the stage for an incident we remember with amusement to this day. One by one, each refused, regretfully, because of some previous commitment: one had to read a paper at a meeting; a second must take the children to the dentist, and so on down the line.

Next morning, my cook asked, in perplexity, as she viewed the bursting larder, "What'll we do, Mrs. Solomon? Who'll eat all this stuff?"

"My sisters and sisters-in-law," I replied promptly.

"But they said they can't come," she objected.

"We'll just set their places at the table," I told her, confidently. "You'll see, they'll be here, every last one of them!"

And sure enough, they were! One by one they straggled in, sheepish and giggling, until every place at the table was occupied. From that day, my cook eyed me a little tentatively, convinced that I was possessed of occult powers. She never quite believed it was purely a matter of my knowing so well the Greenebaum inability to pass up a spontaneous get-together and so golden an opportunity to "talk things over!"

One day, shortly thereafter, my husband gave voice to one of his frequent and generous suggestions which was, in effect, rather like a luscious topping to a particularly delectable cake! I was scheduled to leave shortly to attend a convention of the International Council of Women, in Berlin, Germany. Susan B. Anthony had been elected first delegate at an executive meeting in Indianapolis, and Mrs. Kate Waller Barrett, National Secretary, was second delegate. Since, at the same meeting, I had been made an alternate, I was asked to take Mrs. Barrett's place when she found herself unable to attend. Henry's idea, which was greeted with unanimous acclaim by our family, was that my journey be turned into a sort of glorified silver anniversary celebration, with the entire household sharing in the trip abroad! That he met with no refusal is surely not surprising! And so, instead of my bidding adieu to the family at the pier, we all sailed off together; my brother-in-law, my sister-in-law, Helen, Frank, Henry and I. It proved to be a magnificent adventure of three-fold significance since, added to its delightful and purely personal aspect were implications of civic and religious importance, as well.

Oh, the joy of that first ocean voyage on the Kaiser Wilhelm der Grosse! And how amazed we were at the smooth sailing we enjoyed nearly all the way! Our staterooms were festive with flowers, candy, books and packages of all kinds and sizes, and each day held a specially breathless moment for us when an additional packet of letters and messages, thoughtfully planned for us by friends and relatives, was delivered.

No travel excitement has ever surpassed the enthusiasm we experienced when we entered London! We greeted the River Thames as an old friend, and were sure each bridge we passed must be the famous Blackfriars. How amused we were, after passing innumerable bridges, to find the one we wanted right in front of the De Kayser Hotel, at which we stopped.

One of my most impressive pieces of luggage was a very fine leather satchel, a parting gift of the board of the Chicago section of the National Council of Jewish Women, presented at a lovely farewell luncheon. Since I planned to devote part of my time in Europe to efforts on behalf of this organization, their gift was appropriately stuffed, almost to bursting, with copies of the Council's constitution translated into French and German by Mrs. Ignace Reis, of Chicago. These I expected to distribute to representative women in communities I hoped to visit.

In London, I was honored by a visit from Alice Hen-

Europe looked wonderful to the Solomons, in 1904 . . .
and this is the way we looked to Europe.

riques who, much to my surprise, brought with her a card on which was printed, "The Jewish Study Society ... A general Meeting of the members will be held at 46, Gloucester Square, Hyde Park (by kind permission of Mr. and Mrs. Henry Lucas). Thursday, second June, at 8:30 P.M., precisely. Mrs. Henry Solomon, President of the American Council of Jewish Women, will deliver an address." Mrs. Lucas, a sister of Claude Montefiore, was deeply engrossed in Jewish affairs, and was president, at the time, of the English Study Society, of which Miss Henriques was secretary.

On the evening appointed, about two hundred representative Jewish men and women assembled at the Lucas home to meet us. I told of the work of the National Council of Jewish Women, and Sadie American, who was also in London, made an additional statement. Miss Henriques reported for the English Study Society which owed its inspiration to our Council, as did the Union of Jewish Women, established as an English equivalent of our National.

Following our addresses, Dr. Hermann Adler, chief rabbi of England, and Claude Montefiore spoke. Mr. Montefiore was a nephew of Sir Moses Montefiore who was, I believe, the most celebrated English Jew of the preceding generation, and Claude Montefiore was, himself, one of the especially distinguished men of our day. I had the opportunity of becoming better acquainted with him when he came to America, some years later, and we felt privileged to hold a reception in his honor at our home.

Such fine women were present at the London gathering! Foremost among them were the Honorable Mrs. Ernest Franklin, a sister of Sir Herbert Samuel, later a Governor of Palestine, and Nettie Adler, with whom I had corresponded during the organization of the Jewish Women's

Congress of 1893. My whole trip was destined to become resplendent through unexpected but thrilling contact with world-renowned pioneers in the emancipation of women.

On our way to Berlin, we stopped at Amsterdam, where I dined with Dr. Aletta Jacobs, one of the outstanding women of Holland; a suffragist, well-known beyond the borders of her own country. I spent one evening in Amsterdam discussing the activities in which Jewish women participated, and found that in Holland many were engaged in non-sectarian enterprises, but few were interested in Jewish religious efforts, as such.

The convention of the International Council of Women opened early in June, in Berlin. The delegate body was composed of the officers and representatives from the National Councils of the various affiliated countries. Each day we were called to order at ten in the morning, adjourning at one. Luncheon followed; usually a function of no mean proportions, arranged by the Berlin women. We re-convened at three each afternoon, and the evenings were devoted to public meetings or receptions. It was inspiring to deliberate with women of many countries, consecrated to efforts for improving social conditions. But, alas! It was a man's world in which little could be accomplished as long as the lust for power remained an unchecked human passion! Would woman's suffrage act as a check? We worked — we hoped!

The meetings of the convention were conducted in three languages, German, French and English. Representing the United States, I was placed on the nominating committee because no other person in our group understood both French and German, and I was later elected chairman.

The Council sessions were most illuminating as problems of world-wide interest were discussed. The chairman of the

Women from all over the civilized world assembled in Berlin, in 1904, for the International Council of Women

(Editor's note: Mrs. Solomon is seated in the front row, fourth from the left; Susan B. Anthony at right, along the wall, fifth from the front.)

various committees were heard in questions of great moment, including white slave traffic, political equality for women and the rights of racial groups. Reports were given by the delegates from the United States, Canada, Germany, Sweden, Great Britain, Ireland, Denmark, New South Wales, Holland, New Zealand, Tasmania, Switzerland, Italy, France, Argentine, Victoria, Austria and Norway. A world gathering, in truth!

At the first public meeting, Mrs. May Wright Sewell, of America, the international president, delivered her message in faultless German. It was most inspiring to see the audience assembled at the Philharmonic Hall, all the seats filled with interested and enthusiastic listeners as aims and accomplishments were summarized. At all open sessions, the men were well represented, many giving flattering acclaim to the attainments of women. A great public meeting was held on one of the evenings, at which the beautiful Baroness von Suttner, of Austria, author of "Ground Arms", gave the main speech. The Baroness, a most convincing speaker, was one of the first to advocate the substitution of arbitration for war, and she was the champion, in Austria, of the rights of Jews. Madame Bogolet, of France, and the Scotch Countess of Aberdeen, who became the next president of the Council, also spoke on the Peace and Arbitration program.

At the close of the Council convention, the Congress of Women — an unofficial gathering of women from all over the world — convened. There were no appointed delegates to the Congress, and speeches, discussions and entertainment were each day's meed.

The social functions for both Council convention and the Congress were numerous and were elaborate beyond words! Our Temperance women were greatly distressed when wine was served at a lovely breakfast given by Mrs. Sewell! They were horrified when decanters of champagne appeared at still another breakfast, but they were duly impressed, as were we all, when bon bons were brought in, each wrapped in a paper covering which bore the portrait of Miss Anthony! Susan B. Anthony took Berlin by storm! The most admired of all representatives, she was by far the sprightliest among us; always the center of attraction, she was greeted with enthusiasm and affection wherever she appeared. At the convention, the American delegates always sat together, and mine was the rare privilege of being next to Miss Anthony and acting as her interpreter.

The American Embassy in Berlin gave a beautiful reception for the visiting Americans, one afternoon, and on another occasion we were taken to Miss Willard's School for American Girls. The English women were invited to go there with us, to meet representatives of both of our embassies and many professional persons, including American and English artists. Another day we attended a lovely concert at the home of Frau and Herr Goldberger. The Kaiser had at one time commissioned Herr Goldberger, one of his Jewish friends, to visit the United States in order to gather material for a book. "The Land of Unbounded Opportunities" was the result. I did not read it; perhaps the Kaiser didn't either, for certainly he did not learn that unbounded opportunities would build Americans into an invincible foe.

The Goldberger home was a palace of regal proportions, containing many objects of rare beauty. We wandered into the garden where I visited with Lady Battersea and Mrs. Frederick Nathan of New York. Lady Battersea and Mrs. Ernest Franklin were among the influential Jewesses of London who were in Berlin at the time. Lady Battersea's interests lay in many fields, with special emphasis, however, on prison work for women. Mrs. Ernest Franklin was a leader in England's social and religious movements.

A magnificent reception was held on Wilhelm Strasse, in the adjoining gardens of Gräfin von Bülow and Gräfin von Pasadousky, wives of Ministers of the Kaiser. The houses were built almost to the sidewalk, with only a small grass plot in front. Beyond a courtyard, one entered a gorgeous park of majestic extent with acres of trees and flowers. Thousands of roses were in full bloom when we were there. One of the palaces had been the residence of Bismarck, and although its halls held priceless furniture, gorgeous chandeliers and unique ornaments, as far as I was concerned, an impressive portrait of Bismarck, by Lenbach, outshone them all. The gentlemen of the households acted as hosts, for at every social function we attended they assisted, gallantly, in receiving in their homes.

These were the impressions I recorded for my report on my return: "The question most interesting to foreign women is political rights. The reason for this is that women constitute an enormous percent of the working population, as the armies take the men, and so they feel that greater political privileges will aid them in securing recognition in more fields of labor. The German women, who are supposed to live for "Kuche, Kleider und Kinder" (kitchen, clothes and children), do nothing of the sort! The rich leisure class does none of them. They live like women of all lands, diversified according to station, and the attitude of the men is by no means hostile. At every meeting, men attended; the official Germany was represented time and again, on one delightful occasion by Professor Münsterberg who, like his brother at Harvard, is a great advocate and admirer of woman's work; and the

[123]

men had no hesitancy in approving all the women were doing."

Prominent among the women at the Congress was Mary Church Terrell who headed the National Federation of Colored Women of America. A college graduate, she spoke excellent German, and I had become well acquainted with her when I was treasurer of the National Council of Women of the United States. I admired her accomplishments and valued her friendship. Mrs. Terrell was a guest in a German home while the convention was in progress. There was little discrimination against races of other color on the continent at the time. I was conscious, however, of prejudice against the Jews, in spite of the many who had risen to prominence in business and in the professions, and of those with whom the foremost leaders claimed friendship.

The Jewesses of Germany interested me greatly! A large number attended the Council convention and the Congress, for out of the one hundred and seventy-nine organizations in the National Council of Germany, five were Jewish. Many of them had chosen to be baptized as a matter of convenience, but a prominent Jew told me that baptism would cease altogether in a few years, and that those who had, shall we say, submitted to it, would later regret it. (How woeful a prophecy . . . and how true!)

I made a point of meeting as many Jewish women and men as possible, so that I might describe the work of the National Council of Jewish Women, and promote the idea of a similar endeavor over there. The first opportunity for a public hearing was before a committee of men of the German order of B'nai B'rith, a lodge to which most of the representative Jewish men in Germany belonged. The general topic under consideration at this meeting happened to be "White

Slave Traffic" and a report was given by a young woman who had been sent to investigate this evil in Galicia. It was a sad story that she told, and one all too familiar, because of my own committee work in the United States.

One afternoon I attended a gathering of women who wished to organize a union of Jewish women's charities. There were about fifty present, and many different groups were represented. It was here, for the first time, that I heard the suggestion that the only solution for the Jew was Palestine! When I spoke, I urged that a study of Jewish history and literature be made a part of the program of their organization. This idea was something so new to them that they could not conceive of it, at first. In the end, however, the suggestion was adopted, and when I met one of the women, later in my travels, she told me that it had never before occured to her to read a Jewish work, but that during the summer, owing to our influence, she had studied Lazarus' Ethics, with deep interest. At a subsequent meeting of this group, I was delighted to be of service in helping organize and many women urged me to remain in Germany throughout October, to assist them in other communities. I was greatly tempted, but that was impossible. Nevertheless, I did distribute almost all of the entire first edition of the German translation of the Council's constitution I had brought from home, and many sections were organized later, as a result.

CHAPTER XIV

H OW WE SOLOMONS revelled in that first wonderful European journey! And how I wish I need not pass over so quickly the story of our travels!

We had so much to see in London. At Westminster Abbey, with its fascinating chapels and marvelous statues and tombs of the good and the great (as well as of those who were only titled) my husband almost wept at the memorials to his old friends of literature. We were certain that nothing we were to see elsewhere could possibly equal this — our first visit to the Abbey! There, too, was the Tower of London with its pomp and crown jewels and golden articles of State, on the one hand, and — on the other — reminders of the tragic many who, either noble or ignoble, played their short parts in English history, and met their doom.

We were not privileged to view the Houses of "Lords" and "Commons", in action, though we found the Parliament buildings most imposing, but we *did* see the King! One day, as we walked in St. James Park, opposite Buckingham Palace, King Edward drove up to the curb, and we had a fine opportunity to see his kindly face. He was accompanied by an equerry, and they rode in an unassuming coupe, on the way to the Epsom Races. It was very pleasant to catch so informal a glimpse of the King of England!

Oh, the great art museums of London! Of the National Gallery everyone has the impulse to write volumes and to express his intense delight as he experiences, for the first time, the sight of the originals of the works he knows so well through reproductions; paintings by Romney, Gainsborough, Reynolds, Lawrence and many other masters of schools both English and foreign.

In the British museum we found the famous Rosetta Stone of basalt upon which the same inscription is written in Greek and in Egyptian hieroglyphics, providing the key through which Egyptian writing was deciphered. The manuscript section and the printing room provided our first glimpse of those illuminated pages that tell of the time and patience necessary to create an art that will continue to live and to give joy to multitudes yet unborn. We were lost to the present, and antiquity became the living era. The Golden Age and the inheritance of Beauty which Greece gave to the world, then lived for us! We found, too, the famous marble figures brought to England from Athens by Lord Elgin. Unfortunately, the Turks had used the Parthenon on the Acropolis for a powder magazine, when they were masters of Greece, and a tragic explosion occured. But we annexed the picture of those broken pediment figures, bought by Lord Elgin, to our store of precious memories.

One day in London, I visited Toynbee Hall, where Jane Addams received her inspiration for Chicago's Hull House. Entering through a gate, one came into a narrow court around which the ivy-walled buildings stand. There I spent almost half a day. One of the head residents showed me through Toynbee Hall and I found the work both interesting and significant. There, too, I saw the same types of people I knew so well at home, and one person addressed me in Yiddish.

My next stop was at the Jewish Guardian's Society, which corresponded to our Jewish Charities. I asked innumerable questions, especially about the work-rooms for girls, where instructions were given and money paid for the articles produced. I also visited the Hebrew Free Schools where a Mr. Abrahams had been Headmaster for many years. As we entered a classroom Mr. Abrahams said, "Good morning, boys." The boys rose and said, together, "Good morning, Mr. Abrahams." It was all very formal and mannerly. In one room a rather young lad — a pupil instructor, studying to become a teacher — was conducting the lesson. Classes for girls were also in progress, with manual training and domestic science forming part of the curriculum. There were three thousand children in attendance at the time I visited the schools. The task of supervision had been taken over by the city and some changes from the traditional type of Hebrew Free School instruction had been introduced.

Toward the end of the afternoon, I found the old Synagogue, situated on a narrow street in the most ancient part of London. It looked just like a dwelling, with windows of ordinary transparent white glass. Such interior decorations as there were — chiefly candlesticks and a railing around the ladies' gallery — were of brass. Nearby was the great Synagogue into which I went. Here was a large hall in the center of which was a raised platform for the president who was, at that time, Lord Rothschild. The small carved wooden stand for the reader was approached by a circular stairway. A wedding was about to take place, and the Chuppah (the wedding canopy) was already in place. Obviously, traditional customs were followed, here.

Twice, in London, we witnessed imposing dinners from the balcony of the elegant banquet hall of our hotel. At one, for the Corporation of the city of London, we were provided with printed diagrams so that we might locate, with ease, the important dignitaries as they sat at their appointed places. Even democratic Americans seem to be impressed at contact with nobility and royalty, and Helen and Frank were agog as they watched the Lord Mayor and other high officials at the second dinner. Breathlessly, they pointed out a man in gorgeous regalia whom, they were certain, must be "at least a Duke!" Imagine their chagrin when, as they viewed the banquet, they spotted him stationed behind one of the chairs! Yes, we were dazzled even by the costumes of the butlers as they stood back of their masters, and served them!

Mrs. Nathaniel Cohen, upon the occasion of the debut of her daughter, gave a dance at the Botanical Garden, to which we were invited, and where we were greatly intrigued by the long buffet tables, laden with quantities of delectable food. It was a style of serving to which, in Chicago, we were not yet accustomed. Fashions in clothes, too, seemed different — and more simple. The smartly garbed women we admired on the streets wore hats, coats and dresses of one color. When they went driving, in 1904, they added a feather boa — the approved "accent" of the hour.

Vivid memories of each delightful place we visited during that first London trip remain! The Inner Temple with its Crusader's Church, the Cheshire Cheese Inn, the Old Curiosity Shop of Dickens' fame; great edifices like St. Paul's Church; names like Fleet Street and Piccadilly Circus now, for the first time, came to life for us! Never before had I visited a city with an Old World flavor . . . it made Chicago seem very new and very young.

Holland we found delightful, with its fields of tulips, hyacinths and narcissus, and the river barges loaded with blooms turned the canal into a floating garden! At the roadsides, too, swayed red poppies, blue corn flowers and big white daisies. Of the Hague I mention only two highspots: our visit to Queen Wilhelmina's "House in the Woods" in which the first World Peace Conference met, and the famous picture gallery where we met, face to face, noteworthy masterpieces of Rembrandt and Rubens.

Though we had seen King Edward but once, in England, from the Westminster Hotel, in Berlin, where we stopped, we watched the Kaiser drive down Unter Den Linden almost every day. Two fine horses harnessed to his open Victoria sped by at a furious pace. He passed in a hurry — yes, mercifully, he did, indeed!

We became acquainted with taximeters, for the first time, in Berlin, for they were part of the equipment of the horse-drawn fiacres in which we rode through the Tiergarten and to the suburbs and the gardens where there was always music and where thousands came to dine of an evening. We visited the Reichstag and many other massive buildings and were specially impressed by the huge Pergamon excavations from Asia Minor. Beyond the famed Brandenburg Gate, the trees of Unter den Linden seemed so puny that one wondered whether, perhaps, they were not just a second generation of something that had once been mighty.

Two cousins of my husband lived in Berlin, and at the home of one of them, one evening, was served the most elaborate dessert imaginable! It was an imposing ice cream, called "Gefrorenes", and was brought in on a huge platter on which an electrically lighted boat blazed out the name, "Kaiser Wilhelm der Grosse", in honor of the ship on which we had sailed from America. After dinner another innovation awaited us! It was an evening of delightful surprises! We all made a joint phonograph record. Joe, my brother-in-law, was the first to orate, and he proceeded to tell of his happiness and joy in being in his childhood home, with his relatives, again. Henry followed, and in turn we came after, all playing variations of the same theme, as did our German relatives. It was a sweet and thoughtful plan of theirs, to make this record. Only, unfortunately, though we carted those records all over Europe, swathing them carefully lest they break, we never were able to find a phonograph in America into which they would fit! Truly, it was a "song without words"— in reverse!

The wife of this German household came of a long-lived family, with a father of seventy-five, an eighty-four year old uncle, and an aunt who boasted ninety-two years. All were interested in my mission as a delegate to the International Council, and — as did many others in Berlin — clamored to know all about Susan B. Anthony. The youngest brother questioned me about her age, and I told him she was eighty-four. "Oh!", said he, "That is quite old, isn't it?" The uncle queried, "What did you say her age was?" "Eighty-four", I replied. "Oh", he remarked, "That's not very old, is it?" Later, the ninety-two-year-old aunt put the same question to me, and again I gave her the answer. "Hm-m-m," she retorted, "That is not old at all!" They were all most eager to understand just what Miss Anthony was demanding. When I explained that she wanted the right to vote, one of them asked, "And why do they not allow her to do so? She seems such a fine old lady!"

While I was at the convention, in Berlin, my husband, his brother and sister paid a visit to their birthplace, a small village not far from Colmar. They were thrilled with their experience, and Frank, who accompanied them, said he would not have exchanged it for any other of the whole European trip. In a short account of it, Henry wrote, ". . . what quickening heartbeats when we beheld this old spot of a half-century ago where we lived and hoped, where our parents struggled and toiled. God, I feel, must have had his guiding hand specially over us in bringing us to our new home in the land of freedom and liberty. Naturally, the thoughts uppermost in our minds were of our dear parents and of their lives of labor and sacrifice for their children . . . their aim was to educate us for lives of industry and integrity. The highest tribute children can bestow is to live in the memory of their parents and to emulate their example . . . for the first time since 1856, we slept in our native town . . ."

Henry further describes the newer "more imposing buildings" and "modern architecture" (of 1889!). He told, too, of old friends of their parents still living, and many relatives of persons who were in America, and whom he promised to seek out. His story ended with the words, "Frank was deeply impressed." How much it meant to Henry to revisit, with his son, the scenes of his childhood!

It was a beaten path we took on our tour of the Continent, and one so well-known to European travelers that I shall tell of it in a tempo too swift to permit mention of many rare and cherished experiences.

From Berlin we travelled to Dresden, stopping at the Bellevue, a pleasant little hotel delightfully situated beside the river Elbe. We revelled in the great art museum where hung Dresden's most treasured possession — Raphael's Sistine Madonna, considered at that time the most famous picture in the world. There, too, we went to opera, to hear Mozart's Magic Flute, so rarely presented.

Seeming almost to belong to a fairy-tale era was Nuremberg with its delicious long-ago atmosphere and the old city walls still surrounding it. The houses, too, were very old as were the churches with exquisite stained glass windows and the quaint streets in one of which was located the Synagogue.

We purchased ivories in Nuremberg, as well as many of the toys for which that city was famous. We shuddered at the medieval instruments of torture and the ancient weapons of war which recalled the days when a land was held only as long as it could withstand the onslaught of enemies. Nuremberg was so charming, so peaceful, so serene, we were bound to feel that civilization had really moved ahead, and that other weapons of war would, in a none-too-distant future, all be relegated to museums.

Munich, with its handsome buildings, seemed, in contrast with Nuremberg, a city built for kings! It, too, had great museums and many works of genius. One evening we spent at the opera, and heard "Joseph in Egypt" which I especially enjoyed because in it was an aria I used to hear my mother sing, in her rich beautiful voice. The opera house was jammed and attention was concentrated entirely upon the music and the stage, and not at all on the "diamond horseshoe" or an exquisitely gowned audience, for there was neither! Standing room, at thirty-five cents per person, was completely filled, and between the acts many of the patrons went out into the foyer to walk about or enjoy a drink and a sandwich, in the most informal manner.

At the conclusion of the performance, we went to the famous Hofbrau Haus, the huge beer tavern whose floors were always crowded with beer-drinking men. In my diary, I wrote, "If there was ever an argument for temperance, the Hofbrau is that argument." That was in 1904. How different the brand of desired temperance, now, as we recall Hitler's Hofbrau Haus putsch in the nineteen-twenties!

Leaving Munich, we rode through the Tyrol, toward Italy. The River Inn was surrounded by pine-covered mountains and back of these rise higher peaks; some rising above the line of verdure and breaking into the clouds; others with snow-capped summits. The hills were studded with villas and many convents were discernible. How lovely, the blended colors of woods and flowers, vine-clad mountains and rows of wheat! How peaceful the flocks of shepherded goats!

The Tyrolean costume was much in evidence, especially among the men. Along the road we were amazed to find women in charge of railroad stations! Their uniforms consisted of a man's hat, a blouse with or without a vest and a faded skirt of some washable fabric that seemed to be hung over a hoopskirt. As we passed, they presented arms — usually a club. Truly, a different breed of club-woman!

And now, Italy, the dream, became a reality! Verona, Venice, Florence . . . . . .

Beside the "swiftly flowing Adige", Verona! We walked, in the early morning, to the old market place, once an old Roman forum, where antiquities abounded; we saw the aged amphitheater built by Emperor Diocletian, some twelve-hundred years before, and the tombs of the famous Roman family of Scaliger, as well as that of Romeo's Juliet. In the gardens of the old Francescan monastery was the rude sarcophagus as was, too, a marble tablet marking the spot where Juliet, of the house of Capulet, was said to have lived.

Then on to Venice, where we stopped at the Royal Danielli which had once been a palace. It still bore traces of its ancient splendor in its crystal chandeliers, regal staircases and rich frescoes. Much as there was to see, in Venice, I'm sure we didn't miss a single "sight", and our days there ended serenely, if conventionally, with lovely rides on the Grand

Canal. It was in Venice that we met a dashing Colonel whom all the soldiers saluted most snappily. I hoped that he might be merely a guardian of the peace, all his life! In the course of our conversation about the Church of San Marco, he inquired if we were Catholic. "No," I replied, "We are Jews." "It's all the same, here," he replied. "In Italy everyone is alike!"

Recalling his words, now, I bethink me of Luigi Luzzais, a remarkable man, and a Jew, who became a Roman Senator in 1920. He had occupied high places in public service for many years, and when he died, in 1929, Benito Mussolini extolled him "for his disinterested zeal and devotion, as well as for his profound knowledge." He had served as Minister of the Treasury, Minister of Agriculture, Industry and Commerce, Premier and Home Secretary, and was known as the "Grand Old Man of Italy". To what extent, one wonders, is everyone "alike" today, in Italy?

To Florence, our next port of call, I felt I must surely return some day! Florence — one of the world's greatest treasure troves! Can one still see the wonders there, today? The beautiful Cathedral Square with the church dome by Brunelleschi from which the great Michelangelo is said to have received his inspiration for the dome of St. Peter's, in Rome! The multi-colored marble Campanile, so skillfully planned by Giotto; the magnificent eight-sided Baptistry with its two great doors of bronze, wrought by Ghiberti, of which Michelangelo said, "They are fit to be the doors of Heaven!" And its two other doors of which Pisano was the brilliant craftsman! Memories of "old Firenze" fill one with nostalgia! Florence, where men of genius were protected and encouraged by the lords and ladies of wealth, by the Medicis and especially by Lorenzo, the Magnificent! I was particularly touched when we visited the old San Marco monastery with its exquisite wall decorations by Fra Angelico and Fra Bartolomeo, for here lived Savonarola! Here one viewed the great square where he was burned because he belonged to perhaps the greatest of all brotherhoods; that brotherhood of men who, in all ages, have tried to effect reforms, in a day when ignorance, stupidity and evil stalk through — and master? — the land! Would that the beauty and serenity of the Florence of 1904 might be preserved, as we saw it, for all future generations!

Rome! Even in 1904 the thought of the possibility of war made me shudder! How I hoped Italy would be made neutral ground forever, for the sake of art and history.

We spent hours on the ancient Forum which had a special fascination for my husband, for here the ghosts of the Rome of hundreds of years past still seemed to gaze upon the old haunts whence the Caesars ruled the known world.

Temples and arches, too, make ancient history thrillingly alive! How grateful we should be to the Popes who surmounted the Columns of the old Roman Empire with saints or crosses, thus saving them from demolition! Yet far more significant, to us, was the Arch of Titus with its seven-branched candlestick frieze, commemorating the taking of Jerusalem by the Romans in 70 A.D., and the return, to Rome, by the conquerors with their loot. We drove on the old Appian Way passing the little church of "Quo Vadis" fame, erected on a spot where Jesus is said to have appeared after his death, and on to the Catacombs — those fascinating underground burying places; labyrinths which provided added interest because they served, too, as meeting places at a time when the Christian was the persecuted faith, and his Diety challenged the gods of the country.

But always, my interest in things Jewish took precedence

over all others, and so we visited the Jewish Catacombs and the Jewish Ghetto, much of which had been torn down. The Ghetto in Rome was then an anomaly, certainly, so far as its house of worship was concerned. But just as birds with clipped wings cannot fly far from even an open cage, so, here, a beautiful new Synagogue was in the course of construction. The ancient Synagogue was an amazing building! Since Roman law ordered that only one Jewish Synagogue was permitted in Rome, five different congregations worshipped in different rooms under the one roof. These included the Sephardic, Sicilian, Italian and one or two other groups. The new Synagogue was to replace several of the old ones which had, meantime, amalgamated. The Reverend Professor Vittorio Castiglione was, at that time, chief rabbi of Italy, and we much enjoyed a visit with him. True to my mission, I left with him French and German translations of the constitution of the National Council of Jewish Women, and urged him to try to organize the Jewish women of Italy for religious and philanthropic work.

Great was our excitement when tickets to attend an audience with Pope Pius the Tenth were delivered to us at our hotel! To comply with certain regulations, it was necessary for us to make some purchases for the eventful visit: black lace veils for the women and false white shirt-fronts for the men. We had not carried all our baggage into Italy, and so we were compelled to rent full dress suits for our men-folks, since they were obliged to present themselves in formal attire. This was the first "full dress" experience for Frank, who fairly strutted in his grandeur!

We arrived at the Vatican at a quarter to five, to find the streets jammed with people, because it was the Feast of Saint Peter, one of Rome's greatest holidays.

The marble staircase of the Vatican, up which we walked, was flanked by picturesquely garbed Swiss guards, so privileged because in the French Revolution Swiss soldiers shielded Marie Antoinette until the last man fell. At the head of the stairway we were met by men in crimson brocade livery and ushered into the magnificent rooms of state. Gorgeous tapestries covered the walls and the draperies of white silk were braided in crimson and gold. The floors were of beautiful colored marble and onyx, removed from old Roman buildings; the ceilings rich with handsome frescoes.

About thirty people were granted an "audience", many carrying rosaries and other articles to share in the papal blessing. Accompanied by one of his Bishops, His Holiness appeared. At a sign, all knelt, and as he passed, each one kissed his large emerald ring. For some, this was a religious rite; for others a mark of respect, or merely a prescribed ceremony.

Pope Pius the Tenth was a fine man, majestic in bearing, with benevolence and kindliness shining in his face. One could not but be impressed by his presence, for a profound faith, though it differs basically from one's own, is inspirational to sincere adherents of any religion.

Church bells were pealing as we drove up the Pincian hill to watch the sunset over classic Rome. There were "the hills of Rome" and "the pines of Rome" as well as "the fountains of Rome", with their clear spring waters running into basins dating from the time of Nero and Caracalla! One must throw pennies into the Trevi Fountain, tradition has it, for then one will surely return to Rome. The pennies I tossed in were evidently possessed of the necessary magic, for I was privileged to return many times.

Which is more thrilling? An unexpected revelation or a

personal verifying of sights one has imagined, but never seen?

In Naples, I speak first of a glorious night! Into our rooms facing the Bay, the stars shone brilliantly! The moon was full and, periodically, flames ending in wreathes of smoke, issued from Mount Vesuvius, exactly the way we had dreamed it!

Naples and its Bay . . . the fishermen . . . the crowded streets . . . the cows being milked at the doors of the homes . . . the goats . . . the maccaroni hanging on the roofs to dry, like clothes upon a line — all these, so typical and so picturesque!

And then, Pompeii! It was difficult to feel alive and in the present, as we walked through the deserted streets of the ruins of a once beautiful city that tells, still, the story of an era of pomp and luxury.

On the train to Milan, my brother-in-law asked, "Why are we going to Milan?"

"To see the Cathedral", I replied.

"When was it built?" he inquired.

"Oh, about 1300 A.D.", was my answer.

"Hannah!" he burst out indignantly. "Do you mean to tell me that we are actually stopping off to see a building as recently erected as six hundred years ago?" But before we left Milan, he conceded that we could not possibly have passed it by! The exterior, with its innumerable pinnacles and turrets, has so many rare points of interest and beauty that one might study it for years without exhausting the possibilities for new discoveries! Inside the church, one can scarcely bear to take one's eyes from the exquisite stained glass windows with the heavenly blues and glowing reds sparkling in the sunlight.

Indescribable was the ride from Milan to Como, from

Como to Menaggio! The glorious mountain peaks seemed to point to heaven as the only place where this paradise can be improved upon! The Italian sky, the unrivaled foliage, the perfect blending of sea, sky and land . . . once visioned and forever remembered! In the hotel at Menaggio, complete with porters and servants, galore, we were almost alone, for it was out of season. The grounds were abloom with hydrangeas and magnolias, and as we rested, in luxury, we watched the sun slip away behind the lovely hills dotted with impressive villas, church spires and bell towers. All my life I had yearned to row on Lake Como . . . and now I could! And I did! And I could hardly believe it!

Leaving Menaggio, we rode on Lake Lugano, another delightful body of water sunk in the Alps, with villages cuddling at the base of the mountains, ending our journey, by rail, through the St. Gotthard Tunnel, into Switzerland.

We arrived in Lucerne at the height of the season. In contrast to Italy, here tourists swarmed over the mountains and climbers armed with field glasses and Alpenstocks, adorned with Edelweiss and Alpine roses, clambered up and strolled down the mountains.

We travelled to Interlaken, over the Brunig Pass, and there became acquainted with the Jungfrau as she rises between two other mountains, shining forth brilliantly in her snowy dress and donning, each evening, her rosy "Alpen glow".

We chose to ride, rather than to climb up the mountains. All the way, from the little cog-wheel railway, we watched the energetic mountain climbers as they gathered bluebells, roses and daisies. Our destination was the Eiger glacier, and here I permitted my son the novelty of pelting his unreproving mother with snowballs; an unresistible impulse for both of us, since the month was July, and the situation so unique.

Out of Switzerland we went, by way of the edge of the Black Forest, to Heidelberg, in Germany, where my brothers had gone to school, to enjoy a glimpse of the University and of the ruins of the old and famous castle, overlooking the Neckar River.

We visited my old Aunt Matilda Greenebaum at Frankfort-on-the-Main, where she had gone to live after Uncle Isaac passed away. They had dwelt in Chicago for many years and were much interested in all the family news. Aunt Matilda was a dressy old lady, and so in the evening we donned our most fashionable attire before going to dine at the "Palmen Garten". There, the head gardener informed us that our Garfield Park greenhouse, in Chicago, was reputed to be much finer than theirs ... interesting news, surely! Aunt Matilda, too, was a mine of information for me! Much to my surprise, she even made it known that she had read in an American periodical that I had been nominated Trustee of the University of Illinois, on the Democratic ticket! I had not been consulted, and I was amused rather than impressed because, at that time, the Democrats were so far outnumbered that a Republican nomination assured election, and I was so far away I could relax as I calmly awaited the inevitable defeat.

A pleasant and popular resort called Wildungen was our next stop, and there we met many delightful celebrities from various countries, including our own. From Wildungen, to Wiesbaden, then down the Rhine River with its Lorelei Rock and Mouse Tower, both of legendary fame. There, too, were the "castles on the Rhine" — baronial ruins suggesting the splendor of bygone days, and, most important to us, the city of Bonn where Beethoven was born!

We left the boat at Cologne where, of course, we saw the

Cathedral. The massive bronze doors and portals of this magnificent Gothic edifice were tremendously interesting, but most wonderful of all, it seemed to me, were the windows which might, in truth, be called divinely beautiful! Then on, by train, to Brussels, where we saw all the prescribed sights and had all the reactions a Baedecker could exact of tourists in a foreign land. But the picture of old women, sitting in their doorways, in the outskirts of the city, weaving with bobbin and thread their intricate patterns of lace will remain with me longer than the glories of architecture and of scenery.

Last of all was Paris! To me, Paris is the most beautiful city in the world. Again and again I have visited its galleries, and each time brings, anew, an upsurge of marvel and delight. There is a great temptation to linger in memory over the sights of Paris! No matter how adequate the fine descriptions written by thousands of enthusiastic and well-qualified travelers, each individual thinks of his own reactions, "They may be comparatively 'poor things, but mine own' ". This time, however, I shall not stray into that trap!

France's Grand Rabbi, Zadok Kahn, had given me letters to several Jewesses of Paris, and many of my interviews bore results, later. In the course of our days, there, I enjoyed a most satisfactory visit with Mme. Eugene Simon whom I had met in the United States in 1893, when she came to Chicago with her husband who was one of the French commissioners to the World's Fair. Helen and I were invited to Mme. Simon's summer residence at St. Germain. I remember how nonchalantly we conversed in French, bravely carrying on despite an occasional inaccuracy, such as our amusing statement that we had bought delicious cherries, "a mile of them!" Several other women were present at luncheon, there, and after I had told them of the work of the Council in the United States, they decided to form a similar organization. I agreed to put them in touch with English women who might be of assistance to them, and gave them French translations of the Council's constitution, as well as a file of our reports. They were especially interested in the question of modernization of the Synagogue, and I promised to send them copies of the prayer books used by our Reform congregations. It was not until afterward that I realized I had been, probably, the first woman missionary to the synagogues of Europe!

As we drove through the terraced woods of St. Germain just an hour before train time, they recalled to my mind Alexander Dumas' brilliant description of a butterfly hunt in which he relates the story of the meeting between Louis the Fourteenth and La Valliere. Away from the busy routine of my life at home, I seemed better able to give free rein to my thoughts and memories of tales of the past, written by Dumas, Balzac and Victor Hugo.

We left Paris with especial regret, because our holiday was drawing to a close. At Cherbourg, where we boarded the tender, it was heart-warming to be greeted as old friends by the crew of the Kaiser Wilhelm der Grosse. The goddess of Liberty, too, seemed to be awaiting us with a personal welcome when we reached our own good land.

According to my diary and the memories still lingering so happily, our first European trip was such a success that we hoped for another, five years later. In my diary, I wrote, "But shall we? The future is screened from sight, but we can often lift the curtain of the past to view again, in thoughts, the delightful hours of this beautiful silver wedding holiday which we spent so joyously, together."

CHAPTER XV

"LET US TAKE COUNSEL TOGETHER"
(Nehemiah vi:7)

OUR RETURN HOME after our silver wedding journey, at the end of August, brought no proverbial "let down", for immediately I was plunged deep in preparations for the Fourth Triennial of the National Council of Jewish Women which was scheduled to take place in Chicago, in December. A great deal of necessary groundwork had been done at executive meetings in St. Louis, in 1904, and in Philadelphia, in 1905, and so — on the opening day of the convention — on December 5, 1905, we were ready and eager to evaluate, in the city of its origin, the book of history the Council had written since the day of its birth.

Illustrative of the many phases of Council activity was the program prepared and presented at the Triennial. A splendid paper dealing with religion was presented by Josephine Lazarus, who had represented us so ably in a general session of the Parliament of Religions, in 1893. Miss Lazarus, whose sister, Emma, authored the moving verse inscribed under the Statue of Liberty in New York harbor, was a woman of unusual depth and vision and her message was of inestimable value and stimulus to all who heard her. All of the speeches and papers were remarkable, however, from the standpoints of material and presentation, and each served as added proof

[144]

that the Council was contributing its share of constructive thought to the problems of the day.

The talks on philanthrophy set forth the newest and best methods in social work; the papers on immigration and housing struck straight to the heart of each problem. Participating in the discussions were Dr. Hirsch, Judge Julian Mack, Julia Lathrop and Professor Graham Taylor who was the distinguished head of one of our leading settlements, and founder of Chicago's first school of social service.

Reports were given, also, of the International Council Convention and the International Congress, in Berlin, and an excellent statement for the peace and arbitration committee was made by its chairman, Mrs. Hugo Rosenberg.

The programs were pleasantly varied with interesting social affairs like the reception held one afternoon at the Lakeside Club which was located at Forty-Second Street and Grand Boulevard and was then prominently identified with Jewish activities. That same evening marked what really amounted to an innovation, when a paper on "Looking Forward" was followed by an animated "Round Table". Certainly this was looking-forward toward an era when round tables are the mainstay of our intellectual life and development, but in those days they were rare — almost non-existent.

Friday night was left open to permit delegates an opportunity to attend religious services. The convention program stated that, "Mr. and Mrs. Henry Solomon will be at home, informally, from 9 to 11, to officers, essayists, delegates and alternates." We were grateful, indeed, that our house was large!

Saturday, too, was left free for morning Temple attendance, and in the afternoon the convention-eers visited the University where, said the program, "a reception will be tendered by the Women's Union, University of Chicago, from 2 to 4, 15 Lexington Hall."

The Fourth Triennial found the Council, then, a well-established organization with ninety-seven sections reporting a membership of eleven thousand, two hundred and seventy-nine Seniors and Juniors. Again we noted steady progress. The Juniors had gained a firm foothold; the Seniors had reached maturity and numbered, in their ranks, the leading Jewesses of the country, the value of whose accomplishments was recognized and acclaimed.

Social changes had occurred, giving women an opportunity for more active participation in religious, civic and political life. It was a period of almost miraculous growth and development for all women. Our leaders realized that Jewish women, always interested in philanthropic and Jewish projects, should now participate more actively in civic and legislative affairs.

The philanthropies of the Council's sections had grown tremendously, and there had been general education in advanced methods of procedure. Trained workers were employed, wherever possible, and we encouraged women to take college courses in social service, for they were then beginning to be established. Fifty-six different philanthropic endeavors were listed in our tabulations! New homes for various enterprises had been opened in many sections, in addition to those previously created in Albany, Pittsburgh and Cleveland. In Portland, there was now the Guild House which was a manual training school and settlement; in Philadelphia, a Council Industrial Home for girls; in New York, an asylum for girls and women, called the Lake View Home. In cities where juvenile courts now functioned, sections aided in securing funds for probation officers and in caring for delinquents. Work in prisons and reformatories was undertaken. Many additional clubs, classes, kindergartens and vacation schools had been opened and helpfulness to immigrants was general. Some of the agencies we had originally established had grown to such proportions they could now be turned over to independent agencies and we were cooperating in a number of national movements. Of particular note was the Council's membership, in 1903, in New York's Committee on Household Research, which made a survey of conditions in household service and studied immigration at the country's port-of-entry. The New York section had maintained an agent to act for Jewish women and girls entering the United States, and it was the hope of the National board that this would become a national Council project, since so much work for immigrants was being done by individual sections.

From the beginning, Council dues had been placed at one dollar per annum, so that no women would find them prohibitive. One-half of the dues was to be kept in the local treasury, the other half sent to the National. These sums were for current expenses, only, and if projects were to be undertaken, money for their financing was to be raised by private subscription.

During my presidency, we continued to secure funds, nationally, for special needs, by requesting assistance whenever the occasion arose, and in every instance a splendid response from the sections was immediately forthcoming. Letters sent out in 1903, when we received news of the massacre at Kisheneff, brought us eighteen hundred dollars without delay; over two thousand dollars was contributed, in the same way, to the Russian Relief Fund, and ten thousand dollars had been raised, likewise, for Army and Navy work during the Spanish-American war.

It was obvious that if we were to adopt aid to the immigrant as Council work on a national scale, a greater national income was imperative. The board discussed the advisability of raising the dues to two dollars, one dollar per capita of which would be turned over to the national treasury. The original plan for voluntary subscriptions was of great help, but not sufficient to warrant any project requiring much money, unless we employed a special agent for the purpose of procuring funds.

The board realized all the implications and attendant difficulties. Dual claims had developed! Local philanthropies had been projected, in addition to those undertaken by the National. The local sections, however, could raise money in their communities, while the National could draw only upon its own treasury. A choice had to be made, therefore between an increase for the treasury, or curtailment of national work. Lengthy and heated was the argument and discussion at the Chicago convention before the two dollar dues was finally voted. In consequence, much bitterness developed, but we were nonetheless enabled to establish Immigrant Aid as a national philanthropy. No one questioned the importance of adopting this project, and certainly it proved its tremendous worth during World War I, when our government appointed the National Council of Jewish Women as the official group to be stationed at Ellis Island, to receive all incoming women and children, and to arrange for their departure to various points on American soil.

Up to 1904, no salaries had been paid to Council workers, with the exception of stenographers and those persons employed for similar incidental services. Now, however, the board agreed that the work had progressed to a point where other arrangements were not only feasible but desirable. It was therefore voted to make Miss American — formerly the secretary — the Council's executive secretary, at a stipulated yearly salary. Jeanette Miriam Goldberg who was elected official organizer for the Council, was likewise voted a nominal compensation.

I refused reelection at the Chicago Triennial, and Mrs. Hugo Rosenberg, of Pittsburgh, assumed the Council presidency. Great was my happiness, at that time, to be elected honorary president, in which capacity I have served ever since. That, too, was the delightful occasion upon which I was presented with a beautiful Tiffany lamp — grandeur of grandeurs! — at one of the evening sessions. I was called from the rostrum, I remember, and skillfully detained in an adjoining room until the lamp was installed, in all its glory, upon a table on the platform. I was then recalled to the assembly-room where, with "pomp and circumstance" a memorable presentation was made! As Mrs. Andrews, of Boston, made her charming and heart-warming speech, and I saw the light shining through the exquisite glass shade of the lamp with its bronze placque, appropriately inscribed, I knew that moment would live always, in my thoughts, surrounded by an equal and undimmed radiance. The lovely lamp is still one of my most beloved possessions, as is the handsome silver loving cup, which was the gift from the board when I retired from the presidency.

And now I felt I must try to rest. The Council was always fortunate in its numbers of loyal, efficient and responsible workers, by whom its many arduous commitments would be admirably fulfilled, and I could, again, pick up the threads of tasks, unfinished. I had agreed to act in an advisory capacity in a number of activities; there were innumerable books waiting to be read and promised articles to be written and friends and relatives from whom I had been too much apart. I knew that I should not be idle. My years of devotion to the Council had brought unexpected richness and fulness of life, engendering an eagerness to participate wherever I could, and to contribute, with delight, whenever I was called to service.

The success of the Council was so overwhelming, so far beyond our most optimistic hope, that in my gratitude I could have said, "Dayenu" (it would have been enough!) But, in addition, the unexpected personal returns that brought me such constant joy, taught me that earnest effort in a cause that lifts one out of oneself, invariably brings unsuspected and rewarding by-products.

CHAPTER XVI

"IS IT WELL WITH THE CHILD?"
(2 Kings iv:26)

UNDOUBTEDLY, the years from 1893 to 1905 were the busiest of my life! Hours of each day I had spent at my desk, always with a secretary working beside me. When, in 1905, I gave up the Council presidency, I thought I saw the beginning of lessened labors. Never, however, did I lose contact with work begun, and up to my seventieth year I served actively on boards and committees, of which the greater number dealt with suffering humanity. Whenever I was asked, as I frequently was, "How do you endure all you see and hear?", my invariable answer was, "I believe all sense of horror leaves us when we stretch out our hands to help."

No project ever affected me more deeply than that which came to the Reform Department of the Chicago Woman's Club in 1905; the task of investigating and reorganizing the Illinois Industrial School for Girls. This institution, located in Evanston, just north of Chicago, had been founded in 1876, under a then-new law, passed by the state in the interest of dependent girls. It had become shockingly demoralized because its board did not raise enough money for operation at an adequate standard and the county, therefore, had discontinued paying its pro rata share for the maintenance of the children. I was appointed, by the Club, to serve on the investigation committee, and soon found myself a member of the school's board of which I later became president.

On the first of January, 1907, an entirely new board was formed, of which Jane Addams and Mrs. Henrotin were members. Among the liabilities we inherited when we took over was a large debt which we were able to liquidate during our first year, by means of what was then a unique departure. We arranged, in the summer, a benefit baseball game, for which we were granted the use of the National League Baseball Park on the South Side. It was, I believe, the first time in the history of Chicago, that anyone had staged an athletic event for charitable purposes. Prior to that time, the usual money-raising ventures had been bazaars and an occasional theatrical performance, but I think I am right in stating that no one had ever before held a baseball game to assist a philanthropy. The competing teams, the Gunthers and the Ansons, coached by the well-known Captain Anson, himself, were contending for a cup offered by our Mayor Busse. Our board facetiously referred to it as "Mrs. Solomon's game", and a great deal of effort was expended to make it a financial success. Picture, then, our gratification, when about eight thousand dollars was realized! As a matter of fact, it was a tremendous game we were all playing in our determination to re-form the Illinois Industrial School for Girls!

Our building, which had been an old soldiers' home, was totally unsuitable, for it was bare, big and forbidding, in poor condition and miserably equipped. We had, in our care, one hundred and twenty-five girls; the oldest was eighteen years of age, the youngest only five. These children were in such a wretched state that we all agreed the first requisite was to substitute nurses for teachers! As Dr. Sarah Brayton, who entered into the situation with us, said, "the health and physical assets of the children were much on a par with the financial status of the school . . . . . . there was need of immediate interference and the correction of existing conditions, the most earnest plea coming from the pale anemic faces of the children." She went on to say, "They needed more out of doors and less drudgery. Then we found that warm clothing and shoes were lacking." Thanks to Dr. Brayton and her assistants, within six months, "the weary, hopeless look of the underfed with its sullen discontent, gave way to a happier, healthier tone of mind and body." At the end of our first year, order had emerged from utter and deplorable chaos!

The Chicago Woman's Club fortified us with its original determination to see conditions in the school changed. It provided five hundred dollars from its treasury, and a little later gave us an additional two thousand, five hundred as a loan; the Reform Department then voted us one hundred dollars and individual members contributed still another four hundred. Our new board attacked the problems with vigor! We secured an excellent advisory committee of men, including Judge Tuthill, Judge Mack, Edward Brundage, Louis M. Greeley and my brother, Ben Greenebaum. A group of eminent specialists served as consulting physicians, and we voted into the corporation such outstanding persons in the community as Mrs. Ella Flagg Young, Mrs. Emmons Blaine, Mrs. James Houghteling, Mrs. Andrew MacLeish, and others.

Fortunately, there were several particularly cheering circumstances in our otherwise dreary picture. One was some land we owned, in Park Ridge, Illinois, not far distant from Chicago, and we planned, from the first, to find ways and means for leaving Evanston and developing the school into a model institution on this forty-acre farm. Another bright spot was the income from a legacy of one hundred and fifty thousand dollars, bequeathed to us by a Mrs. Straut, which we could use for our needs. Since this bequest was then in litigation, Louis Greeley and my brother, Ben, represented us with the other legatees.

Even though we did not expect to remain in Evanston longer than necessary, we were obliged to make some improvements in the old building, and we adoped a modernized school plan as quickly as possible. The school then became a fine example of cooperation: the Vacation School committee furnished a teacher during the summer; the Art Institute loaned us members of its senior class in normal training and the School of Domestic Arts and Science provided instruction in cooking and sewing.

In 1907 we sold the Evanston property, and though it held a mortgage of twenty-five thousand dollars, there was equity remaining after the sale, making it possible for us to proceed immediately with our plans for Park Ridge. While the new buildings were being erected our children were placed in private homes where we paid for their care; a teacher was employed to visit them, so that we could continue to keep them under our supervision. Soon all was auspicious for the opening of our new Park Ridge School for Girls, as it has been known ever since.

The school is built on the cottage plan, and at the entrance to the grounds stands the first house, named "Solomon Cottage" at the request of Julius Rosenwald, by whom the funds for its erection were donated. In 1911 the Chicago Woman's Club Cottage was reported as "built, furnished and the planting provided for", and it has been maintained by the organization ever since. The Illinois State Federation of Women's Clubs, which has continued its steady interest in the institution, also presented a building, and provides for its upkeep from year to year.

Today we have a large, important institution with many

buildings upon its well-kept grounds. When last I inquired, I found its staff numbered seventeen persons and its faculty, nine. The children are carried through the high school grades.

The Park Ridge School for Girls has, indeed, developed as we hoped and it is heartening, now, to see a group of healthy, well-groomed young girls working or playing happily together under the supervision of trained personnel, in an atmosphere conducive to the formation of character and the growth of skills. The children find a real home at Park Ridge, as well as a school, and permanent friendships are established between the girls and with the superintendent and teachers.

There is, however, no such thing as a detached project, and one day I found myself on the way to visit our lawmakers, in Springfield. When we first became interested in the Illinois Industrial School, we realized that ten dollars per month from public funds was too small an allowance toward the feeding, clothing and educating of a child who was a public charge. So, we applied to the legislature for an increase, and remained in Springfield long enough to see the law changed to a grant of fifteen dollars, the amount now allotted for each girl in all public institutions in Illinois.

We learned, when we began our investigations, that some of the children had been delinquents. These, of course, should never have been admitted and, as soon as we were able, they were transferred to the institution to which they should have been entrusted in the first place. After that, we were in constant touch with the courts.

This, in turn, led to a deep concern with the problem of juvenile delinquency. The difficulties of the children with whom we worked resulted, for the most part, from the commercialized vice rampant wherever the poor lived in congested districts, and those who practiced it considered the immigrants their legitimate prey. Pennies went to operators of pool rooms, dance halls chiefly owned and run by saloon-keepers or breweries, and to low theaters where the white-slavers congregated. In one such place, little girls were actually trapped! Thanks to Mayor Edward Dunne, we succeeded in having its license revoked and it was never permitted to reopen.

We realized that the causes creating delinquency were many, but one of the worst — commercialized vice — was then treated most casually. Sometimes under the protection of an alderman or a dishonest policeman or a dealer who sold them merchandise, unscrupulous vultures were vouched for as respectable citizens, and allowed to ply their trade. Crimes against children were not punished severely enough, and, at the same time, the cases of delinquent and dependent young people were handled with a complete lack of intelligence. Dependents were often lodged in poor-houses; minors were confined for slight misdemeanors, and placed in police stations and jails, in the company of hardened criminals. Later, the John Worthy School was established. This was an institution where the boys were taught, "not merely the rudiments of a common school education, but manual training, as well, in a well-equipped manual training department."

In 1892, the Reform Department of the Chicago's Woman Club assumed the responsibility for placing a teacher in the city jail and paying her salary. In the Annals of the Club we read, "The Sheriff allowed her the privilege of teaching the boys in the corridor of the jail from 9:30 until 11:30 A.M. The attendance of boys varied from fifteen to fifty, the ages ranging from ten to sixteen years.

More and more did the Club become a factor in education. From its earliest days, the Kindergarten, then a new pedagogic field, enlisted its interest. The Club's insistence that women be appointed to the Board of Education met with success and, for the most part, those who have acted in such a capacity have been members of that body, and have kept alive a most vital interest in our schools.

The constant increase in numbers of women in organization work has added, immeasurably, to their service in legislating for better conditions for women and children. Seeing the advantage resulting from their combined strength, these groups united for joint effort and large practical undertakings were launched. One of the earliest accomplishments was the appointment of a woman physician at Dunning, in the Cook County Insane Asylum. Politics suffered brutality and unscientific treatment of patients to exist in spite of the attempts of excellent physicians to introduce improved methods of procedure, and newspapers of the era tell of many unbelievable situations.

Progress had been made, indeed, since the days when the Chicago Woman's Club had urged that children, many of them under ten, be taken from the jails and a special department be provided for them. Furthermore, a special time had been assigned for the hearing of juvenile cases in court, and as the years passed, still more appropriate methods for dealing with delinquency were developed. Then, two splendid women, Mrs. Lucy Flower and Julia Lathrop, led the fight for the passage of an adequate bill by the State Legislature, and the consequent establishment of the Juvenile Court. This was a field which held my most earnest interest, and I served as a member of the Juvenile Court Committee of Chicago. for many years. Miss Lathrop later became the first head of the Children's Bureau in Washington. My attention was called to an article written by Elbert Hubbard many years ago, in his publication, "The Philistine", in which he urged that a Children's Bureau be established. He suggested a number of women who might be appointed as its head, and I was honored to read that my interest in the plight of unfortunate children prompted Mr. Hubbard to place my name on his list.

It is doubtful that any individual performed a greater service for the reform of our social agencies than Mrs. Lucy Flower, and great improvement appeared in whatever work she undertook. She was the founder of the Everyday Club, and was, for many years, its president. This was a small organization, but very strong in influence, with membership limited to persons who were contributing in one way or another to the public weal. At luncheon meetings we discussed every-day affairs, and many of the celebrated men and women who had participated in the World's Fair Congresses were our speakers. Often the discussions led to practical results. The Everyday Club's effort in behalf of the Juvenile Court was constant, culminating with a large luncheon to which many judges and others who were sympathetic to the needs of delinquent children were invited. History was made when the Illinois Legislature passed the Juvenile Court Bill on July 1, 1899, and Chicago's Juvenile Court — the first in the world — was established!

Let no one think, however, that the Juvenile Court sprang forth, in full growth, as did Athena from the head of Zeus! Indeed, no! At first, we who were interested, were obliged to secure volunteers and to collect funds for the salaries of probation officers. The Bureau of Personal Service financed three, one of whom was paid by the Juvenile Court Committee. In our district, too, many Friendly Visitors served as investigators of the Jewish cases.

If the Juvenile Court has not achieved all we had hoped,

it is only because no such institution can work miracles. We recognize that the *prevention* of delinquency must be our first concern, and the factors that must be dealt with in order to accomplish that goal are many. We must see to it, at least, that housing conditions are bettered; that the care of adolescents is more intelligent and, certainly, we must insist that not only must drastic punishment be ordered for those responsbile for the delinquency of children, but that it is carried out — and promptly!

Judge Tuthill was the first to sit on the bench of the Juvenile Court, and he was followed by Judge Julian Mack, one of Chicago's most eminent men. But it is impossible to think of the Court's development in Chicago without paying tribute to Judge Mary Bartelme who brought to her office, in addition to her professional understanding and rare judgment, the high human qualities with which a superior woman is endowed. I had known and admired Mary Bartelme for years! Her brother, Alfred, worked in my father's business beside my own brothers, and his sterling qualities paralleled those of his sister. Years after my parents had moved to the South Side, Alfred Bartelme walked down Adams Street when our old house was being torn down. There he managed to obtain one of its frosted glass-paned front doors which he placed in his own home to remain for him, as he put it, "a permanent symbol of hospitality."

My thoughts revert insistently to Adams Street. How deplorable the contrast between the misery of some of Chicago's children, and the dear "Adams Street house" where only happy children lived! No life is complete which has not, in its span, consciousness of light taken from the bright places in its own and transmitted into homes of sorrow and gloom, dividing the fullness of earth with those whose portions are nothingness.

CHAPTER XVII

"MAN DOTH NOT LIVE BY BREAD
ONLY"
(Deuteronomy viii:3)

ONE SUNDAY AFTERNOON, in 1905, a dynamic, attractive young woman whom I had never seen before, called on me. Her name was Louise Loeb, she told me. She had moved to Chicago just the year before, to study dramatic art. It had occurred to her that an informal organization for the study of literature would find favor with our Jewish group which, she felt, possessed a background of real interest and education. Since she, herself, had not yet a wide acquaintanceship in the city, she had come to me to enlist my assistance in promoting her idea. To me it seemed not only feasible, but desirable. Not long after, therefore, a group of seven young people, including my daughter Helen, met and agreed upon a plan.

A membership committee compiled a list of one hundred eligible persons, and sent out invitations to an initial meeting, to be held at the home of Mr. and Mrs. Julius Rosenwald.

It was an enthusiastic assembly that foregathered on the appointed evening to launch the new organization, of which Judge Julian Mack was made president and Dr. Emil G. Hirsch, honorary president. Thus the Book and Play Club, of which I am now an honorary member, was started on its way to eminence. Those were before the times so familiar to us today, when our cities are practically glutted with series of lectures and forums, and so the Book and Play Club became a decided and welcome cultural acquisition. All of the speakers were individuals of note, and their talks were concluded, regularly, by open and general discussion, followed by a pleasant social hour, for most of the members were old friends.

The last meeting of each year was a "Gridiron" dinner at which many came in for a share of the "roasting", and our most talented actors and writers blossomed forth with skits of remarkable cleverness. We look back, for example, to one especially delightful moment when Fannie Bloomfield Zeisler, herself, strutted the boards. She appeared as a mechanical doll, and walking stiffly across the stage, she seated herself at the piano and played beautifully. In the midst of the composition she arose from the bench and rigidly marched off . . . but the music continued! She had made a record and placed it in the "piano-player", so that she was able, actually, to press the keys in perfect synchronization with the machine mechanism, and she did such a superlative job that even those members of the audience who were seated close at hand, on the very platform with her, never dreamed it was all a hoax! Another "Gridiron" boasted George S. Kaufman, the noted playwright, among its authors, for he lived in Chicago for a time and belonged to the organization. The Book and Play Club still thrives! It has lost its close personal aspect since the meetings are no longer held in private homes — it met often in ours — but it still contributes much, especially to the men who have not the constant opportunity, as have the women, of hearing the great and the near-great upon the lecture platform. Nothing, perhaps, sufficiently emphasizes the dramatic increase in cultural advantages time brings to each succeeding generations. Now, through press and radio, the finest contributions are brought to us directly and daily. But, as I look back over long years to the many stimulating evenings of the Book and Play Club, each appearance of poets, prose writers and prominent representatives of other fields was an event!

I remember many; among them Tagore, Edna St. Vincent Millay, Van Loon, Lorado Taft modelling in clay as he talked to us, and countless others. None of us who heard him can ever forget Von Luckner who had run a blockade, successfully, in World War I. We sat on the edges of our chairs for over three hours, as he held us spellbound by the drama of his story. Stephen Wise, too, spoke to us some thirty years ago, and he and his wife dined at our home before the meeting. Rabbi Wise was in his prime then, a magnificent speaker, and already a leader of men. But today he seems still in the prime of life, for he has never lost his youthful zest and zeal or his gift of magnetic oratory.

Such delightful activities as the Book and Play Club, however, were but pleasant and stimulating accents to busy days of work. It was but natural, therefore, that by the summer of 1908 I found myself sorely in need of a rest after concentrated effort in behalf of the Park Ridge School for Girls. My sister, Henriette, and her husband were summering in northern Wisconsin, and it was decided that I should join them there.

Camp Franklin, my destination, was situated some fourteen miles from the railroad station, and it was necessary for the hotel management to send a wagon and team of horses to transport me and my trunk. It was obvious, from the moment I first saw the driver, that he had arrived at the station long, long before traintime, and that he had employed that interval in a fairly steady imbibing of intoxicants! I certainly did not relish the ride ahead, in his company, but since the thought of remaining in the uncomfortable and isolated little station was not much more enticing, I climbed up into the wagon, and we jounced off. Sure enough! We had driven but a short distance when my companion began to nod! Another few yards, and he was dozing! Desperately I attempted to keep him awake, and finally decided that perhaps a little sprightly conversation might serve my purpose. I launched forth with the first thought that presented itself.

"My," I exclaimed, as we drove through the burned remains of a forest. "Why doesn't your state pull up those charred trees and plant growing ones?"

"Ur-r-umph!" was the grunted reply. He nodded; he dozed; I looked around for another interesting subject for conversation. We came to a stretch of swampland where the wagon-wheels splashed and moaned through puddles until I was dotted with mud.

"How unpleasant and unhealthful," I exclaimed. "Now why aren't these swamps drained?"

He turned toward me, glaring. Ah, ha! I thought, now I've caught his interest! At last he's really awake! What a blow to my complacence were the next words he sneered out at me!

"Say, lady," he drawled, menacingly, "You'd sure have a lot to do, wouldn't yah, if you lived here?"

That we finally reached home safely was due entirely to the intelligence of the horses. And the moral of this incident is, I suppose, that it's just what the reformer can expect whenever he hurls his ever-active mental agitation against the inevitable stone-wall of the public's apathy!

When I refused to stand for reelection to the presidency of the Park Ridge School, in 1909, Mrs. Henrotin, who had stood by from the first, rendering assistance at every possible point, assumed the office and carried on, heroically, for a long period of time. I served as an active member of the board for many years and have always retained my deep interest in the school. I must admit, however, that the reorganization of the institution had imposed a strenuous and consistent effort in its behalf and, for the first time in my life, I was completely exhausted. So, in the spring at the Easter season, Helen and I went to Atlantic City where my husband joined us, later. How we all enjoyed that wonderful rest together, beside the ocean!

At intervals, in one's journey through life, a pause is important. I cannot say that I spent many moments in conscious evaluation of past experiences, as some people so frequently do, or even in planning for the future. But surely, in days of continuous repose, there comes a revival of the balance and urge so essential for furthering endeavors, and a shifting of emphasis readies one to attack problems, again, with renewed vigor and enthusiasm.

Vacations for pure enjoyment never particularly appealed to me. Music, the theater and literary pursuits as well as pleasant social relationships were a part of our daily living and a strand of gaiety wove its way in and out as we went along. But each summer my husband and I went away together for relaxation and rest. In 1909 we took our third trip to Canada, going through the Muskoko Lakes and returning by way of Toronto.

The room we had engaged at the hotel of our choice in Toronto was not available, to our regret, because the annual exposition was in progress at the time. However, the manager had made reservations for us at another place, some distance away. He offered to send our bags on for us and we accepted the suggestion gratefully, as we planned to spend the evening at the theater. It was, therefore, midnight when we reached our hotel and there, in place of my bag, we found a grip awaiting us that was filled with men's clothing and featuring, in addition, a huge bottle of whiskey! We telephoned, immediately, to the hotel from which it had been sent, informing the clerk there of the error. "Have *you* that satchel?" he gasped. "The person to whom it belongs is the angriest man in Canada! He wanted to leave town on an early train, and was wild because he couldn't continue his trip with a gripful of women's duds!" Poor man! We could be amused, but he had been inconvenienced. Besides, since we were not to blame we need not experience even the slightest chagrin.

We were delighted we had decided to visit Toronto because we found the Exposition there most worth while. My greatest interest centered about the medical section where, in glass cases, lay tube after tube filled with precious serums. What an advance, since the days when vaccination against smallpox was unique! I was convinced that, one by one, all diseases would be vanquished . . . an optimistic conjecture that must wait a long time for fulfillment, I fear!

Never did Canada and the Great Lakes regions lose their attraction for us as a vacation spot, and we returned again and again, from Lake Superior to the Saguenay, down the St. Lawrence to Montreal, to Ottawa, to Toronto, to Quebec, and — often — to Mackinac Island and Niagara Falls.

We are all chemical compounds of geography, animated by psychic influences of history. Time and place are the determining factors in our development, spiritual and physical.

CHAPTER XVIII

W HEN THE INTERNATIONAL COUNCIL OF WOMEN held their
convention in Toronto in 1909, the foreign delegates —
fifty-three of them, from Great Britain, Germany, Holland
and Sweden — took occasion to travel across the continent,
tarrying for two days in Chicago. Jane Addams and I served
as honorary chairman and chairman of the committee that
arranged for their entertainment, and for the first day we arranged a formal luncheon at the South Shore Country Club.
Officials of the city and a number of the foreign consuls were
invited to be present and to address the gathering. Short
speeches, too, were given by women from abroad; Jane
Addams represented our American group and I presided.

A drive through the city, in the afternoon, gave our visitors
an opportunity to see the parks and playgrounds, the fine
residences and public buildings for which Chicago was noted,
even then. But the highspot of the afternoon was, by all odds,
teatime, which we spent with Miss Addams, at the Hull House
Coffee Shop. The shop had been opened in the days when I
was devoting much time to the Bureau of Personal Service
and was important to the district. It provided an ideal meeting place for those of us who were active in the West Side
neighborhood in which foreign groups had settled. Many

were the social and civic problems discussed within its friendly walls. It seemed to us a most fitting place to end the delightful day with our guests from other lands, rounding out our good-will gathering, and making it one long to be remembered.

There was, at this time, a growing civic consciousness among the women of Chicago, and more and more were we participating in all that pertained to our city's welfare. Committees multiplied and we found ourselves engaged in an increasing number of enterprizes. We were beginning to wonder, too, about the management of our city. At last there were men in the community who had come to the realization that our interest would be valuable! In 1910, Medill McCormick called together a group of very busy women and urged that they turn their intensive thought to civic affairs. Then and there we decided to organize the Women's City Club, of which I became a charter member, serving as vice-president.

My first effort for the new organization was as chairman of City Waste, with Mary McDowell and Harriet Vittum as able assistants. Miss McDowell was head resident of the University of Chicago Settlement, and Miss Vittum later held the same position at that founded by Northwestern University. It was my rare fortune to be closely associated with these fine women for many years.

Mary McDowell had the Chicago Stock Yards practically in her back yard and "Bubbly Creek", thick with Stock Yards waste, in her immediate vicinity. I must admit that, at times, the Stock Yards odor reached even our dwelling on Forty-Fourth and Michigan Avenue, many miles away! But it was not because of her own personal discomfort that Miss McDowell labored. She often told of going to court with a large group of her neighbors to attend a meeting of the Finance Committee of the City Council when the waste disposal situation was discussed. It was there that the aristocratic young lawyer for the Reduction Plant to which the garbage wagons daily made their pilgrimage represented the company's interest by pleading for its retention in that neighborhood. The plant had to be located somewhere in the city, he argued. Certainly it was best to keep it where the people were "a less sensitive group." Instead of reacting to this statement with anger, the folks of Miss McDowell's vicinity met it with laughs! Indeed, their amusement throughout his speech was helpfully disconcerting.

Miss Vittum, too, had a repertoire of amusing incidents which she told with gusto. One of them, which she loved to bring forth whenever the occasion warranted, pointed the finger of fun at me. Now, as I think back, I am dismayed to remember how ill-equipped we women were for some of the work we did! Today it seems almost unbelievable that we could be so earnest yet so unprepared; that it just never occurred to us to include, for example, some apparel in our wardrobes, suitable to the jobs we undertook. Yet so it must have been, for surely Miss Vittum spoke the truth when she said, "And there . . . making a personal inspection tour of one of the city's most unsavoury dumps, was our Mrs. Solomon, clad in a trailing gown of white cotton lace and clutching in her white-gloved hands a matching parasol!"

The first report of the Committee on City Waste presented the results of a thorough investigation of the methods employed for handling garbage throughout our city. City dumps, polluted water supplies, open garbage trucks, garbage disposal plants — all came under our fire.

In 1911 the Chicago Woman's Club Reform Department appointed an ordinance committee on which Mrs. Herman Landauer and I served as chairman and vice-chairman. Over

I not only wore white for garbage inspection, but
frequently in the evening, as well

a period of time we selected city ordinances with which we believed the general public should be familiar and arranged to have them appear, daily, in various newspapers, including many periodicals published in foreign languages. Later we collected and printed the laws in a booklet called "City Ordinances You Ought to Know", and these were widely distributed. Thousands were ordered by the Superintendent of Schools for the higher grades and city policemen were also given copies. Perhaps some of them even read them. Who knows?

Regardless of trained skirts and aesthetic preferences, women went marching on! As a law enforcement committee, we investigated pictures shown in the various arcades, finding many that were obscene and unfit for children. We also were given occasional assignments to see plays, making our reports to the police department through which office all public exhibitions were supervised. Advertising material was included, for it, too, was supposed to conform to rules of decency. We succeeded in keeping from our stage performances that were exceptionally vulgar or portrayed vice and we aided in framing a motion picture law which was passed in 1907, and held valid in 1909 by the State Supreme Court.

The office of the Second Deputy of Police was created in 1912 and the censorship of films, as well as of public performances of all kinds, was placed in this department. Constant differences occurred between producers and the department and many pictures were found unfit for public exhibition. In 1919, seventy-five were totally rejected and over one hundred thousand feet of film eliminated from otherwise satisfactory sequences. Our committee continued to aid the censor and, in cases of controversy, was always upheld in the courts. It was conceded that clubs, churches and the public, as well, were effective in preventing the exhibition of pictures violating the law which prohibited showing vice, crime, degradation of women and defiance of laws. Needless to say, situations gave endless opportunity for bribery and corruption. The office of the Second Deputy was later abolished, largely through political pressure, and the censors were placed, again, directly under the police superintendent.

It took splendid cooperation to remain vigilant in behalf of decent pictures. As chairman of the Chicago Woman's Club committee on motion pictures, I called together representatives of the large women's organizations which were interested in the same project and the Joint Committee on Motion Pictures was created. Mrs. George Bass of the Chicago Woman's Club became its first chairman. This committee existed as an influential body for many years and only recently was it dissolved. Many clubs, however, still retain their motion picture committees.

The Motion Picture ordinance was often attacked, but in all cases it was sustained, as there has been a marked change in sentiment toward public exhibitions. The generation after World War I moved far beyond the bounds of decency, but today, although there is no predisposition to return to Puritanism, there is nevertheless a distinct desire to swing back to more wholesome standards as well as to preserve prescribed regulations. The producers, in self-interest we admit, impose some restraint themselves.

The motion picture industry has developed into a high art and has been a boon, furnishing a medium of recreation open to all. During the "depression" many would have been shut out from all enjoyment of play-going had it not been for the "movies". These, with the marvels of radio, have educated the rank and file to high-grade performances definitely advancing the aesthetic cultivation of the arts in our day. It was essential, indeed, that many new ways should be found for distributing opportunity for education and recreation so that privileges should accrue to all rather than to those with healthy pocketbooks, only.

The city of Chicago was becoming a great metropolis. The parks and museums, as well as the public libraries, were open, of course, to all. The Historical Society had its own brownstone building on Dearborn Street, housing relics of old Chicago which already, even to me, seemed to belong to legendary times. In Lincoln Park there was located the Luther Laflin Museum of Natural History, famous throughout the country for the manner in which its exhibits were arranged. Here was reputed to be found the first results of an attempt to combine the skills of taxidermists and artists in portraying animals in their own habitats, and wonderfully successful they were, all agreed.

Our great pride was the Art Institute with its fine old masters procured through the influence of Charles Hutchinson, the Institute's first president. Jules Breton's "Song of the Lark", the piece de resistance from the standpoint of the general public of the day, was a part of the Field Collection where many examples of the Barbizon School were hung. Plaster cases of the Elgin Marbles and of other famous Greek and Roman statues stood in the room in which we had held our Jewish Women's Congress in 1893. And, just beyond, in the corridor, Chicago's Lorado Taft was represented by his beautiful marble concept of "The Solitude of the Soul." Modern art had not yet come into its own, nor had the Institute, in those early years, grown to its present great proportions.

In the city, also, I witnessed the erection of theaters upon whose stages great plays were being performed. There was one we found particularly impressive. Thanks to the renowned genius of Louis Sullivan and Dankmar Adler, wizard architects, we had our wonderful Auditorium, second to none in the country. My husband and I were there at the dedication, when the beloved Adelina Patti sang. At the Auditorium were presented the famous operas and here, too, on Friday afternoons and Saturday evenings through the season, Theodore Thomas and his orchestra presented their glorious concerts. From time to time a new trend in music was introduced and was discussed with the same scepticism or enthusiasm as were later expended upon Debussy, Ravel and their contemporaries. It is true that only tickets for the topmost gallery, which seemed miles distant from the stage, were within the reach of those with slender means. As yet, education in the fields of art and letters, available to the affluent and the so-called "intelligentsia", had not been taken for granted as the heritage of all. But finally there dawned a new day! A day when motion pictures and radio brought to everyone the opportunity to become familiar with the best that the creative genius of man has produced!

Greater museums were now developed. The Art Institute grew more impressive, year by year. The magnificent building for the Field Museum of Natural History was ready for occupancy in 1918; in Jackson Park the crumbling Art Palace of the World's Fair of 1893 —"poetry in plaster"— was being saved by the combined efforts of some farsighted women of the Woman's Club and an appreciative citizenry which felt that so great a glory as it had been must be preserved. It was recreated in stone by the city of Chicago — a dream made real. Knowing that the fruits of industry were, in themselves, an art, and believing that in the galaxy of Chicago's exhibitions there should be one which would tell of the progress that the labors of men had produced, Julius Rosenwald made possible the conversion of this building into the Museum of Science and Industry.

In Grant Park, near the Field Museum, the Adler Planetarium, presented by Mr. and Mrs. Max Adler, was erected, where one might see the stars of the firmament shining in a miniature sky, and watch them move in their orderly procession. Close by was the Shedd Aquarium, while in Lincoln Park a fine new building housed the Chicago Historical Society. Chicago was developing a new social consciousness, becoming increasingly interested in providing the finest possible educational and recreational facilities for *all* of its people. Stronger and stronger was growing the realization that men and women cannot be measured only by the ability and justice with which they administer their own affairs, but by their devotion to the public weal.

CHAPTER XIX

THE FREQUENT RECURRENCE of Council Triennials and executive meetings kept me travelling from one end of the country to the other. Through all my years of Council work I have been deeply appreciative of the heart-warming reception I have been accorded everywhere. Indeed, there are few states in the Union I have not visited, and I have the pleasantest recollections of speaking in synagogues in many cities in which Council sections are located.

In the spring of 1915, I attended an executive meeting held in San Francisco at the time the Panama-Pacific International Exposition was in progress.

One of the laughable experiences of this trip now comes to my mind. Changing cars at Williams, we found the train in which we were to travel through the night, so crowded that no lower accomodations were available. I was a little disconcerted, because the road-bed was rough, but a woman who was much older than I was talking so casually about the upper berth she was to occupy that she made me ashamed. Made courageous by her example, I determined not to be a "softie" and when I finally clambered up to my berth, I found I was really most comfortable. Next morning I told the woman how much her good sportsmanship had helped me gain a fine night's rest. "*I* did? I helped you!" she exclaimed. "Why, I was so petrified with fear lest I tumble out, I never closed my eyes the entire night!" Thus did my heroine expose her feet of clay!

On the way to California, the lure of the Grand Canyon caused us to stop off there. As we drove 'round the rim, looking through spy-glasses, we were enraptured by the magnificence of the scene. How find words to describe the Grand Canyon . . . so astounding, so majestic! Why even attempt to describe it? Speak, rather, of the wonder it engenders; of the awe it inspires! We who dwell within the confines of a city forget to measure our lives in relation to a tremendous universe. But the Grand Canyon is tacit reminder to us of Infinity, Eternity and the Creative Source of all!

Like San Francisco, San Diego was holding a fair in 1915; the Panama-California Exposition, celebrating the opening of the Panama Canal. The Spanish-type buildings, copies of the many old missions of California, were unique in atmosphere which was further emphasized by the superlative landscape gardening with its array of gorgeous blossoms. The Arboretum, with its quantities of trees, displayed varieties fascinating, indeed, to an Illinois inhabitant.

The San Fransicso Exposition was admirable, also. The fine buildings and exhibits, the glorious horticultural display, the lights at nightfall reflected and doubled in beauty by the water surrounding it, brought the fair to a high plane of excellence, making it worthy, in truth, to ᐧake its place with other great world expositions. The high-colored buildings — reds, blues, greens — set the keynote for the brilliance that dazzled one on every side. The Tower of Jewels, feature par excellence, gleaming so brightly in the sun, with its thousands of twinkling glass prisms set in motion by the movements of the air was, if possible, even more resplendent by night. The Court of the Universe, the main concourse, symbolized the union of the eastern and western hemispheres and its imaginative statuary and embellishments accentuated this noble conception. Were the East and West, then, *really* to meet and to clasp hands? Certainly, it did seem that the Panama Canal was to serve in hastening that end! How serenely interested we were. Who guessed, then, how tragic a meeting was to come?

The executive meeting of the Council was most gratifying and again I met many dear old friends and with them discussed the opportunities and possibilities of our National organization. We were all pleased to see an exhibit of our work in a booth in the Palace of Education, at the Fair, and disappointed to note that ours was the only Jewish women's group so represented.

Following the executive board meeting, a party of four of us travelled to the north and we were delighted to find Council sections in so many cities on our way. We gloried in its accomplishments.

We drove along the Columbia River Highway, one of the most beautiful routes I have ever seen, and very reminiscent of Switzerland. And there we were, in the region where Lewis and Clark, pioneers of the far west, met Multnomah, the Indian girl who showed them the way to Oregon. Oh, the roses of Oregon! In what profusion they bloomed! And how wonderful were the famous apple orchards! Through Portland we went, and then on to the State of Washington; still further north, and into British Columbia; to Victoria, that charming English city with its noted homes and fragrant gardens; on to Vancouver which then showed evidences of the end of its building boom. As we continued east, on the Canadian Pacific, that king of railroad routes, each mile showed us new glories of mountain and lake, river and waterfalls!

We stopped at an inn, on our return journey, where we were mystified, for a few moments, by the signs of great excitement. The reason soon became clear, however. Italy had joined the Allies in the European war! Consequently, both the English and Italian national songs were being sung, as intertwined flags waved wildly. We, who were pacifistic by inclination, could not rejoice; we felt only profound pity for both sides. Not until two years later did our own dear land become involved, so at the time we could do little but pray for peace between all nations upon whom war would bring an inevitable harvest of tragedy.

In 1916 I was among those most intensely interested in the reelection of President Woodrow Wilson. Mrs. George Bass, my very good friend, and national chairman of the Woman's National Democratic Committee, was an extremely effective leader; certainly one of the most effective representatives that women of the Democratic party have ever had. I served as a member of the local committee for Wilson, and on the night of the election all ears were glued to our telephones. When a late bulletin reported "the outcome is in doubt", we decided to go to headquarters in the Congress Hotel. All of us feared Mr. Wilson had lost — all of us except Elizabeth Bass, who insisted to the end that the trick would be turned by California. History reveals her a true prophetess!

The President's inauguration, in March of 1917, found me in Washington. On the morning of the thrilling occasion we arrived very early at the plaza in front of the Capitol, to secure seats enabling us to hear the President's impressive speech with ease.

My especial interest in Mr. Wilson's candidacy had hinged

upon his attitude toward peace, for I believed him to be the man who could avert the danger of our entering the Continental conflagration. Consequently, I was both surprised and disturbed to find the inaugural procession completely military. Women, pining for suffrage and peace, were all arrayed in military capes and caps; cannon, soldiers and all implements of war were out in full force! At luncheon I questioned my neighbor, an assistant secretary, next to whom I chanced to sit, about the significance of a military parade, since our election slogan had been, "He Kept Us Out of War!" The official said he was sure we would not fight; that he knew the President believed the United States need not participate in the war. We, who were among the most ardent in our insistence on arbitration, who believed that armed conflicts never settle controversies but create, rather, an urge for revenge on the part of the vanquished, did not realize, then, that war cannot be banished so long as there are still powerful barbarians who force their hateful policies upon unwilling subjects; while there are those who have not the desire for peaceful settlement of differences; while there breathe those who defy humane government!

When we turned toward home, in 1917, I was filled with dread of what I feared would come. And so it did ... on April seventh ... the portentous declaration of war! I had been one who dreamed of our being able to plan a better world; one promising freedom from the tyranny of force, forever. But it was not yet to be, and so America, too, was destined to add her strength of arms, rather than of mind, at this grim point in the world's history.

Women soon were called upon to participate in the gigantic effort necessary for the carrying on of war. In the Council of National Defense, a subsidiary division composed of the large national women's federations had already been formed, and of these the National Council of Jewish Women was one. In February, 1917, after the dismissal of German Ambassador von Bernsdorff by President Wilson, a group of women came together, in Chicago, to consider the steps we might take, locally, to create avenues for woman's service. We sent a representative east to see what activities had been set in motion, up to that time, and upon her return, a meeting was called, "for the purpose of considering the best methods of co-ordinating the work of women's organizations to meet conditions in this national crisis." Before the plans for Illinois were completed, Mrs. George Isham, who had been heading the preliminary setup, died. In May, after the woman's committee of the Council of National Defense met in Washington, our state organization was perfected, with Mrs. Joseph T. Bowen as its chairman.

My special assignment in the Chicago unit was as chairman of the City Ward Leaders Committee. I was appointed in 1917, and we immediately began to make a survey in order to plan for work to be undertaken in each district. I had believed I was acquainted with Chicago, but when I traversed its many wards I realized how superficial my knowledge was, and I regretted that the real familiarity with situations in them was, after all, consigned to politicians to be utilized for their own purposes when election time drew near.

All of our service was effected through wards and every ward was conditioned by varying factors such as type of population, locality and the other inevitable circumstances in a large city where nearly forty nationalities, each living in an area of its own, have congregated in larger numbers, in many instances, than in any but the capitols or largest cities of their mother countries.

In some outlying districts, we found women who never heard a word of English and who took no part, whatever, in community life, some of them scarcely ever passing beyond their own gates. We were able, nonetheless, to create an organization for the persons who were unaccustomed, in any way, to efforts outside their homes, and brought to them information on the essentials of child welfare and food conservation, securing their cooperation for such patriotic measures as housewives must consider important in times of war. Women already proficient in dealing with large projects helped them survey their neighborhoods so that they might induce others to register for service. Often the job was most bewildering, but there was never any thought of faltering. Too much was at stake.

We assisted, also, in the registration of aliens, some of whom, although they had lived for years in this country, had never learned to speak the language. We gave aid to many concerning their boys overseas, and made investigations for draft boards and for men claiming exemption from the army, and were ready to respond to any emergencies that might arise.

I found ward organization useful, again, in 1925, when I took part in the Woman's Division of the united drive for Jewish relief work, and assisted in reaching women's groups, ward by ward. The effort proved highly successful.

The result of our war contribution far surpassed our hopes and we felt we had established a new outpost for cooperation and goodwill. Up to the time of the Armistice the units aided in many ways. Until March 20, 1919, the major part of my time was devoted to this work, and not until July of 1919, was the final report published.

November eleventh, 1918 . . . the greatest day of rejoicing

any of us had ever known! Armistice Day! All together, we participated in the wild enthusiasm marking war's end.

There was victory for our side, to be sure, but permanent peace was not yet assured. Now, after many years of difficulty for the conquerors as well as for the conquered, we face, once more, the terrible spectacle of a world in the throes of mortal combat. We had laid the foundations for a lasting peace in the Kellog-Briand pact to which Chicago's Salmon O. Levinson gave such devotion and assistance through his plan for the outlawry of war. He first read this, before publication, at an evening party given by my sister, Rose Eisendrath. These foundations the totalitarian states have cast aside! Again, peace will come and once more we shall have the opportunity of attempting to establish that golden era when "Nation shall not lift up sword against nation, neither shall they learn war any more."

To say that one nation performs a God-given task better than another — or earlier — would be idle boasting, unless we see therein the message that when Divine purpose is revealed to a prophet and the right path presented to a nation, the *reasonableness* of it does appeal. And the steadfastness with which it is followed through century and age in spiritual exaltation, despite bleeding hearts and tortured bodies, flashes across the path of a despairing humanity a bright ray of hope, thrills like a song of seraphim chanting the Divine consolation that the universal conscience, struggling, climbing, is making for righteousness, and will be crowned with the truth which is harmony with the Eternal and which, prevailing, will "fill the world with its glory."

CHAPTER XX

EMILE LEVY, of Canton, Mississippi, became a dear son to us when, in 1911, he married our daughter, Helen. Many of the qualities we loved in my husband were Emile's also. He, too, was most consistently considerate and responsive, and found his greatest happiness in serving and contributing to the joy of others. Emile had attained a position of note in his town and state which brought fullness of life both to him and to Helen. When, in 1912, their daughter, Frances Hannah, was born, bringing new delight to all of us, my husband told me, confidentially, that no baby ever had seemed to mean so much to him. Unfortunately, this rejoicing was his but for one brief month, for on January thirtieth, 1913, Henry passed away.

The impressive services held for Henry in Sinai Temple were attended by a large gathering, attesting to the esteem in which he was held by the community. His endless deeds of kindness were related by the many whom he had helped, and tears were shed for "the good man", even by the apple woman who had come, daily, to his office. His relatives, his associates and his friends felt that a true nobleman had joined the ranks of those who had passed into the great Unknown.

After Henry's death, Jacob Abt spoke these words at the annual meeting of the Wholesale Clothiers' Association of

Chicago: "Henry Solomon, loyal and untiring in cooperation, friendly and high-minded in competition, a lovable nature and gentle soul, has passed to his eternal home. I knew
him first when I was a child. His almost womanly tenderness
and devotion to his aged mother and widowed sister made a
lasting impression on my mind. With the sweetness and
beauty of his family life, with his ready response to communal
obligations, with his deep interest in our Association's work,
we are all familiar. To have known and to have worked with
such a man is a rare privilege. The memory of his life and
his character must ever be an inspiration for all of us; must
ever keep us mindful of our obligations to each other and to
our fellow men."

How glad I was that before my husband's death we had
published "A Sheaf of Leaves", because it afforded him such
real pleasure. In 1911 I had collected some of the speeches,
papers and articles I had written into a volume I entitled "A
Sheaf of Leaves", and I had dedicated it to my children. In
the foreward I stated the chief reason for printing the book,
thus: "In these pages you will find your richest inheritance,
the religious faith that has come to us through our ancestors
and which I would have you keep strong and pure. In these
days, when we are prone to discard the truths that do not
admit of practical demonstration, we need to treasure the
historic consciousness in our hearts which has been developed
by generations of martyrs who were firm in their trust in a
Higher Power. It is because of the religious note that I
gather these papers for you."

At the time Henry died, Frank was already a young man
and had entered into business life at the side of his father.
On the Saturday afternoon before he became ill, Henry had
taken Frank on a pilgrimage to the west side where he had

lived and worked in his youth, and pointed out landmarks of special interest. Earlier in the day, at his office, he had discussed matters of business and of personal import with his son. It was as if he had sensed a completeness in his own life and was ready, now, to see Frank enter the door which he, himself, was about to close.

Years of restlessness for me followed after my husband's death. Wherever I was, I felt uprooted! I shuttled back and forth between Chicago and Canton. At home, Frank was an unfailing source of comfort to his bereft uncle, Joe Solomon, and to me, but it was not until 1914, when Helen and Emile came from Canton to make their home with us, that the presence of the small granddaughter brought brightness, again, into our home.

During the winter, for several seasons, we arranged a series of lectures in our home for Frank, his young cousins and friends of his generation. These afforded us many interesting times. University of Chicago professors, James Weber Linn, one year, and Ferdinand Schevill, another, were splendid and stimulating leaders, and the audience was responsive and enthusiastic. How well I remember the shock with which Professor Schevill's prediction, that the great clash of interests on the European continent was bound to result in armed conflict, was received! Much emphatic scepticism was voiced on this point, but Professor Schevill insisted he could see no possibility of averting the disaster. He spoke, much, of Russia; the great Russian Bear, which came from its lair for such combat as the Russian-Japanese war, had her fill of struggle, then lumbered back without pressing on to a decisive conclusion. That was the Russia of 1915 — not of 1942!

It was to one of these lectures at our home that Frank brought Helen Bloom, of Brooklyn, who was visiting with relatives, in Chicago. She was petite, dainty and most attractive, as well as an intelligent young woman, and she and Frank soon became engaged, setting December eighth, 1915, as their wedding day. Their first child, Elizabeth Anne, was born in September, 1917, and now I had two lovely little grand-daughters in which to find delight! The Frank Solomons lived not far from us at that time, but soon decided to seek the advantages which the suburbs afforded both for themselves and their baby.

I wish that Elizabeth Anne, who soon became Betty to us, could have had some recollection of our Michigan Avenue home as an "ancestral background". Scene of so much joy, housing us through many years of experience and growth, we found it hard to leave. The appropriate moment had come, however, and so, in 1918, we sold it. The house would remain, of course, in our memories; the large rooms and the appointments typical of the eighteen-nineties; the huge mirror console in the living room, and the mirror-back bench in the hall, with hat-rack devices at either end. And the incidents of furnishing! The dining room walls were hung with the same pattern as that of the tapestry with which the chairs were upholstered; in the "parlor" was the curio cabinet — fortunately not ornate and golden — that has been able to hold its own through years of changing modes. It still contains objets d'art that I have collected on my five trips to foreign lands: ivories from Nuremberg, wee copies of statues of St. Peter, from Rome, a small reproduction of the Kamakura Buddha from Japan and the Taj Mahal from India, a Javanese fan and many more! Today, a curio cabinet is a pleasant and tangible reminder of happy jaunts, but on Michigan Avenue it had been a fashion-decreed and necessary adjunct.

In the parlor, too, was a "Verni Martin" table, charmingly painted with French scenes. It finally went the way of other outmoded incidentals, when more rugged styles began to prevail, and Morris chairs and their companion pieces urged interest in things less exquisite. Not that the "parlor" became vastly changed, ever . . . nor the living room, for that matter. I do remember a day, however, when its mahogany table was daringly moved against the wall! Until that time it was an unwritten law that every living room must contain a massive table which must be placed directly under the elaborate chandelier, in the geometric center of the rug! The fact that it was always in the way, mattered not a whit, and when ours was actually moved it was done in a spirit of pioneering!

There was an evening, too, when some of my brothers and sisters dropped in to visit with us, and one of them suggested that perhaps a different arrangement of furnishings might be an improvement. I can still see my sister-in-law, Rose Greenebaum, sitting upright on the middle of the davenport, clutching a marble bust of Apollo Belvedere in her arms for safekeeping while the shifting of furniture went on! It was a lengthy and hectic performance, and in the end every solitary thing was returned to its original place with the exception of a single picture which had been moved, approximately, one inch. It was, I believe, the Alma Tadema etching, presented to me by the Council board and was the very first etching I had ever possessed. That was the era when it became imperative to appreciate and own etchings. Previously, we all had fine engravings and black-and-white reproductions of great works of art, with an occasional water-color or, perhaps, an oil — good, bad or indifferent.

There hung, in our living room, a copy of a lovely portrait of Mrs. Frederick Freer, painted by her noted husband. The original had been exhibited and greatly admired at the World's Fair of 1893. Once, when Mrs. Freer attended a reception at our home, she stood, talking, beside the picture of herself, entirely unaware of its presence, to the great delight of those who saw her. Cora Freer, sister of Frederick, was also a distinguished artist. She had been one of my girlhood friends, and her portrait of our son, Herbert, has always been one of my most highly prized possessions.

We had first moved to Michigan Avenue at the beginning of the electric-light-and-telephone-for-all era, in what was — we believed — a very modern day! I do not remember, explicitly, the clothing details of that time, but I do know we had passed beyond the slavery of the huge balloon sleeve. The bell-shaped skirts that trailed on the ground were with us, still, however, and I could never forget the real diamond solitaire earrings we wore, or the ubiquitous sunburst pendents. Costume jewelry was foreshadowed by things known as "fads" like the sword pin in a scabbard, or the Trilby heart, for DuMaurier's book was of such moment that it had definite fashion repercussions. We wore hair ornaments, too, some of them jewelled, as well as hair bows, now, once more, in vogue. A chatelaine bag hung at the belt of our shirtwaist skirt, taking the place of the even more comfort-giving real pocket formerly sewn into an inside seam to keep it invisible, but handy. We *all* carried mesh bags of gold or silver and were even beginning to tell time by wrist-watches.

It was on Michigan Avenue, too, that we saw the first automobile driven past our house at what we thought was such speed we would wait, patiently, on the curbstone for one to pass, even though it had just appeared on the horizon, blocks away, before we dared venture across the street. We called them "red devils", and felt not a little uncertain if,

[187]

by chance, we rode in one. Before we left Michigan Avenue we saw the airplane, too, and became acquainted with the game of golf, for we had joined the Ravisloe Country Club. Oh, we felt very modern, indeed!

In the summer of 1918, Helen, Frances Hannah and I went to Denver, Glenwood and Colorado Springs. The companionship of the five-year-old added much to our pleasure, as may well be imagined. She was particularly intrigued by the mountains, and loved "God's Garden", as she called the Garden of the Gods. In Denver, she attended a meeting with us. It was her first experience of the kind, and she sat perfectly still as I made my address. When the woman next to her asked if she liked her grandmother's speech, Frances Hannah replied, "Yes, but she talked very long!" How I hoped the members of my audience did not agree with her! If they did, their adult inhibitions kept them politely silent!

I could not be in Denver and neglect visiting, again, the splendid National Jewish Hospital for Consumptives. We also enjoyed meeting the family of Seraphina Pisko, who was one of Colorado's outstanding Council women. Her work in the hospital for consumptives was recognized throughout the country.

We returned from our trip to prepare to dismantle and move from our Michigan Avenue home. How difficult the decisions we now had to make! How to determine which of our possessions should go with us, which be weeded out, was a task we approached with dread. It was comforting to know that none of our memories would be left behind! Recollections would go with us of all the family visits, the gay parties, my children's happy years carrying on into joyous days for my first grandchild. And the serious times, the loss of Herbert and my husband! These were deeply woven into our hearts, a rich and beloved motif in the pattern of our home. So, again, just as on Lake Avenue and on Morgan Street, we prepared to close the doors behind us, and proceeded on our way. We looked, for a last time, at the bushes and flower beds I had added, year by year; looked long at the catalpa tree to which Henry had been deeply attached because I had planted it in honor of one of his birthdays ... and then ... we left.

The days in our next home, on Grand Boulevard, brought a swift procession of events, many sorrowful. But, day by day, satisfaction came to us because we really lived "in a house by the side of the road." In the apartment above us dwelt Gerson and Elsa Levi and their family. Elsa was the daughter of Dr. Hirsch and Gerson was, himself, an honored rabbi. Dr. Hirsch was still living, and we enjoyed many delightful visits with him and his daughter and son-in-law. Members of our family, too, were close at hand. The Joe Eisendraths and the Mose and Ben Greenebaums were virtually, neighbors, and many of my nieces and nephews, who had married, visited us frequently, with their children. The beautiful, charming and talented Beatrice Welles came to us, often, bringing with her the eight-year-old Orson — precocious and gifted, even then. We loved all these casual visits, whether prolonged or of the "pop call" variety, and each brought fresh interests and welcome diversion into our home.

The terrific "flu" epidemic of 1918 did not spare our clan! Two of our promising young nephews, James Lesem, son of my sister, Theresa, and Gus Haas, Mary's son, were victims of the scourge. Both boys were married and each left a young wife and small son.

The severe emotional strain of that trying year made me especially receptive to a plan concocted by my three intimate

[189]

friends the following summer. It was proposed that "we girls"— Lizzie Barbe, Mrs. Rose Liebenstein, Mrs. Jennie Meyers and I — take a summer holiday together, visiting the National Parks in the West, and recapturing, for a time, the carefree spirit of our youth.

It was a tonic, indeed, to visit the parks, and marvel at the wonders of Glacier, Yellowstone and Estes, and our return found me refreshed in body and mind.

Arriving in Chicago on August twenty-sixth, I was over-joyed to find my first grandson, born just the day before, awaiting me! Much to my delight, he was given the name of Henry Solomon — a name I felt he would learn to carry with dignity and honor into a new generation.

We had need those days for bright spots such as these to illumine our lives, for with the summer of 1920 came the shock of my beloved brother Henry's death, bringing inex-pressible grief to all of us. Esther, his wife, lived gallantly, until 1940, yet always, we knew, in the shadow of his memory. Together, in our thoughts, they constitute immortal perfec-tion, such as is seldom envisioned here, on earth.

Nor was that heart-ache all we were called upon to bear. The following June we lost Louise Eisendrath Nathan, oldest daughter of my sister, Rose. We had just gone to summer in River Forest, Illinois, where we had rented a furnished house for a few months, closing up our own home and transplanting our menage, maids and all. The suburban house in River Forest belonged to the well-known musician, Glen Dillard Gunn, and we loved its artistic atmosphere and the fine pic-tures and autographed photographs of celebrities lining the walls.

It was a quiet, thoughtful summer for us. My niece, Louise, who had just given birth to her third child, became desperately ill, and died. She, too, was of our younger generation and we parted from her with heavy hearts, for in our large united family the sorrow of one was the sorrow of all. The music at the services, as we said farewell to our gay, colorful Louise, included the Brahms "Wiegenlied" which we always asked Louise's mother to sing for us when we gathered together. Strange, that we had scarcely returned to River Forest after the funeral, when Frances Hannah begged us to play the Cradle Song for her on the Victrola. No one mentioned that we had just heard it, but it was as if its echo was still alive, assuring us that this lullaby would never fail to bring back to us the memory of Louise. Now it brings back, also, the memory of my sister, Rose, as she sang it to our rapt and listening family group.

Yes, it was a saddened summer of quiet and meditation. Our poignant new sorrows served, perhaps, to sharpen our perceptions, causing us to take stock more consciously than was our wont, of the griefs and joys that color each one's weaving.

CHAPTER XXI

"AND, BEHOLD, IT WAS VERY GOOD"
(Genesis i:31)

ALL MY LIFE I have loved to travel, and now, in my latter years, I have indulged myself! One trip at a time is the usual procedure, but in transcribing reminiscent experiences, I find myself possessed of the (to me) intriguing details of four major trips, enough for four volumes. I'm strongly tempted to incorporate, here, my diary of descriptions written day by day, in the glow and enthusiasm of the moment. But I remember, too well, what always happened when friends welcomed me home, after my travels. They would say, eagerly, "Do tell us all about it!" And gladly I responded. But in less than five minutes I could sense the wandering of their minds and see a far-away look in their eyes, and at once curtailed my rhapsody so as not to tax their politeness too far.

Decidedly, the joy of travel is to the traveler! No matter how eloquently others have dealt with famous or historic places, each one loves best his own reactions, and wants to verify picture postcards and guide-books, personally. So I shall compromise by mentioning only the unique elements in each adventure.

The first came in 1921, when I conducted four delightful young women — my nieces Helen Kuh and Ruth Greenebaum, Ruth Stein (who later became my niece through her

[192]

marriage to Richard Kuh) and Beatrice Levy, artist and friend — through Europe. We visited England, Scotland, France, Holland, Belgium, Italy, Sicily, Tunis and the Sudan, each country leaving an indelible impress of novelty and high-spots, to be priceless souvenirs for us all.

As we approached England's shore at the end of our first voyage, I wrote, in 1921, "The rolling green, dotted with forts, the half-hidden batteries and war ships gave us a jolt! We were all so peaceful." We lingered in Ann Hathaway's "cottage" of fourteen rooms, and pictured Shakespeare dining at the wooden table, hollowed out with individual depressions for food; unpolished for the main course, then "turned over" to the "pudding side", all smooth and shiny.

We realized how much of the thrill of sight-seeing was due to association as we reveled in the "human interest" element of the birth-places of celebrities and saw the relics that have have been kept to perpetuate their babyhood and youth. But we were just as engrossed with notable architecture and cultural treasures. We did not miss a single cathedral or art collection or theater or concert hall as we delighted in country after country, and evaluated with ever-increasing appreciation how very much each had to contribute to the glory of the world.

The girls were sympathetically indulgent toward my predilection for synagogues and Council possibilities, and they were often rewarded with interesting and amusing by-products of my indefatigable pursuits of all things Jewish. In Paris, for example, they saw Temple ushers in blue uniforms with red trimmings, silver chains and tricorne hats, the chief rabbi wearing a low derby hat with a wide brim, and they heard the familiar service read in French. And in Tunis, in the Ghetto, they watched the women filing in to services, decked

[193]

in sugarloaf hats, with long draped pongee scarfs and very full skirts reaching to their golden anklets, speaking Hebrew and old Castilian — a language inherited from their martyr ancestors who escaped the Spanish Inquisition.

We saw Jews of every color — yellow, brown, black, white; of every shade of belief and every degree of culture. Never again would any of us think of the Jews as a race or a nation.

Yes, we shall always be able to play, at will, the wonderful memory records we gathered on our perfect trip. But some things, like the vision of caravans and palm trees silhouetted against a desert sunset sky, or the Sh'ma intoned by strange people in a strange tongue are knit into the very fiber of our being, and one is conscious of a profound and lasting enrichment.

Returning from Europe, I was overwhelmed with the renewed evidence of my children's desire to spare me all unnecessary exertion and fatigue. For, lo! during my absence, the Emile Levys had moved our household to Chicago's North Side, and there I was comfortably established without any of the inconvenience such a trek usually entails. Such a change of locality was essential, since it was our desire to give Frances Hannah the privilege of attending the Frances W. Parker School, where a number of the other children of our family had gone. The school was outstanding and offered the type of primary and secondary education we so heartily approved. In the minds of all Parker alumni and their parents, there is profound gratitude for close association with such a rare personality as that of the school's first principal, Flora J. Cooke. Her influence in the field of progressive education and upon the personal development of all "her children" is beyond one's power of acknowledgment.

Now, then, we were to be among the "North Side Greenebaums", for the clan had divided into three sections: those on the South Side, those on the North Side and a large North Shore suburban contingent. In this last group were the Frank Solomons in whose household I spent a great deal of time. Frank and Helen had moved to Winnetka when Betty was a baby, because they sought the advantages which it afforded; homes in place of apartments, a certain freedom, a less hurried tempo, clean air and, of course, pleasant companionship. The larger family unit had begun there years before, and from that time on, our colony grew and grew for, as the young folks married, many of them joined the procession, northward, from the city.

When we left the South Side, my brother-in-law, Joe Solomon who had lived with us so long, took up his residence at the North Shore Health Resort in Winnetka. He had been in failing health for several years, requiring constant care, and we were satisfied with his move since a number of his nieces and nephews had homes close by and, always attached to him, these children of his brother, Ernst, brought him cheer and comfort. Harry, the oldest, with the same devotion that had characterized the three Solomons of the preceding generation — Ernst, Joe and Henry — in their attitude toward one another, was like a son to his aging uncle, and we knew he would continue in his conscientious way. I had watched Harry's development through the years. Indeed, he claimed that he had received his start in life as a business man when, in his youth, he had delivered hymn books of the Congress of Jewish Women for us.

At the North Shore Health Resort, in 1928, Joseph Solomon passed away, the last Solomon of his generation, for his sister, Fanny Peyser, who had lived with us, also, died in 1908.

Residence on the North Side was most satisfying to us. We

lived in the immediate vicinity of Lincoln Park and, for several years, we had the zoo and the conservatory virtually in our front yard. The park brought especial joy to Emile and, loved as he was by all children, he often wandered from flower bed to flower bed and from peacock to elephant, surrounded, always, by a group of admiring youngsters.

For me, too, these were attractions, yet their lure was not enough to keep me at home! In the summer of 1922 I went to visit Rose, in Kennebunk. Our sister, Henriette, had passed away in March. Now her piano was closed, but the memory of her musicianship which meant so much to us would never be lost. The influence of her dignity and poise would continue to be with us, as would the quality of her fine intellect.

Joe Eisendrath died in 1921, and now Rose was alone. We, who shared her hospitality in Kennebunk, were grateful for the calm and peace that filled those days we spent together in Maine. During our stay we visited the lovely spot where Mrs. Edward McDowell, wife of the renowned composer, had developed the Peterborough Colony in memory of her famous husband. In what was once a deserted farm, musicians, sculptors, writers, poets and painters enjoy a solitude which enables them to devote themselves to their God-given talents. Here, artists dream and create! We, too, were in pensive mood as we rode along the roads where leaves were turning to red and gold. We passed New England farms and farm-houses with the Colonial doorways we loved, and visited Longfellow's home in Portland and Thomas Aldrich's, in Portsmouth, exploring all the countryside as we rolled along.

Returning to Chicago in Rose's auto, we drove north through New Hampshire via the White Mountains, up to Dixville Notch, where we lived for a few days in the woods; then crossed into Vermont and rode through the Green Mountains, stopping one night at the Beekman Arms, in Rhinebeck, said to be the oldest hotel in America.

On our homeward way we arrived at Indianapolis rather late one evening and decided to remain until the next day instead of continuing to Chicago, as originally planned. Walking along a downtown thoroughfare we were aware of someone following us. Yes, even at our age, his intention to overtake us was evident! What then, was our amazement and delight, at being addressed by the man and discovering that he was none other than my son, Frank, who just happened to be in Indianapolis on business! What a happy ending to a perfect summer, the first of many I spent under Rose Eisendrath's roof!

Many years before, my father said he wished he might possess a home so big that all of his children and grandchildren could be gathered together in it. So, for the first New Year's Eve party after their marriage, Alfred and Rose Haas Alschuler made a huge blueprint of just such an imaginary estate in which each of us had a special niche, a domain appropriate to our individual talents or pursuits. Henriette's for example, was the music room; mine, the kitchen! This fanciful estate the Alschulers dubbed "Villa Garnix" (Gar nichts, German for "nothing at all"), a name sister Rose adopted for the house on the farm she bought, near Torrington, Connecticut. And a true gathering place of the clan, her Villa Garnix became! From hither and yon we arrived, to spend a few hours or days en route to other destinations, or for prolonged visits with Rose and her children and grandchildren.

How cheering our experiences at Villa Garnix!

There was much music, of course; piano, voice and violin. And painting! Rose engaged a teacher and each of us set up an easel and went to work. To me this was no new interest, for when I was young, the copying of certain standard pictures with pencil or crayon was a prescribed accomplishment for a lady. In fact, I had gone on to a second stage and the smell of oil paints could often be detected in our Morgan Street house — an activity to which lillies, on a shiny black placque, still bear silent testimony. But a parrot on a background of pale blue satin was my chief pride, as it hung in elegance, functioning as a "splasher" over a washstand, to protect the wall from water spots. The Villa Garnix artists, however, were something quite different, and latent talent of impressive proportions was disclosed.

The eminent lecturer, Earl Barnes, had a home near Rose's, and our association with him and his charming wife afforded us many pleasant hours. Often Mrs. Barnes read poems of New England to us. What a wealth of joy is added to living when one finds time for poetry! There were other interesting neighbors whose association enriched those summer days! The celebrated violinist, Ephrem Zimbalist, and his wife, the noted Alma Gluck, lived not far away. I have just finished the novel by Alma Gluck's daughter, "The Valley of Decision," and my interest in Marcia Davenport's achievement is by no means lessened for thinking back to her lovely mother and the pleasure she brought to those beautiful Connecticut summers.

Rose's was the marvelous power of giving joy to old and young, alike, and her glowing spirit warmed every place in which she lived. Certainly it carried over into the lovely home she built, later, in Tempe, near Phoenix, Arizona. Here, in the winter, members of the family gathered just as they did at Villa Garnix, and we roamed the out-of-doors, revelling in the way Nature and man worked together, under God's sunshine, to create loveliness. There were daily walks and long rides to see the Arboretum, the Dam and other beauty spots and many were the jaunts our indefatigable hostess arranged for us. How we loved the house, the patio in which we ate our noonday meal, the welcoming porches and the spacious living room! Every corner spelled enchantment, and I am grateful that through Rose and her house in Tempe I came under the spell of the desert and the great open spaces underlined with sand.

But the Wanderlust was again upon me! So successful was my first "personally conducted" European tour, that in 1923 I ventured forth again, this time with Helen Bergman, daughter of my cousin, Lina (always counted one of the clan), and her friend, Celia Elbogen. My companions proved a desirable choice, for our journey consisted of a cruise around the world, and sympathy of taste is a necessary asset for consistent sight-seeing. In addition, both girls were unfailingly considerate and appreciative.

We landed in Liverpool, and started most auspiciously, being just in time for the Shakespeare Festival, at Stratford, and a remarkable performance of "The Taming of the Shrew". To us, Holland will always mean flowers, grapes and Rembrandt! Brussels, on the Day of Atonement, at a "Reform" Temple, more Orthodox than any in America! Paris, for two weeks, with French lessons and everything one "does", in Paree; Lourdes — Biarritz — Burgos. Madrid . . . a Bull Fight, tortoise shell combs and mantillas and the famous Del Prado full of old masters! Toledo, home of El Greco, wondrously picturesque fortress city of rocks and bones of martyred Jews of the Inquisition; Cordova's Mosque and the home and synagogue of Maimonides. Seville, and the Alcazar. Tangiers, and a Mohammedan feast and our first ride on "mule back". Granada — and the first breath-taking view of the glorious

Alhambra; lacy architecture and gardens and leafy balustrades and trickling water and famous vistas — spirit of Washington Irving! Then, Barcelona, and after the Land of Mañana, back to France and the glory that is still Italy, with "The Last Supper" in our eyes and Toscanini's "Magic Flute" in our ears, and Mussolini's iron hand over everything!

Cairo — and, at last, Jerusalem! Zionist and non-Zionist unite in deepest tribute to the magnificent achievement in Palestine. Again, our visit there was timely, as my birthday was celebrated by a group of distinguished friends: Mr. and Mrs. Nathan Straus, Henrietta Szold, Sophie Berger, Mrs. Judah Magnes (wife of the head of the University), and Miss Day. Miss Szold introduced us to the wonders wrought in Palestine, and perhaps our most poignant memory of our World Tour was the revelation of the "Promised Land", present and future. Of course, we were prepared for great accomplishment, and found it, but there were unimaginable surprises, everywhere: Pagliacci, sung in Hebrew; a Jewish Woman's Club, advocating "equal rights for women"; the silk worm as a possible future industry; Jews still practising polygamy; Arab children married at eight and ten years of age and having children at fourteen; graduate Hadassah nurses and most progressive institutions of all kinds; acres of tobacco plants and citrus groves; the wonderful National School for Farm Training!

Since my visit, I believe in a Zionist state less than ever, but I *do* hope all the persecuted may find sanctuary there, under adequate protection. And I admit that what the Zionists already have done is the greatest adventure of the century. To take a country, a wasteland, and make it bloom again in the hope of its becoming a resting place for hunted people, with the ideals of Jewish education and culture; to spread this ideal throughout the world, is an unmatched goal in human history! Most of us are satisfied to let destiny guide, believing God holds the reins. Now, we know we must act, as well as pray.

Egypt, again, and the Pyramids; Thebes and all the Biblical persons and places restored to life for us! An almost uncanny verifying of the stories that seemed Sabbath School fiction, before. It wasn't always a serious quest, and as our guide pointed out the spot where Pharaoh's daughter *may* have discovered Moses, we gaily picked out a nice clump of bulrushes as our choice; our guess was as good as his!

Then the whole scene was enlivened by my sister, Rose, who joined us for the rest of the tour. Time and space were forgotten as we set forth, merrily, to encircle the globe. We saluted the Colossus of Rhodes and steamed through the Suez Canal and settled down comfortably on the *S.S. Samaria*, our home for several months. There were provided all the diversions of steamer life, but best of all we loved the ever-varying sunsets and moon-rise with resplendent night skies and clear evenings, bright as day.

India, next! Bombay and the matchless Taj Mahal; Ceylon; the Indian Ocean, all permeated with the spirit of Buddhism; Calcutta and Benares, and ghastly as well as beautiful sights to remember. Questionable travelling comforts, as when I found a huge lizard in my bath-tub! I gave him right of way, and went to bed to dream of Burning and Bathing Ghats and the teaming, streaming mass of humanity so crowded with beggars exploiting their hideous deformities; the living seemed more gruesome than the dead. Religious practices were both fascinating and disgusting!

It was good to return to our ship and sort out our confused impressions. We crossed the Equator with traditional pranks;

then, on to Sumatra and Java! Indulgence in purchases of batiks and orchids; Singapore, Manila and meeting old friends; Shanghai and Peking; rare specimens of jade, lacquer and cloisonne; innumerable native dishes (but we preferred "American duck"); and a visit to the Calhouns, our Ambassador. Of course, we did justice to all the really wonderful sights of China, including theaters, palaces, show places of all kinds, and enjoyed acquaintance with new customs. Rose insisted on riding on the Chinese Wall in a riksha, though a murder had just been committed there. I reluctantly consented and lo! the only man we encountered was a resident of Chicago! We returned safely. On to Korea; then to Japan, charming in its apparently picture-postcard make-believe: dwarf trees, pagados, cherry blossoms; Yokohama and the snow-capped Fujiyama in the distance; Tokyo, enlivened by a native wedding in our beautiful modern hotel. The bride wore a blue kimono tied in with yards and yards of "obi", and her face was whitened with chalk. Then, back to our home on the *Samaria*.

The last two weeks were filled with grateful reminiscence as we steamed toward Hawaii. Honolulu, like a dream, with its music and leis and brilliant flowers; sunny hours on the beach at Waikiki; graceful 'Hula" dancers; the strains of "Aloha" blending with the notes of "Auld Lang Syne" as our ship pulled anchor. A barge-ride to Kilaua and the Hilo volcano with its huge multi-colored pillars of smoke and deep fissures overgrown with grass and fern.

As we turned toward our ship for the last time for a leisurely voyage to San Francisco, regret at the inevitable termination of an unforgettable chapter was happily tempered by the anticipation of a joyous return to home and family — the best of all endings to a complete and glorious adventure.

In the summer of 1925, the Frank Solomons rented a charming house in La Jolla, California, where I was with them much of the time, revelling in the loveliness that is so peculiarly California's own. Betty and Henry were in the delightful years of their childhood, yet old enough to be companionable, and it was, indeed, a satisfying interval. When we started home, Frank, Helen and Henry drove to San Francisco by automobile, and Betty travelled with me, on the train. With what an air of complacence did she settle herself at my side in the Pullman, saying in a tone of gratifying content, "My family will just have to get used to being without me, because I'm always going to go travelling with you!"

When, several years later, I returned to the far west, I visited with Tress' son, Alex Lesem, and his wife, Myrtle. Alex, alone, of the Lesem children, remained in California, becoming a doctor, and the head of the San Diego Health Department. With them, I went to their cabin in the mountains. Snow had fallen and a log fire was kept blazing all night; so blazing, as a matter of fact, that the andirons actually melted! I wore my fur coat over my night clothes and learned, first hand, what it is like to be a California eskimo. I loved it all, though, and proved to my own satisfaction that I still possessed the capacity for new thrills.

And thrill is the only word for my reaction to my trip through the Panama Canal, when, in 1929, Rose Eisendrath and I went by boat from California to New York. The story of the Panama Canal is an astounding one, but fascinating, also, is the canal trip! A Mississippi friend of Emile's had charge of the locks at San Pedro Miguel and he afforded me the privilege of turning the key which opened the gates to admit water for the entrance of a ship.

Helen and Frank had moved to Baltimore, in the meantime,

and there, in 1928, Frank Solomon, Jr., was born! How we rejoiced in this new baby boy! And well we might, for he has brought us sheer happiness, ever since. Such a trio of children as we now had drew me to the South, ever and anon, and often Baltimore swung within the orbit of my travels. (If such an orbit wasn't always quite logical, I wasn't in the least averse to doctoring it up, a bit, now and again!)

Later, Cleveland claimed the Frank Solomons and, after the marriage of Frances Hannah, in 1936, I added Charleston, West Virginia, to my port of call.

Now, I don't think I'm an unreasonable or complaining woman, but, really, it does seem that for the constancy of my railroad patronage, a decoration of some kind should have been forthcoming from their companies! Just once, however, did I merit recognition on a train, and that was en route to a meeting of the Denver, Colorado, Council section. I had been invited to stay at the home of a woman whose husband was one of the partners in the company providing the dining car service. A realization of my regal status was thrust upon me when I was served with eclat in the diner, and informed that I was the guest of the management! How I preened myself, as I wondered just how they discovered I was I! I should dislike to confess to the florists of our country that I felt every bit as elegant, then, over delicious oysters, as I do, ordinarily, when wearing a corsage of orchids. Never let the florists believe for a moment, however, that I haven't been duly appreciative of the exquisite corsages it has been my good fortune to wear from the east coast to the west! Why, I often ask myself, should one be so rewarded for treading in paths that, in themselves, have always been pure joy?

CHAPTER XXII

THE FIRM THREAD of the National Council of Jewish Women runs unbroken through the fabric of my life. I devoted myself to its spinning while I was in active leadership and watched its progress with no less satisfaction as the presidents who followed after me seated themselves at the distaff.

The women elected were all persons of distinction with large club and civic experience in their own communities, and had served brilliantly in both local Council sections and as members of the national board or committees. Their names and accomplishments are inextricably woven into Council history: Mrs. Hugo Rosenberg, Mrs. Caesar Misch, Mrs. Enoch Rauh — who was able to act only a short period — and Mrs. Nathaniel Harris; illness prevented Rose Brenner from completing her term, and she was succeeded ably by Mrs. William Dick Sporberg. Mrs. Joseph E. Friend, Mrs. Arthur Brin and Mrs. Maurice L. Goldman followed, in turn, and each brought sagacity and initiative to her task. Though vastly different in personality and technique, all were as one in their devotion to and understanding of their grave responsibilities. Each was impressed by the realization that we, as a band of workers pledged to "Faith and Humanity", must cherish the altruism that brings us strength

[205]

to aid in the organization of the best social development, when moral and intellectual forces have conquered materialism and when wealth, knowledge and power are put to their legitimate uses for that development of the individual which best redounds to the advantage of society at large.

Thus, the regimes of all of the presidents were marked by steady progress, both nationally and locally.

In the life of the Council, its almost phenomenal development is landmarked by its successive Triennials. That there were issues which, at times, disturbed the accustomed harmony was not surprising. The Triennials were forums for the discussion of points that were debatable and problems that demanded solution. Only once, however, did matters reach so intense a point that drastic action was imperative if the principles and purposes of the organization were to be maintained.

Little did we know, as we prepared so busily for the fourth Triennial in Chicago, in 1905, that the question of a raise in dues from one to two dollars was destined to become a burning issue threatening to ignite and consume sections near and far! The conflagration started so mildly — with a number of the sections feeling that such a raise would work hardship upon many of their members, causing them to resign. A majority, however, favored the idea and the change in dues was effected. The Cleveland section struck the initial spark, for it had already increased its dues even beyond the two-dollar figure, in order to carry on its own local philanthropic enterprises, and was unwilling to conform to the sum established in the national by-laws. Therefore, between the time of the Chicago convention and the fifth Triennial, held in Cincinnati, the affiliation between Cleveland and National was severed. This unprecedented situation was, naturally, a focal point at the Cincinnati conference, and the "Cleveland incident", as it was termed in the President's report, came in for a lion's share of concern and discussion.

The Cincinnati Triennial was the first held after I left the presidency. I had presented a paper on "Industrial Education", but this seemed of exceedingly minor importance when I found myself the chairman of the arbitration committee appointed to attempt a solution of the heated topic of the moment — the "Cleveland incident." Cleveland, feeling it had been dealt with in a summary and arbitrary fashion, refused to rejoin the National despite all pleas and, in truth, the National had displayed certain headstrong attitudes so obviously that the Chicago section had been among the first to make protests, all of which had been disregarded.

During the Triennial period following the Cincinnati convention, dissatisfaction on the part of some of the other local sections was expressed in no uncertain terms, and before the Philadelphia meeting, in 1911, the Baltimore section came forward with a scathing letter, sent to all local sections, protesting vigorously against what it termed, "arbitrary and extravagant administration." Toledo withdrew from the National before the Philadelphia convention where the Baltimore letter became a paramount issue, and during the period immediately following that meeting seven other sections also seceded: Baltimore, Boston, Chicago, Denver, Savannah, Washington and Youngstown, and none of these was represented in 1914, at the Triennial in New Orleans.

We, in Chicago, were fortunate in having for our president, Mrs. Israel Cowen, who proved herself to be a wise and tactful leader during a most difficult and trying time. Our Chicago organization, during the period of its disassociation with the National, called itself the "Chicago Association of Jewish

Women". We had seceded merely as a protest, and pledged ourselves to return to the Council at such time as the national organization would again function democratically. We rejoined in 1915 and by 1917 all of the sections were reunited with the exception of Cleveland, which rejoined our ranks later.

To me, this entire incident has always been most regrettable. But, as I look back, I am cheered by the realization that, despite differences, we had always identical objectives. Like our fingers, each section is capable of functioning individually, but we need the National — the whole hand — to do the happiest and most efficient work for "Faith and Humanity."

The twenty-fifth anniversary of the Council was celebrated in Chicago, in 1917, and our local section gladly made ready to receive, once more, those women from far and near who were the Council's "stay and staff". Mrs. Felix Levy, a woman of unusual ability and with a rare gift of oratory, was president of the Chicago section; Mrs. Nathaniel Harris, efficient, genial and beloved, was our national leader, and as chairman of the local committee on arrangements, it was with deep personal pleasure that I carried on my share of the proceedings. Headquarters were the Congress Hotel, and here our daytime meetings took place. For our evening programs Chicago's large Temples were our hosts.

The first formal session was a "President's Evening" and the three past presidents, Mrs. Rosenberg, Mrs. Misch and I, presented a panel on "The Development of Jewish Women During the Past Twenty-Five Years." For that occasion we met in Sinai Temple. Dr. Hirsch gave the opening address and many of his words, referring as they did to the first World War, were strangely prophetic of the scene today: "Out of this cataclysm, terrible beyond all expression, will be born a new world where justice will be enthroned. That word 'justice' is a summary of all that the Jew suffered for, of all that Judaism has taught. . . . Go, ye Jewish women, into your cities, into your counties, into your states; go with the nation and let the whole world learn through you and from you that the highest glory of a nation is to be exalted in and through justice."

As I travelled, from time to time, in the interest of the Council, I found outstanding rabbis everywhere, who represented the Jew magnificently in their communities. But none ever surpassed — if, indeed, they reached — the pinnacle scaled by Emil G. Hirsch. Chicago sustained an irreparable loss, in 1923, in the death of this great leader, stern martinet, cherished friend. At memorial services held in tribute to him, the honor of representing the women's organizations was granted to me. The women's associations owed much to Dr. Hirsch and his influence was direct and vital to them. As I spoke of him on that twenty-third of February, many were the memories that crowded my mind, of aid given me in various undertakings, and of advice and guidance in my religious studies. How well Dr. Hirsch knew that, to be of service, the synagogue must be an active social force, giving its thought and placing its members in the stream of living, moving force and fire which is working in our civilization for a better, juster, higher economic and moral standard of life!

When we wonder how much a single individual counts among myriad human beings, history reminds us how often the thought and the work of just one man has revolutionized the whole trend of phiiosophy or of science. Without doubt, Dr. Hirsch contributed, to a marked degree, in raising the standards of our whole generation. Liberal Judaism was inspired by his leadership and became the greater and more lasting power because of him.

One of the most heart-warming tributes of my life came at the 1917 Chicago Triennial, with the establishment of the Hannah G. Solomon Scholarship Fund. The convention left to my choice the field in which this annual award was to be granted, as well as the first recipient. My decision to ask that it be turned into the channels of social service was reached, partly because of the crying need for trained social workers and, partly, because this was a sphere open to women and one in which they function so tellingly. In 1924, the Council's Juniors took over this project and they have maintained it, superbly, ever since. Today we may count many fine additions to the ranks of professional workers as a result of this scholarship fund.

It was at this Triennial, too, that a resolution was presented by Mrs. Alexander Kohut, for the New York section, concerning the raising of a fund in honor of the Council's twenty-fifth anniversary. This fund was to further a plan for aid in after-the-war reconstruction. Representatives of the Committee on Reconstruction, which was appointed in consequence, were sent to make an exhaustive study of the condition of the Jewish woman in Europe, and "to look into the general immigration situation in the various countries, particularly in the port cities." Recommendations for future effort were to be based on this study.

At Denver, in 1920, and in St. Louis in 1923, the accomplishments of the Committee on Reconstruction were set forth, in detail, and constituted highspots at both Triennials.

In every respect, the Denver convention reached the exemplary standard of other Triennials. The program was excellent, with one of the principal addresses delivered by the Honorable Ben. B. Lindsey, Judge of Denver's Juvenile Court. Council women spoke in the various Temples on the convention Friday evening, as did Mrs. Taylor Phillips, of New York, and I, at Dr. Kauvar's Synagogue.

The St. Louis Triennial was extraordinary, also. Rose Brenner, the Council president, was ill and unable to be present, but my good friend, Mrs. Israel Cowen of Chicago, who was national first vice-president, made a splendid presiding officer. I was on a cruise around the world at the time, and so was obliged to miss the Council's celebration of its thirtieth anniversary, but Lizzie Barbe read the message I sent from abroad. The Triennial program included an address on "War or Peace" by Mrs. Carrie Chapman Catt, one on "Women in the Courts" by Judge Florence E. Allen, and one on "The World Today: Woman's Opportunity" by the Honorable Mrs. Ernest L. Franklin of London, England. Three remarkable women, indicative of the long road the "weaker sex" had travelled since those days of our 1893 congresses when men considered programs their exclusive prerogative!

The statement to the convention by the Committee on Reconstruction was most impressive though, unfortunately, Mrs. Kohut, the chairman, was unable to deliver it in person. The Reconstruction Unit went to Holland in April, 1921, following the survey on the condition of the Jewish woman in Europe which we had agreed upon in 1917. It functioned, principally, in Amsterdam, the Hague and Antwerp. "Through the ports of Rotterdam and Antwerp especially, there poured thousands of Jews, waiting their chance to embark for America", the report read. "The tremendous problems of immediate social and legal service which this floating transmigrant population presented were worked out by the Reconstruction Unit in conjunction with the women of Holland and Antwerp, affording infinite opportunity to put into practice American methods of social service. Councils of Jewish Women were organized in Rotterdam, the Hague, Amsterdam and Antwerp. When these Councils, by the aid of our instruction, advice, organization and re-organization, were well able to take care of their own problems, the Unit left. . . . But there was another call for us. The floating Jewish refugee problem grew worse; famine and disease were raging in Russia and those who could, escaped, arriving at ports and frontier cities in indescribably pitiable condition. European organizations who had watched our work in Holland and Belgium, asked for a return of our workers."

Accordingly, a second Unit was sent to Europe in March, 1922. It was composed of two women, one of whom was paid by the Joint Distribution Committee, the other by us. They established headquarters in Riga, Latvia, on the Baltic Sea, because this was the nearest neutral city which had both an American Consul and banking facilities. Hundreds of absolutely destitute Jewish refugees herded together, here, and the situation must have been unspeakable. The Unit worked for about eight months, effecting an organized method of handling the problems and establishing a Latvian Section of the Council of Jewish Women to take over and carry on.

At the conclusion of this part of our program, we decided to undertake a second major project: the calling of a world convention of Jewish women. Accordingly, Mrs. Kohut made "a tour of the continent gathering together and selecting from the various organizations and individuals, a group of women who came to Vienna in May, 1923, and constituted a Congress of Jewish Women which not only realized and fulfilled our highest ambitions and hopes, but crowned our work in Europe with such brilliant success that the Congress will not be forgotten for many years."

Mrs. Kohut was elected president of the Congress, and serving on the executive committee were, "that fine pioneer in Jewish social service in Germany, the noble Bertha Poppenheim, a woman who had devoted her life and fortune to her work; at her side the fine-spirited and noble-hearted daughter of the former grand Rabbi of France, Mme. Zodac Kahn; beside her, Mrs. Spielman and Mrs. Eichulz, representatives of the best of English-Jewish womanhood; Anitta Muller-Cohen, the brilliant young Austrian Jewess, a dynamo of energy in child welfare all over the continent, and Mme. Rosa Melzer Pomeranz, who has the distinction of being the only Jewess in the Polish Parliament." Representing the United States, with Mrs. Kohut, were Mrs. Nathaniel Harris, Estelle Sternberger who was executive of the Council, and Mrs. Sachs-Barr, the leader of our Reconstruction Unit.

The last of the many splendid resolutions passed by the Congress in Vienna, suggested that a permanent World Union of Jewish Women be formed, for now had been born a realization of the possibility of mutual helpfulness and a great desire to coordinate work. So, finally, a World Union of Jewish Women was to be planned! That the women of Europe have been prevented from achieving this unity is cause for disheartenment, surely, but not surprise! Perhaps, after World War II, we will see it consummated?

Washington, D.C., was the locale of the 1926 Triennial, and I was happy to find myself in the United States at the time, and again convention-minded. It was a brilliant gathering of brilliant women, representing a membership of fifty-three thousand, and there was, in addition, the aura of glamour with which a meeting in our national capitol is always surrounded.

A visit to the White House was a privilege extended to us; a formality that never fails to make each of us glow with pride as we sense our stake in our great Democracy. We were graciously received by President Coolidge, and one could not but feel that such a reception, with its endless hand-shaking, was too great an ordeal for our heavily burdened Chief Executive.

One day the convention delegates made a pilgrimage to Mt. Vernon, and I was humble as I was accorded the honor of placing a wreath upon the grave of George Washington. Reverently our Council women stood, while the iron gates of the vault were opened. I was admitted alone, and as I placed the symbol of our deep respect upon the tomb of the Father of our Country, saying a few solemn words, I was more deeply stirred than ever before. We were all filled with inexpressible gratitude to the Creator for the life of that first President who bestowed upon our country the priceless gifts of his greatness.

Mrs. William Dick Sporberg was Council President during the Washington convention, and her gracious presence and ability added much to the Triennial's distinction. As the convention ended, her gavel was placed in the capable hands of Mrs. Joseph E. Friend.

At the closing session, it was suggested that we sing "Auld Lang Syne" before disbanding. Immediately, a need for an accompanist arose. Dead silence greeted the request. Finally, since no help was forthcoming, I stepped over to the piano. Such applause as I have seldom been accorded, greeted me when I said, reproachfully, "At the least, there is probably one million dollars worth of music lessons represented in this assembly, and I am the only one to volunteer."

Returning to Chicago from Washington, we stopped off to see the Sesqui-Centennial Exhibition. Philadelphia was not particularly happy about its fair, for it did not reach the anticipated heights and, at many points, it maintained an unfinished look, to the end. "High Street", a replica of colonial dwellings, was delightful and perfect, however, and a collection of Rodin sculptures made the art gallery worthwhile, in spite of the fact that the building seemed a mere hollow shell. No place housing works of art should seem flimsy in construction, for there is something disturbingly incongruous about the ephemeral background contrasted with the enduring quality of art. Philadelphia, on the other hand, possesses one of the most perfect settings that I know. To Sam Fleisher, who developed the Graphic Sketch Club, great appreciation is due. A museum connects the school building with the "Sanctuary", which was originally one of the old Philadelphia churches. When Mr. Fleisher purchased it, long after it had fallen into disuse as a place of worship, it had become a warehouse, of sorts. Cleaning disclosed enchanting murals and fine stained glass windows through which filters a "dim, religious light". The Sanctuary — where occasionally one hears heavenly organ music — is a retreat for meditation, and Mr. Fleisher has told me that, open though it is, to all who wish to enter, none of the treasures it now houses have ever been stolen or disturbed. Man, it seems to me, is in essence reverent and possessed of innate integrity.

As I returned home from this Triennial trip, I reflected that it was not alone in women's sphere that fundamental changes were occurring. Through the miraculous inventions and discoveries of this century, countries were being drawn closer and closer, physically. Could this be made true, also, in political and economic life?

It was in this questioning mood that I started on my next journey, when, in 1927, I redeemed my pledge to take Frances Hannah to Europe.

When we sailed on the French liner, S.S.Paris, our congenial companions were my sister Helen and her husband, Henry Kuh, and with them we travelled from Paris to Avignon. The beauties of the Riviera, Monte Carlo and Mentone all measured up to — and even surpassed — our imaginings. Italy, too, held us in its indescribable and unfailing spell, as we revisited my favorite haunts.

In Germany, Frances Hannah and I left the Kuhs, to go to Prague, where the historic relics played second fiddle to our interest in the "Old-New Church" in the Ghetto. This underground synagogue, with its thousand-year-old foundations, its iron ark, its Hebrew-lettered clock tower with numerals reading from right to left, moved us deeply as, once again, we recognized how changeless are the bases of our faith. Impressive, indeed, was the old Royal Palace in its new conversion into residence for President Masaryk. Tea-dancing was, evidently, a daily custom in Prague, and I enjoyed tea-ing while Frances danced.

Then, off to Carlsbad and Nuremburg and reunion with Helen and Henry. Once more, in Paris, we began a daily round of French lessons, music and visits with old friends and new, continuing after the Kuhs departed for England. Suddenly, one day, we decided to leave our delightful old Pension Jules Janin, in Passy, and combine a surprise farewell to the Kuhs, in London, with attendance at conferences of the Union of Jewish Women and the Society for the Protection of Women and Girls, about to convene in England.

While Frances saw the sights, I enjoyed the conference, meeting again, with great pleasure, friends of twenty-five years before. The meetings were highlighted by a series of remarkably fine speeches and delightful social functions: dinners, receptions, garden parties.

It was like going home to return to our Parisian pension, and exciting, indeed, were the following weeks in France, when Lindberg arrived on his epoch-making transatlantic flight, and when Chamberlain and Levine attended the light ceremony under the Arc de Triomphe, on July Fourth.

My brother Mose and his wife spent ten halcyon days with us which included trips to Barbizon and Fontainbleau, "nightlife" at the Moulin Rouge, much lovely music and everything "Paris" means to every traveller. When we bid adieu to France, a tremendous experience lay before us. Italy, and then — Greece and Turkey!

Oh, the wonders of Athen's ancient glory! The mellowed marble of the Parthenon bathed in silvery moonlight; the Acropolis (city on the heights) at midnight; the old Attica where once roamed Plato, Aristotle, Socrates. The National Museum with its countless treasures; the glorious Bay of Salamis, the Marathon mound, Apollo's Temple now but suggested by ruins outlined against the sunlit water.

Sailing on the scarce-rippling Aegean Sea from Piraeus, through the Dardanelles, into the Bosphorus; and then, though we never quite believed it could happen, Constantinople!

No fez, no veil to greet us in Turkey, for Moustapha Kemal Pasha had just decreed the westernizing of the country, and even the English alphabet would henceforth replace Arabic writing.

Constantinople and its Mosques! Constantinople and thick, sweet Turkish coffee; amber beads, perfume and Oriental rugs; three hundred and thirty-five streets of bazaars where once the Sultan housed only his horses! Aroma of water pipes which the Turk prefers to cigarettes; the Imperial Museum with antiques dating back to 3500 B.C.E. The marvelous sarcophagi, dug up in Asia Minor — one of them said to have held Alexander the Great — to me, the most beautiful objects in all the world.

The Sultan's Palace with glittering throne room and fragrant garden; blazing jewels and rare aigrettes. Galata, Pera, Stamboul; endless streams of human beings; the Koran and covered heads.

We could have lingered on indefinitely, but we had already been ten months abroad. As we sped, in our de luxe train, toward Paris, on our homeward lap, I felt poised between two worlds, and as we tore through space I pondered . . . about "change" . . . about "progress" . . . and I knew the two were not, necessarily, synonymous.

PART III

TEXTURE

"Until He Cuts the Thread"

CHAPTER XXIII

"THREE SCORE YEARS AND TEN"
(Psalms xc:10)

WHILE WE WERE IN EUROPE, our household had been moved, once again; this time to a larger apartment on Lincoln Park West. The reason? Well, the family said, it was to provide a comfortably adequate home for a very special occasion. And, sure enough, there it was! Looming over the horizon, for me, was the large round number, seventy! Had I but known, this January 1928 birthday, the seventieth, ushered in the first of a succession of elaborate celebrations, each more wonderful than the last; all of which I managed to survive with equanimity. That I have done so has been due, in part, to an objective viewing of them; but even more to the realization that I seem to have become, perhaps, a kind of symbol as founder of the National Council of Jewish Women, and am, thus, but the tangible recipient of tribute vouchsafed the organization. Never think, though, that the objectivity of which I speak has in any way lessened my complete joy in the warmth and spirit each occasion has engendered as it comes along!

Oh, those amazing seventieth birthday parties! When I state that the piece de resistance of the Council's birthday play, "A Biography", was a most impressive cake so large it was hard to believe it actually was meant to eat, I am in no way minimizing the histrionic ability of the rest of the cast.

The skit was utterly delightful, for it was at this point that my sister-in-law Hattie, wife of Ben — so whimsical in mind and so clever with pen — entered upon a career of playwriting and producing in my honor that should certainly place her in the professional category!

"A Biography" was presented in a number of scenes, in which many members of my family took part. Some of our younger generation were the children in the first act, faithfully portraying a nostalgic scene in our Adams Street home when Greenebaum sisters and brothers were small. The family has often since teased me for practicing on them my penchant for organization, at a time when they were too young to resist, for the episode enacted carried us back to the day when I formed my sisters and brothers into a "club" of which, in some unexplained manner, Hannah was always the president. I had one staunch disciple, however, in my baby sister, Rose, whose sole but continuous contribution consisted of one repeated question, "Ain't we gonna have a constitution?" In the second act, I was taking a piano lesson from Carl Wolfsohn, with one of my nieces portraying my mother and Frances Hannah as I, playing a Haydn Rondo. There followed, next, the founding of the Council; then, the Berlin International Council convention, and in both, my daughter, Helen, represented Hannah G. Solomon. One scene was called "The Life of Hannah", in which Lizzie Barbe spoke, and during the last, entitled, "Hannah, Herself", I was given the opportunity of stepping into the picture to express, in person, my appreciation. At that moment I felt as did Browning's Rabbi Ben Ezra when he said, "The best is yet to be, The last of life for which the first was made." Now, however, after the passing of additional years, I know that seventy is really much too young to philosophize about old age!

On January fourteenth, a large dinner in our own home was attended by my brothers and sisters and nieces and nephews, and all the next day, in a veritable rose garden, I rested in order to be equal to the occasion of that evening, when Chicago Sinai Congregation and Temple Sisterhood celebrated my birthday at the Standard Club.

After Dr. Hirsch's death, in 1923, Sinai Temple was obliged to seek a new rabbi. It found, in Dr. Louis L. Mann, a leader of distinction, an able speaker, a splendid executive and so genial a personality that immediately he won the affection of the congregation. He had been Sinai's rabbi for about five years at the time of my seventieth birthday and his friendly spirit and personal interest were evident in the beautiful atmosphere of the celebration that had been arranged.

Again there was a play, "An Evening in Michael Greenebaum's Home, 1878." Again, my niece portrayed my mother, and Frances Hannah was I. My relatives had a way of liking to participate in the skits and I, for my part, was correspondingly pleased, and glad that persistence in family theatricals had given them poise and histrionic proficiency. My cousin, Moses E. Greenebaum, son of Elias, was then president of Sinai Congregation. We had grown up together, and it was good to see the place he had attained in our city as he proceeded in his earnest and helpful career.

The Sinai Temple Sisterhood, of which Louise Loeb Hamburgher was president, gave me a most wonderful birthday present that year, by establishing the Hannah G. Solomon Peace Fund! No recognition I have ever received has been more sincerely appreciated, and no occasion brings me greater joy than my annual visit to Sinai Temple Sabbath School, on the Sunday nearest Armistice Day, when I am privileged to address the children and personally present the Hannah G.

Solomon Peace prizes, awarded each year to those who have written outstanding essays on Peace.

I seem, indeed, to have come to the "honorary" and "award" period of my life. The Sigma Delta Tau, a college sorority for Jewish students, presented me with a beautiful plaque at the Council Triennial in Pittsburth, in 1938, selecting me as the recipient of their first award to a Jewish woman. That they felt I was worthy of this honor pleased me, of course, but in my heart the feeling has grown through the years, that I was but the humble instrument of accomplishment rather than its embodiment. How, then, could one respond adequately to such an occasion? Only by voicing the belief that devotion to great principles, energetic pursuit of means to achieve purposes which will benefit others, lead some of us into one path, some to another. That Judaism, in its development in prosperity and in adversity, has planted some of the strong foundation stones upon which rest the ethics and morality of the world. We will, perhaps, add our share of glory to our religion. And, in time to come, let us hope they will say, "They builded better than they knew."

There is a divided opinion as to the desirability of college fraternities and sororities, many people feeling that they run counter to the democratic spirit. Some argue that the organization of Jewish groups is unfortunate in that it emphasizes divergences which therefore become more pronounced. The Alpha Epsilon Phi sorority with which I am best acquainted, because I was made an honorary member in 1931, gladdens my heart with its groups of intelligent, educated, thoughtful young women I have met at chapter gatherings in various cities; I rejoice at the promise held for a future in which they — and others like them throughout the country — become participants in the activities of their own communities.

A sorority may bring opportunities for service and for the development of loyalties that are of abiding value, but if they serve merely to promote exclusiveness, the results are wrong and the bases unsound. The college sororities and fraternities in which I am personally interested have rendered praiseworthy aid to many educational and philanthropic causes.

That the University of Chicago should strike in me a particularly responsive chord is not surprising, remembering as I do its early years on the Midway, when I was privileged to know it so well. It is a magnificent institution, and I have always delighted to realize that when John D. Rockefeller's interest was enlisted, and he agreed to contribute a very large sum of money to the University if certain conditions were met, our Jewish group was among those accepting the challenge. A mass meeting was held at the Standard Club in 1890, and a letter from J. W. Goodspeed, secretary of the University, emphasizes a point probably unknown to many today:

"Gentlemen: I am reminded that a year ago, when we were in the utmost danger of failing in our efforts to secure the establishment of the University of Chicago, your Club came to our relief. The subscriptions your committee handed me aggregated $28,350, and enabled me to meet the conditions imposed upon us and thus secured the establishment of the University. It has been felt by the denominations that inaugurated the movement and by the Board of Trustees of the University that the action of the Standard Club was one of notable public spirit and liberality."

I have watched the University grow until now its quadrangles have little space for more structures. Some of the beautiful buildings were presented by our friends, Mandels, Epsteins, Rosenwalds; and I always delight in the exquisite Hilton Chapel, gift of the Henry Hoyt Hiltons.

When the handsome Rockefeller Chapel was opened, in 1929, I was, regrettably, out of the city. Of the events scheduled in connection with its dedication, none would have interested me more deeply than the service in Recognition of the Leadership of Women. With the imposing new edifice filled to capacity, women who had achieved a certain status for accomplishment marched, in impressive processional, down the aisle, each gowned in a University robe. There were many with whom I have worked throughout the years, as well as a younger group, among them my niece, Rose Alschuler, so honored for her outstanding pioneering in the realm of the nursery school, and my daughter, Helen. The services were read by four women: the president of Milwaukee Downer College, our Chicago sculptress, Nellie Walker, Miss Burton, daughter of a former president of the University, and Helen. The address of the evening was delivered by Jane Addams.

I consider Jane Addams the greatest woman of our century. She affected social service throughout the entire known world, and we who worked beside her in Chicago were privileged to see her proceed calmly, simply and with directness and certainty as she faced the problems of the day.

Tragic, indeed, the passing of this great heart and mind. When Jane Addams died, no funeral could have been more stirring. In the open courtyard at Hull House stood hundreds of sorrowing people. The casket rested upon the verandah of the main building so that it might be viewed by all. My daughter and I were asked, by Mrs. Robert Morss Lovett, to stay with Mary McDowell for whom the day was particularly difficult. And so, in Miss Addams' own sitting room on the second floor, looking through Miss Addams' window, we participated, with a group of others, in the service that marked the passing of our greatest citizen.

CHAPTER XXIV

THE RAPID CHANGES occuring everywhere in the world
focussed attention and interest, at this time, on Russia's
experiment. I, too, had been most desirous of seeing how
Russia fared during the process of developing her five-year
plan. The auspicious moment came in June of 1930, and so,
with Frances Hannah and my niece, Ruth Greenebaum as
choice companions, I sailed on the *S.S. Bremen*. The boat
was so gorgeous and so enormous in size that we lost our way
one day and were a whole hour late for a tea engagement!

Aboard, there were many groups of college students; a
large number, like ourselves, Russia-bound, under the auspices
of the Open Road Tourist Agency. Our leader, Carl Borders,
of the League for Industrial Democracy and resident of Chicago Commons, Miss Phillips, of Quaker training and Dr.
Colston Warne, economist, gave us daily informative lectures
and were well-equipped to be our guides in the study of
U.S.S.R. development.

We landed at Bremen and were transferred to a beautiful
Finnish boat. The Baltic Sea was new to us and we caught
interesting glimpses of piers and towns and picturesque sail-
boats and high schooners and fishing craft on the blue waters.
At sundown they were silhouetted in black against the rosy
afterglow, leaving a memorable experience in scenic glory.

The food was so lavish and so delicious that everyone helped himself to too much — and then ate it!

Rocks and pine trees, powerful men and women were the impressions left by Helsingfors and Sibelius' musical descriptions would henceforth have, for us, a new significance.

Soon we arrived in Leningrad and were delighted with our first view of the Neva. Attractive young Russian women, suitably garbed, were our guides and we were introduced to all the well-known places that heretofore had been merely words to us: Nevsky-Prospekt, Catherine the Great's "Winter Palace", the home of Peter the Great and the ornate homes of the Czars, much less wonderful to us than the remarkable institutions for children. The famous Community Kitchen was most typical. Here eight hundred people were employed to feed thirty-six thousand, daily, at a cost of fifteen cents for breakfast and twenty-five cents for dinner. Potatoes were peeled and dishes washed by machine. We marveled at the "new Russia."

In the market place we expected to see caviar and borsch; instead we found blackberries, home-made butter, cooked sausage and thin waffles with creamy filling.

At Moscow our interest centered in the Kremlin, of course, and its great golden domes were as we had pictured them. Here Stalin reigned supreme! Here is evidence of incredible power and wealth! In one room, set aside for armor and military relics we saw swords of mother-of-pearl, gold, silver; ornaments of jade and ivory; precious gems; gifts to the Czars representing fabulous value like Easter eggs set in diamonds. The thrones and trappings for both men and horses would clothe a nation! It was all a startling contrast to the thatched-roof cottages we visited; evidence that the collective plan idea, thus far, had demanded stoical sacrifice of men and women and children. But we were awe-struck at the thought given to childhood as we watched the five-hundred youngsters in the "Park of Culture and Rest". There we found trained kindergartners and fine equipment and there was the best of care for each child, as parents enjoyed their day of rest under the five-day plan for workers.

In the Museum of the Revolution and Anti-Religious Gallery were pictures graphically portraying wrongs done in the name of Religion. Movies of pogroms we witnessed, also, and everywhere we saw hundreds of children being taught Communism and a contempt for old superstitions.

While Frances and Ruth visited the Criminal Colony and gathered information about its revolutionary treatment of prisoners, I had an interview with one of Julius Rosenwald's workers, Mr. Graver, who was assistant to Mr. Rosen. "No country," said Mr. Graver, "is less anti-Semitic than Russia is now, and none is more helpful to the Jews."

In Kiev we visited the Agricultural School and the Schools for Adults in which students are subsidized while studying. We saw the Dnieper River where whole families live on rafts, and felt, everywhere, the worship of Lenin, which seemed to have taken the place of discarded religion. All homes had a "Lenin Corner" instead of the old shrines, and yet in some houses we saw Icons! In our surprise, we questioned one woman, asking the reason for the Icon in an irreligious home. "Oh," she replied, "Of course we don't believe in religion, but the Icon can do no harm, so to be on the safe side we just leave it there."

We sought out Jewish institutions and found them well run and with modern techniques and policies. The Russians appeared a mild and kindly people, deeply engrossed in their great experiment.

Next came Odessa, where we heard about the "declassed Jews" who were rehabilitated for some work. They were taught and given a dollar a day, and allowed to choose their trades. There were six thousand souls there, each one allowed three weeks for recuperation. The soup kitchen and Polyclinic won our admiration.

If the Russians carry out all their plans they will reach the summit of proper care for all workers. Laborer and peasant are free and though not very comfortable, now, will be so when their country is further industrialized. The favorite quotation, that "Religion has been an opiate for the people", was certainly true. This was the tale of Russia trying to dig herself out of merciless despotism into a new dawn. Czars had been dethroned, nobles, whether cruel or kind, banished; rivers of blood had flowed because of fear of those in command.

The lasting impression of our visit to Russia was not one favorable to conditions there. The people worked hard and said, "It is difficult, but when we have finished, the land will be ours!" They have made a brave beginning, but accomplishment seemed very far away.

Budapest was delightful, but we left it excitedly, to speed on to the Mozart Festival, at Salzburg. There we heard a most magnificent production of "Don Juan" and were pleased to sit next to our old Chicago friends, the Max Oberndorfers. In spite of a steady downpour,we "did" everything prescribed, I contenting myself with Tyrolean music and heavenly views of the Bavarian Alps, while the girls did the traditional "Shoot the Shoots" into the famous salt mines.

Then, on to Munich, which we enjoyed as a meeting with an old friend. In Berlin we divided our time between Frederick the Great and Frederick Kuh, with a decided preference for the latter, of whom we are very proud. And last, Cologne

. . . and, once more, Paris . . . and happily back to America!
It was good to be home, where the contrast offered by democracy gave me much food for thought.

As the Council grew in stature and importance, the Triennials became more and more significant. Never were they
perfunctory, and each one was colorful and constructive.

Los Angeles was Triennial host in 1929. It was the first
meeting on the Pacific coast, and for the first time attendance
of members from the western states was thus made possible.
This Triennial found the Council functioning with many national departments and committees: Community Cooperation,
Education, Extension and Field Service, Farm and Rural
Work, Immigrant Aid and Immigrant Education, Legislation
and Civics, Peace, Religion and Religious Education, Social
Service, Vocational Guidance and Employment, a sub-com-
mittee on the Blind and Sight Conservation, and one on the
Deaf. Our Junior Auxiliary was thriving, as were the Hannah
G. Solomon Scholarship Fund and "The Jewish Woman",
the Council's publication for its members. Our splendid national president, Mrs. Friend, had reason to view the organization with utmost gratification.

One of the Triennial's evening highspots was a magnificent
pageant entitled "Hear, O Israel" in which Mrs. Lillian B.
Goldsmith, president of the local section and co-author of
the production, took the leading role.

Los Angeles has a Council House of its own, a building
that greatly redounds to the credit of the section and Mrs.
Goldsmith, to whose effort the accomplishment was largely
due.

Probably the most notable contribution of the Council's
work for humanity lies in the field of Immigrant Aid. Certainly, at the dramatic and vital moment when hundreds of

[231]

our suffering brethren came to America for sanctuary from Hitler's persecution, the Council was prepared, through its previously well-established "set-up", to take over the gigantic task of their rehabilitation in a strange land. We had trained and volunteer workers devoted and well-equipped, to meet them at ports and docks, to arrange for transportation and visas, to place children, to unite families and to follow through with a complete program of orientation. The dramatic story of thousands of grateful repatriated Jews testifies, today, how well that obligation was fulfilled. Our government recognized the excellence of our work and asked the loan of our representative at Ellis Island, Miss Cecelia Razovsky, to assist in its overwhelming task. We were fortunate in having Mrs. Maurice Goldman as our national president during this emergency. Through her former chairmanship of our committee on Immigrant Aid, she brought to the new problems not only familiarity with the need of the moment, but also a rare ability and quality of leadership. At the Detroit Triennial of 1932, she announced the change of name from Immigrant Aid to Service to the Foreign-Born. This department has grown steadily in importance, until today we are a recognized force all over the world. We have included in our work international service, stimulation of interest in legislation affecting the foreign-born, deportation cases and the relocation of divided families.

The Triennial of 1935, took me to New Orleans, the hospitable city where, with special pleasure, I always enjoy visiting many good friends; among them, Mrs. Joseph Friend, a valued worker and not without honor in her own community. The general theme of the convention, "What Do We Owe Our Next Generation?", was brilliantly expounded by eminent Jewish leaders, both men and women, and a panel discussion by representatives of the National Conference of Christians and Jews was most enthusiastically received.

No organization has done more to promote the great ideals of justice and brotherhood for which we strive than the National Conference of Christians and Jews. Created for the purpose of bringing together Protestant, Catholic and Jew, in the belief that friendly and easy association and reasonable discussions will result in mutual understanding and respect, it holds out hope and inspiration for the future. It is too much to expect, however, that in a short span of time we can abolish prejudices and differences in religions and races.

I have belonged to the executive board of the Chicago Round-Table of Christians and Jews, and I am convinced, as are the other members, that human advance can, and will, be made! To me, this splendid organization represented the flowering of years of association with women of other faiths in groups, clubs and classes. A number of barriers had been broken through since the days of the Parliament of Religions, and divergences in religious belief became less disturbing. We found ourselves able to discuss questions freely and we saw how closely our thinking, for the most part, paralleled. Now, the Round Tables, as the local groups affiliated with the National Conference are called, are able, increasingly, to spread their message to a much larger circle than that reached before. Surely, in time, their message must be heeded!

At the Juniors' Council Biennial in October, 1935, I was happy as I spoke to them about "The Daily Adventure." What great promise for the future that gathering held! How eagerly we watch our young people as they start out on their great adventure and how we rejoice in those who, from the beginning, choose the right pathway. We are eager that the years of study may be passed profitably, and that an education may fit them for the challenges life presents. American youth, by and large, possesses courage, honesty and kindliness, coupled with an intelligent social consciousness. That, one felt, was especially evidenced at the Juniors' convention.

My days with these young Jewish women were a source of great joy and satisfaction as I remember so pleasantly their kindnesses. Their eleventh convention, in Chicago in 1939, afforded me another splendid opportunity to observe and glory in their capabilities, and I was touched by their insistence that I be the guest of honor at their luncheon.

Important as the Triennials are, however, as a means of gauging the Council's growth and scope, it was at executive meetings and conferences that national officers and board members set the policies, outlined plans and carried on the detailed business of the organization. A complete record of these many consultations would read like a travelogue encompassing the entire area of the country. As I travelled to one or another, finding new stimulation and encouragement in each, I took advantage of the opportunities presented, to visit sections in every locality. On each such tour, I was glad that — unlike the "old woman who lived in the shoe",— I had no desire to spank my many children, or to put them to bed; I was far too proud of every one of them!

It was recognized that most was to be gained by frequent discussions of common problems, and so the Council organized State federations and, later, regional conferences in some areas.

The North-Central group of the regional conferences, which includes the Chicago area, is of course the one I know best. It has flourished and we have had excellent meetings in our mid-western cities. One of the most noteworthy was held in Chicago Heights, in 1939, where I sat beside young Clifton

Utley, at dinner. Mr. Utley, who was then director of the Chicago Council on Foreign Relations, was the speaker of the evening, and he painted a vivid and unforgettable picture as he spoke on "Toward the Next War!" Yet another such conference, in 1932, was that held in Minneapolis, home of Mrs. Arthur Brin, who has made a telling contribution not only to the Council, but to the National Committee on the Cause and Cure of War, as well. She was then chairman of the Council's national committee on Peace which was the special theme of the Minneapolis conference discussion. As intelligently as we could, we weighed the alternatives which might lead to rational settlement of disputes by the nations of the world. Alas! our message did not reach the ears for which it was intended! When I was given the opportunity of speaking on "The Expanding Universe", I voiced the conclusion that ruin from war is universal. Victor and vanquished, alike, are blighted and the victor should beware lest his gains provide the basis for a next war. Victory should mean more than a medal pinned on the empty coat-sleeve of a martyr. It must denote that right has triumphed, and that saying "Peace where there is no peace," cannot count in the forward advance of the human family.

Mrs. M. C. Sloss was Inter-State president of the Western-Regional Conference which I attended in San Francisco in March of 1936. There the serious work of the meeting was lightened by entertainment which I especially enjoyed, for I never cease to delight in the opportunity of drawing closer to and knowing well the outstanding representative women of our faith with which Council membership automatically endows one.

Toronto extended to me an invitation, in 1937, to attend and address the annual meeting of the section, which I found a thriving organization, doing admirable work, civically. It had established a remarkable community center and gave evidence of inspiring leadership. My visit coincided with the coronation of the King and Queen of England, and Canada was in festive attire. In shop windows were displayed figures of the royal family in their regal robes, and the people were enthusiastic in their celebration and show of patriotism. The Toronto Section of the Council, too, gave a lovely "Coronation luncheon". Today it is functioning effectively in work directed toward the war effort.

Each Council section I have visited, and they have been legion, has thrilled me, anew, with the usefulness of its members. The eagerness of Jewish women to contribute to the general welfare is apparent on every hand, and their devotion to the tasks undertaken has indeed been consecration. Because of them, the story of the Council is a glorious record of achievement. Nor do we forget the signal accomplishment of the Temple Sisterhoods all through the country and of auxiliaries such as that of the B'nai B'rith. Hadassah, organized by Henrietta Szold in the early nineteen hundreds, has brought to Palestine the devoted interest and effort of thousands of women. Stirring and vital, indeed, is the role played by Jewish women in America.

CHAPTER XXV

"BEFORE HONOR GOETH HUMILITY"
(Proverbs xv:33)

THE YEAR 1933 brought to Chicago one of its most significant experiences; one so extraordinary, in fact, that another star was added to our city's flag. Up to that time it
had possessed but three: one for the Fort Dearborn Massacre,
one for the Chicago Fire and one for the World's Fair of
1893. But now there was to be our second great Fair, the
Century of Progress Exposition, celebrating the hundredth
anniversary of the city's incorporation. We, who remembered
so well the magnificent "White City" of 1893, were overwhelmed by this modern day with its new utilitarian type of
architecture, its amazing and effective uses of color and light
and the remarkable exhibits proclaiming advances in every
field. Now, too, we incorporated the word "streamlined"
into our vocabularies.

The World's Fair of 1933, like that of 1893, was built upon
Chicago's lake front, but not in Jackson Park, this time. Instead, it was located practically in the heart of the city. For
this great exposition almost all of the land providing the
brand-new site was man-made! The entire lake front, beginning at Twelfth Street, and extending as far south as Thirty-
Ninth Street, had been filled in and, lo! there was land where
no land had been before! The Adler Planetarium was within
the Exposition's gates, and just outside the entrance were the

Shedd Aquarium and the Field Museum. Thus an interesting contrast in types of architecture was presented between the classic older buildings and the ultra-modern ones that characterized the 1933 Fair.

All of us had season tickets, and a general going and coming to and from the Fair grounds became almost routine in our household. Frances Hannah, with two other young women, had established a Children's Guide Service which delighted us, since it became necessary for her to know the Fair in all its aspects and phases, thus bringing to her an additional educational advantage. These girls arranged a series of special tours for children whose parents otherwise could not afford to send them to the Exposition at all, and expenses for these jaunts were defrayed by groups of public-spirited individuals and organizations.

Thanks to its remaining a second year, the Fair was not a losing venture, financially!

There were many spectacular features of "The Century of Progress", but nothing exceeded the thrill of the moment when, on the opening night, as if by magic, the grounds suddenly became illuminated. We were told that a beam of light which had left the star, Arcturus, forty years before, when the World's Fair of 1893 was opened, had just reached the earth, producing the energy to set in motion the machinery which dispelled the darkness of that first evening of the 1933 Exposition. Nevertheless, to those of us who were not scientists, it *was* magic!

There was an advantage in being over seventy years old! I could appreciate, fully, the great strides made in all the sciences so graphically set before us at the Fair. I thought of the old Exposition on the lake front which we had known years before, where new trends and accomplishments had been apparent, also. I remember that my father's perfected ice-box was exhibited and looked upon with favor. It had some special cooling device for drinking water, and there was a faucet on the outside from which it could be drawn. My father, who was inventive and far-seeing, said once that he believed the day would come when "a door would be made which would be open and shut at the same time." I wish I knew what his mind pictured then, and I wonder if it could possibly have been like the revolving doors we take so for granted, today.

Nothing at the Fair gave us more pleasure than the music! The wonderful open-air concerts, free to the public, were, I am sure, the impetus toward a much greater appreciation of good music, generally, in our city. The Art Institute, too, made history with its borrowed world-renowned collections. Whistler's Mother, straight from Paris, serenely "received" thousands of visitors, daily, and was probably the most popular woman at the Fair!

True to my devotion to expositions, I spent much time at the "Century of Progress," and through appointment of Governor Horner served as one of the hostesses in the Illinois State House which, in itself, played the role of hostess building at the Fair. It was a delightful place and its charming auditorium was in constant use. The Chicago Woman's Club had arranged a series of weekly lectures on "The Progress of Woman", and I was assigned the subject "Woman in Organization," a topic which afforded splendid opportunity for taking note of the great contributions women had made within a century toward the achievement of high goals. All of the talks in this series emphasized both the specific contributions individual women had made to the advancement of civilization, and the aid given to the larger purposes they had espoused by their ability to awaken group consciousness. When we remember the great fear of earlier days, lest woman lose her position as queen of the home, lest her children be neglected and the family mending left undone, we have tremendous admiration for the pioneers who started, quietly, the trend toward emancipation so long ago that already, in the "gay nineties" era, woman's new status was unquestioned. Even her desire to wear short hair, if she chose, was not branded as an insistence upon the right to trespass on masculine prerogatives.

A splendid International Congress of Women was held in Chicago in July, 1933, under the auspices of the National Council of Women of the United States, bringing together members of its component organizations, and persons of note, from all over the world. The stated purpose of the Congress was,"to concentrate the thinking of the representative women of fifty countries upon problems of world moment — and to release that thinking into action." The general theme was "Our Common Cause — Civilization." Lena Madesin Phillips, president of the organization, was a woman of striking personality whose strength added dignity to every meeting.

A most unique feature was arranged for the banquet. Telegrams, cablegrams and radiograms were sent directly, from the hall, to internationally famous women in many parts of the world. A huge map covered one end of the banquet-room, and in electric lights the courses of the various messages were flashed upon the map as, travelling by land and sea, they were received by the personages to whom they were directed. One of these went to a passenger on a ship in mid-ocean! Suddenly, and thrillingly, replies actually came back to us in time to be read to the assembled banquet guests. That, too, seemed a bit of sheer magic!

Among the delegates was Frau Beth, the first Austrian woman to become a lawyer, and winner of the coveted Emmanuel Kant award for the best book on comparative religions. She is now a resident of Chicago, and we delight to number her among our friends. We did not then know the anguish the future would bring to her, to the Baroness Ishimoto of Japan and to other fine and noted women who were with us at this meeting. There was, however, at the convention, an uneasy consciousness of the black cloud hovering over Europe, for Hitler had but recently come upon the scene and one could sense repressed fear.

In the exhibition hall of the Palmer House, next to the ballroom where the larger Congress sessions were held, the participating organizations had set up displays, of which my daughter was in charge, and it was interesting to see what each was contributing to the general good. Here, at frequent intervals, a recording I had made told the story of the origin, development and scope of the National Council of Jewish Women. Rose Alschuler, who established Chicago's first nursery schools, led a round table discussion on "Opportunity Through Education", during the Congress, and each session provided real inspiration to all present, as well as a meeting ground for old friends.

Though the International Congress of Women and the series of lectures arranged by the Chicago Woman's Club would have made 1933 a noteworthy year for our city, even had there been no World's Fair, I believe that by the linking of these three outstanding events, each added to the stature of the others.

The year that added a star to Chicago's flag, marked for me, too, a milestone of personal import when, in the first month of 1933, I celebrated my seventy-fifth birthday. It was difficult to believe I could feel so little change between the ages of fifty and seventy-five, and I made tacit apology to those whom I had previously considered old at that age. I could still travel alone, and keep up quite as lively a gait as my dear companion, Lizzie Barbe, one year my senior, whose vigor I had always ascribed to her Quaker ancestry.

It really required endurance, both physical and emotional, to live through the series of delightful seventy-fifth birthday parties that followed one another in close succession. My, how I loved them all! But I felt I had more than my quota! How often I wished my mother could have shared them, for whenever she was asked what she most wished for her children, she replied, "that they may find favor with their fellowmen." In some way, for me, Fate had fulfilled her desire, but I could not understand why. Could it be that love begets love, and thus perhaps is reflected back to an individual some portion of his outpouring to those who surround him? To me, like Solomon, "an understanding heart" would be my expressed wish. If, from that yearning, have sprung opportunities for service, then I can only feel that the compensatory joy far outweighs any accomplishment; a joy which cannot fail to make one humble.

The Chicago section of the Council celebrated this birthday most beautifully with a luncheon and reception at the Standard Club. Mrs. Arthur Brin, the National president, came from Minneapolis for the occasion, and Jane Addams was the other special guest. It had been arranged that Mrs. Brin and I send messages by radio throughout the country, to over two hundred Council sections which were observing the day in their own cities. It was truly awe-inspiring to feel that a bond was, at that moment, almost tangibly uniting so many groups of women.

The presence of Jane Addams made even more memorable
my seventy-fifth birthday party given by the Council

The after-luncheon program was a playlet entitled, "Dinner for Hannah", which closed with a clever parody of a then-popular song. The name was "Of Thee We Sing, Hannah", and the message it carried was to the effect that the first hundred years are the hardest, but that I had made a very good start! Having attempted play-writing myself, and having produced two skits, "Jews of Illinois in Story and Tableaux" and a parody on "The Yellow Jacket", I was in a position to appreciate the time and effort involved in so delightful a dramatization as "Dinner for Hannah."

The observance of my "real birthday" we have always kept at home, where the comings and goings of family and friends, the letters, telegrams and all of the attendant excitement make each anniversary eventful. This year, the day began at break-fastime, with the arrival of a group of Alpha Epsilon Phi girls who came, serenading. Guests all through the day kept me oblivious to the fact that, for the evening, the family, repre-sented by three generations, was arranging a surprise party. The apartment adjoining ours was vacant, and in it all the secret preparations were made. Imagine my complete sur-prise as I was ushered next door to be greeted by my nieces who were garbed in the charming costumes of my youth. In gala mood we sat down to a royal banquet and added another happy page to the Greenebaum album.

The series of seventy-fifth birthday celebrations was cli-maxed by a supper at Sinai Center, given jointly by the Men's Club, the Sisterhood and the Temple's senior and junior con-gregations. Lizzie Barbe and Jane Addams were special guests and Lizzie and I felt most "elegant" in our costumes of the period of 1893, and the piano solo with which, upon request, I favored my audience, was of the same vintage. Among my most cherished treasures is the exquisite diamond-studded watch presented to me upon that occasion. Sinai Temple has been close to my heart throughout the years, and I am now grateful for the privilege of sitting upon its board.

Among those entering most sympathetically into all my experiences was my son-in-law, Emile, and I have always been glad that his presence made this celebration complete, for it was in the following year that he died. Although we were greatly concerned about his health at that time, he had joined in the observance of the Passover Seder Service with his usual self-forgetfulness. Our distress was, unfortunately, not without cause, for his death followed in a very few days. We were stunned. Our family circle of four was broken. Again, a period of sorrow and of readjustment.

I welcomed the second year of the "Century of Progress" Exposition because Helen, Frances Hannah and I were able to spend a good deal of time there and the impersonal activity helped my daughter through an exceedingly difficult period. We went our way quietly and calmly, but very sadly. The Frank Solomons were now living in Winnetka and each of them brought us solace. However, we lived in a more or less minor key until Philip Angel, a fine young lawyer from Charleston, West Virginia, came to spend a Christmas holiday in Chicago. He and Frances Hannah met! A new happiness was brought to us, as was an awakened appreciation of the good in life, when they were married the following December.

Lizzie Barbe and I travelled west, together, in 1939, to attend the Council's Western-Interstate Conference at San Francisco. We enjoyed rest and recreation at Palm Springs and Los Angeles, too, but the highspot of our trip was a visit at Rose's Tempe, Arizona, house with her and sister Helen. Henry Kuh was no longer living, and my two "little sisters", who had been close companions all their lives, spent much time together. It was always a very special joy to me to be where Helen was. There had been a particular bond of affection between us from the days when, as a child, she had followed me about.

Our days in Tempe had a certain eerie quietness. We were saddened because Rose was ill and to find her so depleted in strength brought a chilling consciousness of the threat we sensed but could not mention. Before the following January — her birth-month, as it was mine — Rose had left us. Death came also, to sister Helen in the next year while she was travelling in Vienna. A son and daughter were with her there, but she seemed very far away from the rest of us.

I had survived many of my younger sisters and brothers. Again and again I had to learn the heart-breaking lesson of life: one must pay in too-exacting ratio the price of the joys life gives us. But I learned, also, that the blessing of human companionship, when removed by death, should entail no aftermath of bitterness. The great awareness of our loss is our tribute to those who have gone.

On December 22, 1937, we had planned to celebrate the fiftieth wedding anniversary of my brother and sister-in-law, Mose and Rose Greenebaum. How tragic that on that day, instead, our Mose was laid to rest! During the year 1941 my brother Gus also died. His wife, Leah, had passed away when she was still young, and some years later Gus had married Blanche Mainzer of Grand Rapids, whose sweetness and devotion endeared her to us all. Their daughter's beautiful wedding took place shortly before Gus's death, and that he had lived to participate in it in his inimitable and joyous way, had added a point of completion to his life. I remember Gus as a most lovable little boy, and his fundamental cheeriness never left him.

So many of us now had gone! Theresa, great in her courage, was away from us when she closed her life's book. Henriette, Mary, Helen and Rose; Mose, Henry and Gus; Henry Frank, Charley Haas, Henry Solomon, Henry Kuh, Joe Eisendrath, Esther, Leah ... one by one we had said farewell to them. Too many of the next generation, too, had died! Herbert, Louise Nathan, Gus Haas, James Lesem, Henry Arthur Greenebaum, Emile Levy and Alfred Alschuler ... each so fine and so beloved. To some this may seem but a list of names, but back of it lies a family saga. Inevitable, these breaks in the ranks; these heart-wrenching moments of parting. Yet, never in our grief did we forget our gratitude for the great privilege that was ours in building a family life so completely satisfying and enriching.

And now sad New Year's Eves for us followed. By this time our elaborated performances had discontinued and we were becoming accustomed to thinking of ourselves as a diminishing troupe. Nevertheless, in unbroken succession, each year's end found many of us congregated at one or the other of our homes, with the third generation dropping in to visit for a bit and share with the first and second generations in this night of memories. New Year's Eve would always be difficult in the future, but we knew we must not mourn. We remembered, with thanks, the many bright days of the long ago when all our lives were interwoven into brilliant blending patterns of joyful living.

CHAPTER XXVI

"AND MY GOD SHOWED FAVOR UNTO ME"
(Testament of Joseph i)

I HAD THOUGHT that no birthday festivity could surpass my seventy-fifth, but by a happy coincidence of date, the seventy-ninth, in 1937, joined itself to the forty-fourth anniversary of the Council, and, lo! I became an international figure! Yes, that is quite literally true, and I wish I could do justice to the wonder and joy I experienced when I was informed that an international broadcast had been arranged in honor of the day, in which seventeen women from seven countries would participate.

Mrs. Marion Miller, executive director of the Council, introduced the program. Mrs. Rebekah Kohut and Mrs. Carrie Chapman Catt spoke from New York, as did Nina Strandberg, president of the Federation of Business and Professional Women's Clubs of Finland. A quotation from a leading newspaper that day will suggest the unprecedented scope of the broadcast: "Mme. Leon Brunschweig, Under-Secretary of State for Education in France, will speak from France. Mme. Frantiska Plaminkova, member of the Czechoslovak senate and chairman of the women's council in that country, will speak from Prague. Mme. Sonja Branting-Westerstahl, daughter of the late premier of Sweden, will be heard from Stockholm, and Mrs. Israel Zangwill, wife of the British novelist, Miss Harriet Cohn, British pianist, and Mrs. Ernest L. Franklin, former president of the National Council of England, will be heard from London. Miss Marie Ginsberg, Polish member of the Secretariat of the League of Nations, will speak from the library of the league. Mme. Gertrude Van Tyne, head of the Jewish committee for German refugees in Holland, will be another speaker, and so will Winnifred Kydd, dean of women at Queens University in Canada. From the west coast will be heard Mrs. M. C. Sloss, honorary vice-president of the Council; and Mrs. Maurice L. Goldman, who will speak from the Rose Bowl of the Palace Hotel in San Francisco." Mrs. Barbara Blackstock Cody was heard from Canada, and Mrs. Brin and I spoke from Chicago. Meetings and social gatherings were scheduled throughout the country, and in all Council sections members came together to listen to the "International Birthday Party", of which the general theme was "Woman's Place in World Progress Today."

Mrs. Brin and I left the luncheon at the Standard Club to go direct to the broadcasting station, taking with us a very excited and jubilant Frances Hannah. It was awe-inspiring to hear the voices of women from all over the world come through the microphone, and it was thrilling beyond words to feel that so many persons were sharing my birthday with me. But far more than any element of personal pride, was the knowledge impressed upon me that day: the Council had "arrived!"

The members of the Chicago section made me happy, as always, with their evidences of affection, and I was grateful to its officers for making their part in the celebration so especially heart-warming. I tried to express this in my letter of acknowledgement to the sections: "The kind messages sent to me from the various sections on the occasion of my seventy-ninth birthday and the forty-fifth year of the Council brought to me one of the greatest joys I have ever known. The International broadcast was the most thrilling experience of my life. Through it we, the heirs of one of the oldest religions, have by the aid of the latest discoveries in science, heard voices blended in sympathetic chorus for all good purposes . . . May we hope that a time will come when all men will be led, as is an orchestra, in unity and harmony. I cannot express, adequately, my thanks to the national board of the Council and to those whose strenuous efforts made the broadcast possible. To the participants, my thanks are due for the privilege they conferred upon their listeners who were thus able to hear the voices of women known throughout the world for their sacrifices and efforts in behalf of a happier humanity. And to all who brought a tribute of love and friendship, I would convey my deep appreciation, for I realize that it is proof of your loyalty and devotion to the Council. In it, too, your homage is given to the memory of the work of the pioneers whose faith in the power of Jewish womanhood created this band of workers. My birthday wish for each one of you is that she may experience such happiness as I have known through this birthday celebration."

There followed a whole series of parties, honoring pioneers in the "woman's movement". (It really was no handicap to be eighty!) The Chicago Woman's Club and the Women's City Club remembered their founders in beautiful spirit, and younger organizations, such as the Alumni of the College of Jewish Studies, proved in their spontaneous tribute that consecration to Jewishness is ageless.

The celebration of my eightieth birthday brought an awareness of a milestone of unusual significance. I was the delighted recipient of hundreds of messages and it was good to know that many dollars were added to charity coffers as a mark of the day.

Sinai Temple devoted a Sunday morning service in its recognition, with all of the members of my immediate family, present, including children and grandchildren, as well as many others who were dear to me. Dr. Mann, Mrs. Brin and Mrs. Gerson Levi spoke, and I responded. I never think of the occasion but as a holy day. It was one of the most beautiful tributes I have ever known, and though many tears were shed, there were none by me. A deep peace seemed to possess me, and I felt profound gratitude for the health that had made it possible for me to live and work.

The following press release appeared in the newspapers just before the National Council's 1938 Triennial:

"When Mrs. Hannah G. Solomon, founder of the National Council of Jewish Women, appears as the honor guest at the Fifteenth Triennial Convention of the organization to be held in Pittsburgh beginning January 23rd, she will be presented with a list of 100 new members for every one of her 80 years. 'Founder's Day', which marks the birthday of Mrs. Solomon, will be celebrated through a series of simultaneous meetings held by 200 Sections of the Council throughout the United States and Canada through January, Mrs. Joseph M. Welt, program chairman of the Triennial Convention announced on her arrival in New York this week to conclude plans for the conference . . . . A nation-wide campaign to add 8,000 new members to the Council's roster of more than 50,000 women is in full swing throughout the country, Mrs. Welt announced." (This goal, incidentally, was almost reached.)

"The 'Birthday celebrations' will begin in Chicago, Mrs. Solomon's birthplace, with a city-wide birthday party sponsored by the Chicago Council section. Mrs. Maurice L. Goldman, First Vice-President and Chairman of the executive committee of the National Council of Jewish Women, will

What a glorious joint celebration was the Council Triennial banquet in Pittsburgh, in 1938, marking the organization's forty-fifth year and my eightieth birthday!

be one of the chief speakers on that occasion. The birthday celebration will culminate with a banquet to be held at the William Penn Hotel in Pittsburgh on Wednesday, January 26th, with more than 1000 delegates and visitors assembled."

In spite of the fact that I had not been well during the summer, and that the days before my eightieth birthday had been difficult and the functions strenuous, I felt quite equal to going to Pittsburgh. In fact, I seemed so brisk that my daughter-in-law, who attended the Triennial as a Cleveland delegate, said to me quite wisely, "You really don't need a doctor or nurse when you are ill, Mother. What you need is a convention!"

The Triennial was most inspiring. It was gratifying to see the fine young women who had joined the ranks with Council's first and second generations. Many were daughters and grand-daughters of the founders in their communities. We of the older group spoke together of the problems encountered during the forty-five years in which we had worked together, of the difficulties we had surmounted and of the great tasks confronting those whose years of active service lay just ahead. The distressing condition of the Jews in Europe immeasurably saddened us and we realized how heavy would be the burdens we must assume if we would be of constructive assistance. A huge program for the rescue of refugee children was projected at that meeting.

The opening session of the Triennial was "Founders' Evening", but even more gala was the convention banquet at the William Penn Hotel, our headquarters. James Lawrence Houghteling, National Commissioner of Immigration and Naturalization and the Honorable George J. Messersmith, Assistant Secretary of State were speakers of the evening, following my invocation.

The Council's Service for Foreign Born formed the basis of the banquet program and its outstanding feature was a broadcast over a national hook-up, which began with the announcer who told of the founding and growth of the Council. He stated that "delegates from Canada to the Gulf" had gathered at the banquet to celebrate its forty-fifth anniversary and the eightieth birthday of its founder.

Then followed, over the air waves, an incident in dramatic form; one that never fails to evoke interest in Council achievements. It told how, in 1924, when stringent exclusion bills kept aliens from the United States, a number of ships were caught on the high seas. One bound for America had just set out as the new law was enacted, and on board were between one and two hundred Russian Jewish immigrants. The captain, learning that his passengers would not be accepted at their port of destination, attempted to land them elsewhere, but none of the countries to which he appealed would receive them. When, out of the Athenian harbor near Piraeus, the boat lay at anchor, a young Russian Jewess, a passenger, managed to make her way past the guard and go ashore. She could speak a little English, but no Greek, and she was immediately picked up by the police and taken to a social service organization. There she told her story of the stranded Russians and begged assistance in their plight. The agency sent a wireless message to the New York office of the National Council of Jewish Women in which the names of the individual marooned families were transmitted, and the Council was able to make provision for their landing in such ports as could be obtained for them. At that time, Mexico and Argentina both offered shelter in the western hemisphere. Similar stories of the efficacy of Council's Service For Foreign Born could be multiplied indefinitely.

The convention banquet, with all the traditional appurtenances from birthday cake to speeches, was held just twelve days after my eightieth birthday, with almost one thousand people gathered to help in its celebration.

From my dear Greenebaum family I received the princely birthday gift of a trip to Florida. My daughter accompanied me, and together we revelled in all that such a vacation could afford. We chose Passa Grille as our loitering spot, and there for six weeks we spent restful, relaxing days, brightened by the presence of many friends, many of whom were in near-by St. Petersburg. Among them were our dear friends, Judge and Mrs. Samuel Alschuler. In my mind, I always think of Samuel Alschuler as an outstanding and perfect blending of staunch Americanism and Jewish constancy.

Our homeward trip was revelatory of our versatility in enjoyment as, after the serenity of our stay in Passa Grille we travelled on, seeing the sights and visiting Council sections of the southland.

Tampa's Council brought admiration by its lovely luncheon meeting and the excellent quality of its communal work; in Orlando, the Fountain of Youth tempted us — albeit a little late, in my case, I suspected. St. Augustine and Jacksonville were enchanting in scenic beauty and thrilling in historic interest, as is so much of Florida. Next came the lakes of Winter Park and a visit at Rollins College; the wonderful Sarasota Art Palace, gift of Mr. "Circus" Ringling; the Boston Red Sox busily practicing and the celebrated Bok Tower and the Lake of Wales all shared our enthusiasm, with what is perhaps forgivable emphasis on the Tower and its beautiful carillon. In Savannah we combined Council business with a visit at the home of a nephew and his wife, and enjoyed viewing the old Jewish burying ground with its old-world brick-walled graves topped with marble slabs bearing lengthy inscriptions. Charleston, South Carolina brought us to delightful relatives and a Council supper meeting, as well as a pleasant drive with Mrs. Octavus Cohen who, with her eighty-plus years, made me feel quite juvenile! In Richmond, we paid homage to Patrick Henry's Church of his speech-making fame, and then . . . Charleston, West Virginia . . . and a beaming Frances Hannah and hospitable Philip Angel waiting to greet us!

I was visiting my children in Cleveland when I received word that I had become a great-grandmother! I was deeply stirred. It seemed wonderful to know that a new generation was beginning in the person of little Philip Angel! When my daughter-in-law drove me to Charleston, after his arrival, I did not need to learn to "rave" about my great-grandson, as I had perfected the art by constant practice on my four grand-children. Small Philip proved to be a golden-haired boy of such charm as one finds pictured, usually, only in the imagination of hopeful parents. His little brother, Henry, arriving on January tenth, 1941, is equally winsome. No, I don't think I'm at all prejudiced!

And now there has been added to our family group another fine young man; a psychologist by the name of James Birrin, who is going to marry my grand-daughter, Betty.

Now, I felt, I might put aside the seven-league boots that had carried me from one end of the country to the other, and across the water, too, and allow myself the luxury of rest and contemplation rather than continuous action. Now I might devote myself to the books I had long wished to read, and I could be at home when came the hour for afternoon tea. So it would be!

Amazingly soon, it seemed to me, 1940 was at hand, and

here again was January! My Cleveland family came in a body to Chicago, and shared, with us, our New Year's Eve. Then, a few days later, Frances Hannah and Philip arrived, bringing the dear great-grandson, and I knew it was no small matter to have become eighty-two!

What a privilege to have lived actively through a span of years which saw Chicago change from a small community to a huge and complex city. How good to have watched the Council develop from an idea to a great, functioning organization which, one knew, was destined to win a future as glorious as had been its blessed past!

The Council's birthday celebration was one of the loveliest it had ever prepared. Seated at the speakers' table were a number of organization representatives and colleagues with whom I had worked through the years.

From the raised platform I looked out upon the assembled members, contrasting them mentally with my memory of the Council's founders. I smiled as I thought how groundless were the fears of the men about what women would lose through participation in communal and world affairs. Never have I seen a more alert, dynamic and, withal, a more chic and attractive group of women, many of them surprisingly young! I felt secure in the knowledge that they would carry forward the Council's high aims and purposes.

Before me, too, at the tables, were my children and grandchildren and my fine young nieces, and I felt rich in the certainty that they would carry to a new generation the ideals and strength of Sarah and Michael Greenebaum. How grateful I was for the years that had been granted me!

Hattie Greenebaum, my prolific sister-in-law, had once more turned authoress, and so there was presented a delightful pageant, picturing some of the early scenes from my diary —

this very account of my life which I had already begun. The play's program stated that it was "The Days of Her Years . . . a dramatization of the autobiography of the founder of the National Council of Jewish Women . . . . to celebrate her eighty-second birthday." On the stage was an enormous book, and from its pages the actors stepped, as the episodes in the life of Hannah G. Solomon, which could be made to seem dramatic, were presented. These episodes were joined together by a beautifully told narrative.

My inexpressible appreciation of the Chicago section's repeated celebrations in my honor was inextricably blended with my consciousness of its loyalty to the National organization, for I always felt that in so honoring me it was giving evidence of that loyalty. My relationship to the local section is unique; the child had measured up to its mother's dreams! However, several of the Chicago's section's achievements merit special praise.

An office maintained for its Service to the Foreign Born, with a staff of paid and rarely faithful volunteer workers is an outstanding accomplishment, as is the "Council Camp" at Wauconda, Illinois, which provides a summer vacation for tired mothers and children who need the out-of-doors. During the past summer it brought rest and happiness to six hundred and ninety-five different women, girls and little boys who would otherwise enjoy no vacation of any type. It is Chicago section's most important project and to most of us Council Camp is synonymous with the name of Lizzie Barbe, for she has devoted herself to it with untiring zeal and has been, in truth, the builder of its strong foundations. After many successful years, it is a source of gratification to the Council and Mrs. Barbe that her cloak has fallen upon the shoulders of Mrs. Ella K. Alschuler, so well fitted to perpetuate her work in spirit and in execution.

Only once was I obliged, through illness, to forego one of the Council's January parties. However, by way of compensation, Rose Alschuler brought a houseparty of six from Chicago to Cleveland, where I was recuperating under the devoted ministrations of Helen and Frank. The Solomon house was ingeniously converted into the semblance of a small hotel, complete even to numbers on the bedroom doors, and nothing was omitted to make the eighty-third birthday another beautiful memory.

Again, I was grateful for the fulness of life that had been vouchsafed me.

CHAPTER XXVII

NOW HAS COME THE TIME for retrospective meditation. The mood for cooperative service is strengthened by the war now raging; but it is no longer a joyous mood.

As delegates gathered, once more, from all over our country for the 1941 Triennial in New York, able, clear-thinking women demonstrated the Council's increasing value in the careful and wise planning of their program and discussions. My own interest was muted by the shocking and untimely death of my beloved nephew, George Kuh. But more than ever, the work must go on.

In my summing up, I am profoundly impressed by the Council's size as well as its comprehensive activities. I found the organization thriving magnificently, proceeding in an ever-widening circle of influence. The Senior membership now numbered 48,899, and in our splendid Junior Auxiliary were 8,500 young women of great potentiality who, taking their places effectively in their own activities today, will augment, in time, the Senior ranks. We now rejoice, too, in the Councilettes, girls of fourteen to eighteen years, who enroll with enthusiasm under the Council banner and carry on as sub-Juniors. In Chicago and in a number of other cities we have, in addition, a Career Group, composed of busy young women whose professional life keeps them from daytime meetings. Together, all go forward in fine cooperative spirit.

At the New York Triennial, the Council's progress with world trends was obvious. While its fundamental interest has always been the study of Judaism and Jewish affairs, it is significant that each successive convention finds greater stress laid upon social legislation, social welfare, international relations and all probems of aliens. Our broader scope was, naturally, partially inspired by the formation of Councils in Holland, France, Buenos Aires, Johannesburg, London and many other countries. Dr. Fanny Reading, of Australia, was so impressed by Council work in America that nine sections were organized in her country upon her return from the United States. Only recently the following cablegram was received by our national office:

"National Council of Jewish Women of Australia profoundly stirred America's splendid leadership Pacific Peril. Have supreme confidence magnificent General McArthur. Inexpressibly grateful President Roosevelt and American people. Britain and America always citadel of Liberty."

The Council today is facing the completion of half a century of service. It has been diligent in pursuing its purposes and with a sense of deep gratitude I see it steadfast to its trust, "Faith and Humanity".

In the warp and woof of my own story, the strand which constitutes my interest in our city stands out colorfully for me, but even beyond it, with the exception of those cords which define my personal relationships, the National Council of Jewish Women assumes major importance, for into it are woven my attitudes and aspirations as a Jewess.

[259]

The motivation for the enterprises and activities in which I have engaged has come, it seems to me, from the Biblical injunction "to do justly and to love mercy", and through the Jewish concept of universal brotherhood posited upon the belief in one God over all. With thousands of my contemporaries, I have participated in movements to improve social conditions, and to us continuing advancement seemed evident and inevitable. Men and women of good will were striving together toward the achievement of high and inspiring goals. Then, suddenly,within these last months, has come the treachery at Pearl Harbor, and America finds herself, again, at war! Helpless and bewildered we see our whole concept of world brotherhood shaken. How dreadful! How unspeakable! And yet, in the clarity of perception retrospect always brings, how naive and irresponsible our amazement now appears.

It was as long ago as 1929 that I first learned that an anti-Semitic group in Chicago was holding meetings and publishing scurrilous anti-Semitic pamphlets. In great concern, I communicated with Louis Marshall, who replied: "The organization concerning which you have written, is affiliated with the National Socialist Party of Germany which is under the leadership of Hitler and Ludendorf. It has become quite formidable and is engaged in all manner of pernicious activities . . . . . Unfortunately, civilization has not yet reached that stage when fanaticism has been eradicated . . . . . . .designing men seek to stir up hatred against fellow-men."

Hard to believe, is it not, that more than thirteen years ago so obvious a menace had appeared and was recognized by only small isolated groups as a world menace! Then, it was construed by the majority as of minor import. Minor import! Why should anti-Semitism, one of the rungs of the ladder upon which the Nazi Socialist party climbed to ascendency, ever have seemed of minor importance? To the Jew, certainly, it assumed vast proportions, even then!

In all histories of my people, whether written by Jew or Christian, the woeful story of maltreatment throughout the centuries has been told. We Jews, who have borne persecutions patiently down the ages, have come to know how little they avail when our oppressors have tried to raise their standards by elevating themselves over our dead bodies. Nowhere, can any nation prove a gain when it has murdered and plundered.

What can be the answer of the Jew? Can it be other than that he has the same right to choose his habitation as have other men? Yet, persons who have no thought of justice have challenged that right whenever they find it to their advantage to rob and destroy. Can these despoilers not realize that the attempt to eliminate Judaism is preposterous? The religion of the Jew has survived, in spite of the destructive measures employed against it, because of its inherent rightness and fitness to exist! It has proved its ability to adapt itself to any honorable environment where it could remain true to its spiritual bases. The Jew has been an asset in countries whose underlying desire is the creation of a state of well-being for its citizenry, with an opportunity for the participation of all in its benefits. He has brought a high sense of responsibility and altruism to the land in which he lives, and he claims a right to be judged as an individual within its framework, rising or falling on his personal merits.

Many have been the lasting contributions the Jew has made to the world. He points to his understanding of evolution in religion; to the development of the concept of a Higher Power, from a tribal god to a national god, and then to a realization of the Oneness of Deity which embraces the correlative of the brotherhood of man. The ethics of Judaism are contained in the Ten Commandments, which are basic in law and government. Through the Old Testament is traced the thought life of the ancient Jews and the evolution of their efforts are therein crystallized. Forms and customs that have come down through the years are but incidental; those which the Jew has preserved express his deep devotion to his forefathers and appreciation of the faithfulness with which they carried forward their trust.

Most of us, today, maintain that not any one sect, or creed, or book holds all the truth. Many Jews and Christians now share a common point of view, considering religion an interpretation of life; believing in the singleness of humanity as it strives toward the perfecting of a human race in harmony with itself. If Jew and Christian, Mohammedan and Buddhist, white, black and brown, cannot live together, in accord, then Judaism and Christianity, with their messages of righteousness, of justice and of love are both failures. But, in the end, right will triumph, I know, and men "shall beat their swords into plowshares, and their spears into pruning-hooks; nation shall not lift up sword against nation, neither shall they learn war any more", and "they shall sit every man under his vine and under his fig-tree; and none shall make them afraid."

Of the war, itself, I shall not write. It is a chapter I cannot complete. Let me think, rather, of the days to follow, praying that wisdom, fearlessness and honesty may guide those into whose hands will be given the responsibility of remaking the world. Behind our leaders, we must play our part, insisting that continued peace and justice shall be mankind's possession, forever. The words we speak in our Synagogue come to me, for in my profound faith I cherish, with Judaism, the belief that a time will come when "the Lord shall be One and His name shall be One."

*　*　*

"In Chicago, where I have lived eighty-four years," I wrote when I began this chronicle, "I have known five generations: the pioneers among whom were numbered the contemporaries of my grandparents, as well as of my parents, Michael and Sarah Greenebaum. There followed my own generation, now overtaken by those of my children and grandchildren." How soul-satisfying that there is now still a sixth; that of my great-grandchildren whom I have been privileged to see! I contemplate the continuance of this on-going procession and in my thoughts life and eternity blend. As for me, the paths I trod were "ways of pleasantness."

The fabric of my life is now spread out . . . the threads, uncut . . . the spindle not yet stilled. And through it all, sometimes submerged, again predominant, two golden strands appear and reappear . . . pointing, accenting, making strong the elsewise fragile stuff. Two endless golden strands . . . the family . . . the Council . . . back and forth they've shuttled through the years! How calmly one may consider the inevitable ending of one's personal pattern, buoyed by the certainty that thest two precious threads will yet go on. From generation to generation they continue . . . weaving newer patterns . . . enriching other fabrics . . . the spindle guided, ever, by the Unseen Hand.

YEARS OF PROGRESS

T HE NATIONAL COUNCIL OF JEWISH WOMEN, the oldest major Jewish women's organization in the United States, was founded during the Parliament of Religions at the World's Fair held in Chicago in 1893. When Hannah Greenebaum Solomon painstakingly brought together for this occasion ninety-five representative Jewish women from the whole United States, she could hardly have foreseen Council's future achievements. What she must certainly have known however, was that through Council, American Jewish women could accomplish together what no one woman could do alone, and that, with faith and with love, Council would act to further the goals and ideals that would move Jewish women in every succeeding generation.

From the beginning, Council has stood for sensitivity to human needs and to democratic values, for leadership in pioneering needed services, for training of volunteers, and for cooperation with other groups. It is not possible here to detail the history of Council's programs. These however, are some of Council's achievements as it worked its way through eighty years of history.

The Eighth Decade

At Council's biennial convention in 1973, ten National Resolutions were adopted by the delegates. These Resolutions set forth the organization's position on important domestic and international issues and are the bedrock for 1973–1975 program development. Four were singled out for special emphasis: *Justice for Children, Protection of Constitutional Rights of the Individual, NCJW Center for Research in Education of the Disadvantaged in Israel,* and *Strengthening the Quality of Jewish Life.*

The Nashville Presidents' Institute, a unique educational program for volunteer leaders, took place in August, 1973, at the Graduate School of Management, Vanderbilt University. For the first time, NCJW volunteers committed themselves to an intensive management training course usually reserved for top, corporate management. NCJW was aware that critical personal skills and cognitive knowledge required for successful careers in business are ultimately the same demanded for successful management in the voluntary sector. NCJW and the Graduate School of Management, V.U. jointly designed and developed the course to sharpen leadership skills and instill the confidence necessary to handle the challenges that exist in volunteerism, and in our changing society.

In 1972 NCJW initiated a survey, "Justice for Children," which was sparked by Council's awareness of inequities in laws affecting children, ineffective rehabilitation efforts, and inadequacies of institutional care and treatment on local, state, and federal levels. Over 130 Sections of Council studied their local juvenile justice system and submitted findings to the national office. The results of these "Justice for Children" surveys have been: the current compilation of a national report; the production of three program pieces in response to Section choices for action—"Children's Rights," "How to Set Up a Group Home," "Coalitions for Action"; and the efforts of Sections throughout the country to develop community service projects and legislative programs in the area of juvenile justice.

Within less than one year, more than 50 Sections were involved in community service projects and legislative activities as a result of their study findings. These included: volunteer services to children in shelters and detention facilities, court-monitoring, walk-in centers for teenagers, setting up group homes, acting as volunteer probation aides, and working to reform state juvenile codes.

In July, 1973, NCJW received an achievement award for "Service to the Children of America" from the National Council of Juvenile Court Judges for "making the most outstanding contribution in communicating the needs of youth and the juvenile courts to the public."

The Justice for Children project followed immediately upon "Windows on Day Care," an NCJW survey of day care needs and the first definitive nationwide study of its kind. Published in April, 1972, and widely acclaimed as a significant contribution to our country's understanding of day care, the report has been incorporated in the Congressional Record, and used by congressmen and day care specialists around the country.

In 1971, NCJW Week was inaugurated so that Sections across the country could simultaneously tell Council's story to the public. Each successful year has generated increasing enthusiasm for this nationwide effort.

For almost a decade NCJW has sponsored "Schools for Action," where volunteer leaders gather to explore methods for best implementing Council programs. The Sixth Community School for Action, "Forging Our Jewish Future," launched in 1971, is the most recent and reflects Council's intensified programming thrust in the area of Jewish affairs.

Within its education-for-action structure, School VI aims to make Council women more knowledgeable in Jewish issues and, following the learning situation of the school, better able to stake out areas of action for Council in Jewish communities locally and worldwide.

This pattern of education-for-action has never deviated since the first NCJW School for Community Action was set up at Council's Seventieth Anniversary Convention in Minneapolis, Minnesota, in March, 1963. The topic was "Equal Opportunity for Youth," and Council's experience and knowledge of problems of out-of-school, out-of-work youth, public education needs, racial discrimination, and social welfare facilities all applied in the curriculum of the three-day school program carried out by Sections throughout the country.

The Pearl Larner Willen Institute, which became the Fifth School for Community Action, was developed in 1969 as a prototype for Section schools, to convene members, other broad-based women's organizations, and representatives of the urban and rural poor to explore new ways of working together in local communities.

The 1967–68 NCJW School for Community Action, "Spotlight on the Family," encouraged Council members to look beyond the individual and to take a new look at their own and other families, including the disadvantaged, with an eye to stimulating new ways of providing needed education, service, and social action in the community. During the same year NCJW published "Blueprint for Day Care," a guide to Sections moving to meet this desperate national need.

The 1965–66 NCJW School for Community Action, "Women on the Move," proposed that middle class women take up the cause of "the other woman" living in poverty and often struggling against insurmountable odds to manage both job and family. In community forums co-sponsored by Council Sections and other local groups on an interracial and interreligious basis, NCJW spearheaded efforts to aid a group largely ignored by society and statistically even more numerous than impoverished men and children.

"The Immovable Middle Class" was the 1964–65 topic of the NCJW School for Community Action. It provided a new and harder look at the Council woman's own attitudes and actions which might be factors in perpetuating poverty and segregation. Raising questions about the effects on children of the middle class as well as the poor, the school helped students recognize the degree to which self-concern and blind spots immobilized middle class liberals.

Women in Community Service—WICS—is an interracial, interreligious, intercultural coalition of six national women's organizations. NCJW was one of the parent organizations, along with Church Women United and National Councils of Catholic and Negro Women, when WICS was born in 1964. In recent years, two organizations of Spanish-speaking women, the American G.I. Forum and the League of United Latin American Citizens, have added their woman-power to the WICS coalition. In its work to combat poverty in the United States, WICS offers services to young women, age 16-21, from low-income backgrounds. Although many services have been given, WICS works primarily with the Women's Job Corps, a federally funded program that offers job-training, remedial education, medical care, and training in social skills at residential centers across the country.

Service for Older Adults is a major concern of Council, and its task force is currently devising new methods of meeting their problems. In 1962 Council's publication of "No Time To Retire," a guide to the formation of Senior Service Corps in which older adults put their skills to work for the community, stirred reaction from educators, welfare specialists, and public officials leading to a bill in Congress to establish a National Community Senior Service Corps. Councils's newest publication, "How to Publish a Telephone Directory," is a guide to Sections for compiling urgently needed services in a directory for older adults in communities throughout the country. "Council Good Neighbors" is a four-point program to assist Sections in serving older adults in their own homes.

The NCJW Center for Research in Education of the Disadvantaged in Israel marks an important milestone in Council programming. It was established in 1968 at the School of Education of Hebrew University, which Council supported for over twenty years. Organized as an action-research pilot project, the center became a permanent Council program. It is designed to develop and evaluate new educational methods, materials, practices and services for the educationally disadvantaged in order to speed their integration into Israel's modern society. The center's findings hold promise for the disadvantaged all over the world.

The Council-built Hebrew University High School, which opened its doors in 1963, has been the seat of a five-year NCJW project to help solve the learning problems of socially and economically disadvantaged youth. The 1970 statistics on the first graduates show the project's worth, with nineteen out of twenty-seven potential school drop-outs having successfully passed their college entrance examinations.

Grants for graduate study in American universities were awarded to experienced social workers and educators from abroad between 1946 and 1971. Council has granted 261 fellowships to persons from 18 Jewish communities in Europe, South America, and Asia; of these, 200 were awarded to

[269]

Israelis. Council Fellowship alumni hold key positions in ministries, municipalities, universities, schools, and agencies throughout Israel. Several Israelis are currently completing their graduate studies in the United States on Council Fellowship grants. Council also offers a training program in the United States for volunteers who are leaders of affiliates of the International Council of Jewish Women.

In June, 1963, NCJW was hostess to the Sixth Triennial Convention of the International Council of Jewish Women in Cleveland, Ohio. The ICJW's 1966 Convention was held in London. In 1969 the triennial was held in Jerusalem, and an ICJW seminar was held in Israel in October, 1970. An ICJW seminar in November, 1973, devoted to "Jewish Identity in the Modern World," was to have preceded Council's second summit conference in Israel. Both events were cancelled because of the Arab-Israeli War.

The Seventh Decade

Creative expansion in program and scope of activity marked this decade. In 1961 NCJW celebrated its fiftieth year of social action in a joint celebration with the Young Women's Christian Association. Both organizations adopted a ten-point Code of Personal Commitment. The code is a guide to actions and attitudes for the individual.

Leadership training in this decade was developed to reach NCJW volunteer leaders throughout the country. Two Presidents' Institutes, in 1960 and 1961, were followed in 1962 by training for 1,000 Council women at ten regional conferences. These, in turn, were followed by Section Board workshops for training. This executive training program was a follow-up of the Community Leadership Training Program, launched in 1957.

In a dramatic outgrowth of its traditional services to children and youth, NCJW launched a nationwide survey of out-of-school, out-of-work youth and their needs in 1960. As a result of the survey, in 1961 Council issued an eighteen-point action program, "A Start for Youth," which outlines service and social action to meet the needs of youngsters.

NCJW also extended its services to the aged during this period, and played an active role in planning the first White House Conference on the Aging in 1961. Council's President, Mrs. Charles Hymes, served as a member of the advisory committee for the conference and as Chairman of the Conference Committee on Voluntary Services and Service Organizations. In addition to NCJW's national representatives, many Council women were appointed to state delegations for the conference.

Another major area of NCJW activity was mental health. Council published a guide, "Promoting Mental Health," and Section services branched out into rehabilitative services for former mental patients, community education, and action for mental health facilities, as well as expansion of direct services in mental hospitals.

NCJW services to youth, the aging, the handicapped, and its coordinated service and social action activities were recognized in 1960 when the Council of Jewish Federations and Welfare Funds awarded NCJW the William J. Shroder Memorial Award—the American Jewish community's highest honor for service.

In 1961 for the first time, all of Council's services were catalogued in a "Directory of Community Services," which reported that Sections maintained over 1,000 services. That same year Council's national president was appointed to President Kennedy's Commission on the Status of Women.

In 1960 NCJW sponsored publication of *The Citizen Volunteer,* a book edited by Nathan E. Cohen, Dean, School of Applied Social Sciences, Western Reserve University, in which the role of the volunteer in America is presented in its historical perspective.

From 1961 on, a major and continuing effort of Council has centered on services and action in behalf of children and youth to achieve equal opportunity for all. NCJW service and action programs are aimed at upgrading public education so that it may be effective for all children. Educational programs for preschool children from deprived backgrounds who would otherwise start school at a disadvantage were piloted, and served as the prototype for the government's Opperation Headstart. Remedial reading and tutorial programs directed at the potential school dropout have been carried on by Sections across the country.

During this biennial period, the Council also established the NCJW Hannah G. Solomon Fellowship to stimulate research in American Jewish culture. The grant is made through the National Foundation for Jewish Culture.

In 1959 Council's support of education took an unprecedented turn when the organization undertook to build a half-million dollar campus for the Hebrew University High School in Jerusalem. The school was dedicated in December, 1962.

With the beginning of the 1961–62 academic year, the number of educators and social workers trained under the Overseas Scholarship Program rose o 177, and the Overseas Program extended to 19 countries. Thousands of Ship-A-Box parcels were shipped to insti utions in Israel and Morocco every year.

[272]

The Sixth Decade

After having assumed active leadership in support of the United Nations, Council was invited to send an accredited observer to the UN.

The professional Service to the Foreign-Born Department of NCJW, engaged in casework on a large scale, was merged with the National Refugee Service in 1946 to become the United Service for New Americans. Council continued and expanded its port-and-dock, resettlement, and Americanization and naturalization services. By this time it was also clear that the activities of Council members in behalf of the foreign-born for half a century had helped create a nationwide pattern of service of profound importance.

In 1946 Council opened the Athens Home, for girls who were victims of Nazi persecution, and in 1947 opened a similar home in Paris. Both institutions were closed when the need for the service no longer existed.

The postwar period was probably the most hectic in Council's history, and the most creative since its first decade. Among the new programs launched were: Ship-A-Box (1945); Overseas Scholarships (1946); Golden Age Clubs (1946); Support of Israel Education (1948). Section services to children developed rapidly, and mental health education began.

Council launched its "Freedom Campaign" early in 1952—the first major membership organization to undertake a public drive to combat a growing danger to civil liberties. The "Freedom to Read" project, opposing censorship, followed.

The Fifth Decade

"The tragedy of the German Jews has darkened the lives of Jews in the remotest corner of the world," declared NCJW

President, Mrs. Arthur Brin, at the fourteenth Triennial Convention, New Orleans, 1935.

German-Jewish children were rescued and placed in private American homes through German-Jewish Children's Aid, which Council helped form in 1938. In 1939 NCJW Port-and-Dock workers served 16,225 refugees.

To combat anti-Semitism and discrimination and to fortify Jewish women with a knowledge of Jewish history and culture, Council undertook a new program in 1935 known as "Contemporary Jewish Affairs." Among the projects of Council Sections in this era were neighborhood houses, summer camps, kindergarten schools, infant health clinics, birth control clinics, vocational guidance, scholarship awards, Big Sister activities, opportunity shops, and services to prevent deafness and blindness. Council toyeries grew out of depression needs.

In World War II, Council again bent its energies to the war effort.

The Fourth Decade

With the deepening of the depression, Council Sections were engaged in job placement, the creation of employment, financial relief, lunches for undernourished children, and a number of special activities to insure the continuance of children in school. A report by the Women's Division of President Hoover's emergency unit for employment recognized Council's contributions in these areas. NCJW also sponsored special free classes for the unemployed in typing, stenography, singing, dancing, and art. Nearly three hundred scholarships were granted between 1929 and 1932.

In 1933 Mrs. Solomon declared: "The Council continues, as it began, to train volunteers as assistants to professional workers, for we are very far from the goal when social agencies can do justice to . . . needy persons."

The Third Decade

Membership grew from 10,800 in 1910 to 48,000 in 1923, plus 8,000 junior members. During World War I, NCJW served in the Council of National Defense, and other war-service agencies. Of the 70 agency representatives at Ellis Island all were ordered off, except six men and the representatives of Council who were responsible for the care of all women and children on the island.

Two units of social service experts were sent abroad by Council after the war to establish services for Jewish refugees. Americanization classes were set up for refugees in Holland. In Riga, Latvia, Council established workshops for war sufferers, found homes for orphaned children, and helped many immigrants to South America, South Africa and Australia.

At home Council joined with other organizations to promote America's entrance into the League of Nations and the World Court, and to urge the development of international agreements to prevent war. Sixty-five thousand immigrants received Council assistance at the eastern port cities from 1920 to 1923. Investigations for war orphans, deportees, and disunited families were among the services for thousands of others.

The Hannah G. Solomon Scholarship Fund was created to enable girls to receive graduate training in social service. The Farm and Rural Work Program was launched; nearly

3,000 farm families were assisted through community projects and religious study groups. Council turned over this program to the Jewish Agricultural Society when it was formed.

The Second Decade

In 1904 a permanent station for immigrant aid was established by Council on Ellis Island. Several Sections established correctional institutions, employment bureaus, and dispensaries. Council made the first organized effort for the Jewish blind and pioneered penny lunch stations in schools. A Council probation officer for Jewish delinquent children was accepted in a municipal court in 1906. By 1911, Sections were providing this service.

In 1909 Council participated in the White House Conference on Child Welfare, where the need for social legislation was driven home. Council's program for social legislation was formally established at the Sixth Triennial Convention in 1911, which called for federal regulation of child labor, the provision of adequate housing for low-income groups, food and drug regulation, extension of civil service, uniform marriage and divorce laws, and federal anti-lynching laws. Council women have determined that remedial services alone were not enough, and would have to be supplemented by basic reforms.

Council aided victims of the Kishineff massacre of Jews in Russia in 1903, and the San Francisco earthquake and fire of 1906. A Committee on Peace and Arbitration was formed in 1908. The International Council of Jewish Women was organized in May, 1912, at a meeting of the International Council of Women in Rome.

The First Decade

Towards the close of the nineteenth century, demands matured for social reform, including political equality for women. Born in this creative ferment, Council immediately launched activities so sound and advanced in concept that they created a firm base for the organization's outlook in the future. Among early projects were service in settlement houses, remedial work in connection with juvenile and other local courts, adult study circles, vocational training for young girls, free health dispensaries, school health inspection programs, day nurseries, and assistance to poverty-stricken immigrant families.

A permanent constitution was adopted at Council's First Triennial Convention, held in New York City in 1896 with fifty Sections represented.

In 1903 the United States Government asked Council's assistance in preventing the white slavery exploitation and sweat-shop labor that were the lot of many girls and women arriving alone and penniless in America. Council responded immediately. Girls on all incoming boats were met and cared for by Council's Port-and-Dock Department; relatives were located; technical details of immigration were adjusted; and many women and families were assisted.